BOY ON ICE

BOY ON ICE

The Life and Death of Derek Boogaard

JOHN BRANCH

W. W. NORTON & COMPANY

NEW YORK · LONDON

For information about permission to reproduce selections from this book,
write to Permissions, W. W. Norton & Company, Inc.,
500 Fifth Avenue, New York, NY 10110

For information about special discounts for bulk purchases, please contact
W. W. Norton Special Sales at specialsales@wwnorton.com or 800-233-4830

Manufacturing by RR Donnelley, Harrisonburg
Book design by Ellen Cipriano
Production manager: Devon Zahn

Library of Congress Cataloging-in-Publication Data

Branch, John (Sports reporter)
Boy on ice : the life and death of Derek Boogaard / John Branch.
pages cm
Includes bibliographical references and index.
ISBN 978-0-393-23939-3 (hardcover)
1. Boogaard, Derek, 1982–2011.
2. Hockey players—Canada—Biography.
3. Violence in sports. I. Title.
GV848.5.B669B73 2014
796.962092—dc23
[B]
2014015731

W. W. Norton & Company, Inc., 500 Fifth Avenue, New York, N.Y. 10110
www.wwnorton.com

W. W. Norton & Company Ltd., Castle House, 75/76 Wells Street,
London W1T 3QT

1 2 3 4 5 6 7 8 9 0

To Joe and Ally

CONTENTS

BOY ON ICE

PROLOGUE

DEREK BOOGAARD DID NOT have to fight.

This time, all he had to do was skate onto the ice. He could keep his thickly padded gloves on his hands, rather than theatrically flick them aside. He did not have to curl his mangled fingers into fists and raise them with malicious intent. Instead of dropping his stick, he could hold on to it with two hands, as if he fully intended to scramble for the puck and shoot it into the net, just like all the other players, just as he did as a boy.

He could glide past the bad guys, the ones Derek was paid to fend away with the constant threat of savagery and the occasional use of violence, and do nothing more than smirk and shrug. He was a hockey enforcer, maybe the scariest one in the league, with a reputation for scattering opponents with a look and shattering faces with a punch. But now, Derek simply could be a child, beloved for doing nothing but being himself, sliding effortlessly in little curls.

Boo-gaard, Boo-gaard, Boo-gaard, Boo-gaard . . .

The sold-out crowd at the Xcel Energy Center in Saint Paul, home of the National Hockey League's Minnesota Wild, chanted his name. The voices of nearly 20,000 people echoed from the rafters to the ice, from the seats against the glass to the concession stands on the concourse, building into a loose and chaotic chorus.

They pronounced his name the way all strangers had in recent years. When Derek was a teenager, first being molded into a hockey fighter by professional coaches, the men who discovered him in the small prairie town in Saskatchewan dubbed him "The Boogeyman." Soon, the first syllable of the boy's last name was transformed to something more frightening, too, with a simple tweak of pronunciation: Boo, not Beau.

Boo-gaard, Boo-gaard, Boo-gaard, Boo-gaard . . .

It was Derek's second NHL season. He was 24. He had scored no goals and recorded one assist the entire year, on a forgettable goal in a February game against Florida. Of the 32 men who suited up for the Wild that season, Derek averaged the fewest minutes of ice time. Yet Derek's replica jersey, No. 24, was the best selling of all the Wild players.

He was listed in the game program at six feet, seven inches, one of the tallest players in the league, but Derek was closer to six foot eight. With his skates on, to the top of his helmet, he was roughly seven feet tall. The height distorted his shape and disguised his strength, stretched him out into something almost lean and gawky. Teams listed him at 260 pounds, but it was wishful thinking. Derek usually arrived at training camp weighing at least 10 pounds more, and occasionally approached 300. His arms and chest and shoulders were oversized, but not chiseled. Derek's center of gravity rested low, in his thick thighs and massive seat, more like a speed skater or a cyclist than a hockey star.

He had little of the outward menace of other enforcers, those desperate to intimidate with snarls and sneers. Derek rarely looked angry on the ice. His lean face was in a constant position of indifference, as if to cloak what he was thinking behind the sad eyes with heavy lids. His nose, repositioned too many times to remember, descended down, then left, then down again, as if following a detour. For some players, missing teeth were a badge of honor. Not Derek. But his full set of white teeth was only partly real.

Under his own oversized jersey, Derek wore the flimsiest of shoulder pads, the same ones he had worn when he was a boy, playing in a small-town rink with aluminum siding and three rows of bleachers. Then, the only sounds echoing through the building were those of the puck smacking the base of the boards with a thud, the hand-me-down skates carving the ice, and the volunteer coaches shouting instructions and encouragement. The bleachers were empty except for smatterings of parents and siblings. When there were road games, the family van or his father's police sedan cruised through the frozen black night of the impossibly flat prairie. The trips often ended long after bedtime on a school night, the bright light of the warm garage awakening the boy balled up and asleep in the back seat.

When the boy dared to dream, he dreamed like this.

Boo-gaard, Boo-gaard, Boo-gaard, Boo-gaard . . .

There was no opposing player's jersey to grab with the left hand, no face to smash with the right. There was no fear of getting his nose broken, or of having the frayed muscles of his shoulder shredded, or of feeling the bulging disk in his back send jolting waves of pain up his spine. There was no worry over having his raw knuckles explode in blood against the helmet or jaw of the other man. There was no risk of another concussion, or of that one perfectly timed blow that can rearrange a career, the kind that Derek had already built a reputation for delivering. There was no thought of a quick and embarrassing fall to the ice to deaden the crowd's enthusiasm and end the fight, which is the way so many of them go, because boxing is hard, but it is harder still while standing on ice with quarter-inch-thick blades attached vertically to the soles of lace-up boots, knowing your job and reputation are on the line.

The moment was just that, a moment in a life made up of millions of them. But to Derek, it was never forgotten. Four years before this night, he had played for a low-rung minor-league team in Louisiana, getting paid a few hundred dollars a week, drinking cheap beer in a ground-level apartment that he shared with his first girlfriend.

Four years after this night, he would be a millionaire living alone in a 33rd-floor condominium overlooking Central Park in New York City, a player for the famed New York Rangers, given nothing less than everything he had ever wanted and silently longing for something else.

Boo-gaard, Boo-gaard, Boo-gaard, Boo-gaard . . .

There was 1 minute, 48 seconds left in Game 4 of Minnesota's first-round playoff series with the Anaheim Ducks. The Ducks had won the first three games of their best-of-seven series, each by one goal. Derek had missed Game 3 two nights earlier with the flu. And in Games 1 and 2, he had spent about nine minutes on the ice and 16 minutes in the penalty box.

Now Minnesota coach Jacques Lemaire wanted to add a desperate dose of Derek's feistiness to the series. Derek had "all the subtlety of an armor-plated Zamboni," reporter Jim Souhan wrote that night for the *StarTribune* in Minneapolis.

Late in the second period, with Minnesota trailing 1–0, Derek corralled the puck in a corner behind Anaheim's goal. He was a good skater for a man his size, but his strength was in straight-ahead momentum rather than ice-carving agility. He was able to build speed with his long strides, and opponents tended to give him a wide berth, the way cars peel aside for an oncoming fire engine.

Given room, Derek flicked a pass that slid between two Ducks players and arrived on the stick of teammate Pierre-Marc Bouchard, standing in front of the goal. Bouchard's first shot was blocked and returned to him. His second tied the game.

Derek was credited with an assist. It was the only postseason point he would ever score in the NHL.

The game was tied, and Minnesota carried the momentum into the third period, scoring three times in about eight minutes. The final goal prompted an immediate scrum, an angry knot containing most of the players on the ice. Five penalties were assessed, including two for a fight between Minnesota's Brent Burns and Anaheim's Corey Perry after Perry launched himself into a group of players.

Derek watched helplessly from the bench, precluded by rules from joining the fray on the ice. And he was on the bench again with 1:48 remaining, when Anaheim's Kent Huskins and Minnesota's Adam Hall stopped the game with another fight. Anaheim's Shawn Thornton skated half the length of the rink to jump in.

The crowd, electrified by the fights and the imminent victory, cheered lustily. Other players paired off and traded barbed words and threatening shoves. Anaheim's Brad May gave mild-mannered Wild defenseman Kim Johnsson a push and then punched him in the face with his right hand. Johnsson collapsed to the ice with a concussion.

Derek leaned over the rink's half-wall, which reached only partway up his thigh. He calmly challenged all the Ducks to a fight.

Anaheim players shouted back over the din. Superstar Teemu Selanne looked at Derek incredulously, and even a novice lip reader could see that the Finn had full command of the vulgarities of the English language. Others tried to shout Derek down, too. Anaheim coach Randy Carlyle dismissively motioned to Derek with a flapping hand, like a man with an invisible puppet.

And that is when the moment came, seeping up through the commotion.

Boo-gaard, Boo-gaard, Boo-gaard, Boo-gaard . . .

"Now the fans are calling for Boogaard!" television play-by-play announcer Dan Terhaar shouted to viewers.

The officials were huddled to the side, sorting penalties and trying to restore order to the final 108 seconds of the game. The series would head back to Anaheim for Game 5, but the immediate con-

cern was ending Game 4 without further violence. Fans were intoxicated with a cocktail of joy and bloodlust.

Boo-gaard, Boo-gaard, Boo-gaard, Boo-gaard . . .

Lemaire, the Wild coach, hollered from behind. Derek glanced
back over his left shoulder and nodded. In one motion, without
expression, he spun over the boards on his right hip. He glided onto
the ice with a couple of small steps atop his size-12 skates.

The noise surged like thunder, a slow rumble quickly overwhelmed by a crescendo of cacophonous energy.

"If the roof wasn't screwed down, it would have flew off," said
Derek's mother, Joanne.

Derek casually held his stick in front of him, across his sturdy
thighs, his right hand near the nub and his left hand near the blade.
He slid to the left, then curled back to the right, toward the Anaheim
bench.

With a look of nonchalant amusement, Derek caught someone's
eye. And, with a smirk on his lips, he shrugged. In the most heated,
electric moment of Derek's career, he did not have to fight.

As a boy, he wanted to fit in, not stand out. Like nearly all enforcers, Derek dreamed of playing alongside everyone else, stick in hand,
skating and passing and shooting and scoring. He could not help
his size, and he grew to understand that, if he continued to play, he
would be expected to stand up for his teammates. There would be
honor in that.

But nobody dreams of playing hockey so that they can hurt other
people. It just goes that way. Players are shaped into puzzle pieces that
fit with all the others. A boy is stripped to a set of skills at the whim
of coaches and scouts. To keep playing hockey, do more of this and
less of that. The untalented and undedicated are discarded, swept
away at the end of each season. Survivors plug away, baited by hope.

No one ever told Derek directly that his primary mission in
hockey would be to fight. Not the scouts who discovered him at

14, when he ripped away from referees and attacked an opposing bench. Not the coaches who limited his playing time, trying to mold him, improbably, into a suitable balance of caged benevolence and unleashed ferocity. Not the general managers who plucked him and pulled him ever higher in hockey's hierarchy, a goon on the ice and a boon at the box office.

To admit to any of that would demean the player and the role. Instead, motivation was wrapped in euphemism and vaunted esteem. To be the "tough guy," to serve the vital role of protecting your teammates, took a special sense of duty and selflessness. There might be twelve forwards and six defensemen and two goalies, but there was one enforcer. It was a void that no one else could fill.

Of course Derek would do it.

He knew deep inside that he would not be there at all if not for his ability and willingness to both throw punches and withstand them. If he wanted to keep playing hockey, Derek would have to take a different route than the other boys. If he wanted to play in the National Hockey League, he would have to use a side-door entrance reserved for those willing to do what most could never imagine.

The late-game discord between the Wild and Ducks settled to a simmer, and the clock eventually expired to secure a Minnesota victory. Derek was named the third star of the game, rare recognition for an enforcer. He had played 8 minutes, 28 seconds of the 60-minute game, more ice time than he had received in all but three regular-season contests.

"Boogey makes an impact because they're looking for him," Lemaire said afterward. "Not to fight, but they're looking for him when he's on the ice."

The scare tactic worked only because of Derek's budding reputation as a fighter. In his first two NHL seasons, he had become one of the most feared players in the league. He fought 26 times in 113 games, more than all but four other players. He won most of those fights, knocking down some of hockey's fiercest men. And when he shattered the right cheekbone and eye socket of plucky middle-weight Todd Fedoruk with a single punch in October 2006, forcing surgeons to rebuild the crater with metal parts, Derek became the scariest enforcer of them all.

Suddenly, Derek had it all: fame, admiration, money, respect, and a job playing hockey. He was not good enough to do it with his stick or his skates, but there was a role for him and his fists, if he was willing to dutifully distribute punishment and quietly absorb pain.

What no one calculated was the slow toll. There were the arthritic hands, the nose broken too many times to count, the balky back that kept him up nights, the right shoulder that acted like a piston during fights but ached so much that Derek often struggled to get shirts on and off. There were the swollen, scabbed hands that bled after fights and ached at night, numbed only with submersion in buckets of ice water.

Derek kept most of that to himself. Players who played fewer than five minutes a game, if they were in the lineup at all, were unwise to provide excuses to be replaced by the reservoir of young men looking to have the job. They were thankful to be part of the team.

What Derek could not comprehend was the cumulative damage in his brain, the tau proteins gathering in tiny brown spots in his pink frontal lobe and other recesses of his mind, strangling the cells, one subconcussive blow at a time.

When the Wild and Ducks reconvened in Anaheim for Game 5, Derek did not wait for the game to begin. In pregame warmups, as teams glided over separate halves of the rink and with no officials on the ice, he elbowed veteran defenseman Chris Pronger. That quickly got the attention of George Parros, a six-foot-five bruiser who had replaced Fedoruk during the season as an antidote to Derek.

"He crossed over the red line, so I got in his way just on their side of the ice and then he shot a puck at me," Derek said of Pronger to the *StarTribune*. He had a habit of understating the bedlam that surrounded him and his role. "And then Parros came flying over the line. It just escalated from there."

The players swarmed near the middle of the ice. Anaheim fans, still settling into their seats, instantly adopted the same thirst for fights that fueled the fans in Minnesota.

Anaheim won the game that night, and the teams lined up and shook hands, a proud hockey tradition of end-of-series sportsmanship. Derek was told to stay away, to avoid trouble.

The Wild re-signed Derek that summer to a three-year, $2.63 million contract that kept him away from other teams hungry to have him on their side.

"Derek's development is a testament to his dedication, discipline, and the emphasis he places on team above individual," Wild general manager Doug Risebrough said. "Through his style of play and his personality, he has made himself a valued player and person in the organization."

But no position in hockey was as fickle as that of the enforcer. Reputations could be burnished or demolished with just one fight— even just one punch. There might be only one primary fighter on the roster, but there were countless, faceless players toiling in lesser leagues, eager to do anything to play in the NHL. Enforcers, usually the lowest-paid players on the roster, were interchangeable parts.

Most of the physical pain was hidden, but some could be seen— in the dazed expressions, the lost teeth, the bleeding faces. The emotional toll—the stress, the worry, the expectations—was masked behind a charade of showmanship and a false display of fearlessness. Like most enforcers, Derek never saw any of that coming, the constancy of pain and the coldcocking of emotion.

Emboldened by the playoffs, Derek got into a fight in the first game of the next season, a 60-second slugfest with Chicago's David Koci. Derek lost his helmet early and absorbed several blows to the face. Most of Derek's punches struck Koci's helmet, which surely had Derek wishing that the unwritten rules of his teenaged days applied. Back then, combatants would remove their helmets before a fight as a gesture of respect to the other fighter's knuckles. When junior leagues outlawed that, the boys would gently remove one another's helmet before throwing punches.

Derek was 25, just starting his third NHL season. Within a year, Derek would have teeth knocked out and be prescribed vast amounts of painkillers by team doctors. In another year, he would be in substance abuse rehabilitation. In another year, he would be in New York, rich and miserable and alone. And in another year, he would be dead.

Maybe it all turned on that spring night in April, when Derek led the Wild to its only victory of the postseason. A rare assist. A bout of intimidation. A smirk and a shrug. It was the apex of a career that no one could have predicted, a hopelessly shy boy from Saskatchewan being cheered for doing nothing but gliding on the ice. It was the night that Derek Boogaard was cheered loudest. Strange that it should come on a night when he did not have to fight.

PART I

SASKATCHEWAN

1

THE ICE WAS COVERED with five-year-old boys. The goalies were immobilized with padded equipment, weighted like firs under heavy snowfall. The others, like Derek, glided in slow-motion packs, cautiously and unsteadily following the puck.

Their sticks, nearly as tall as the boys, were handy to keep balance, either leaned upon like canes or held horizontally, like the balancing poles of tightrope walkers. They swung wildly when the children lost their balance and twirled to the ice, spilling like tops that had lost their momentum.

The little rink had the usual smatterings of family members, there to provide enthusiastic cheers and a quiet wave of recognition. Joanne Boogaard, pregnant with the family's fourth child, had stuffed Derek into his first hockey uniform. He was not yet old enough to dress himself, but he was big and strong enough to make it hard to wrestle his limbs into their proper holes.

His mother slid the boy's legs through the shorts and pulled the oversized blue-and-white jersey over his head. She tugged on the socks that stretched to his knees. She laced the hand-me-down skates that teetered under his weight. She buckled the helmet that protected his head.

Derek was always taller than the other kids, perennially found in

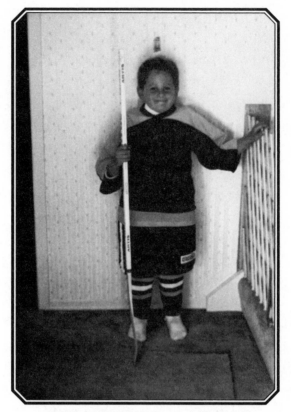

Derek dressed for his first day of hockey.

the back row of the team picture. And as a young boy he was chubby, his round face crowned by dark, curly hair.

It was the winter bridging 1987 and 1988. Joanne, a tall woman with sad eyes, was married to Len Boogaard, a sturdy and stern policeman.

They had met at a Regina bar on New Year's Day, 1981. Len was a cadet at the Royal Canadian Mounted Police Depot Division, the training academy for the national police force, a well-manicured campus on the west side of town. He and some fellow cadets walked into Checkers, an English-style pub inside the nearby Landmark Inn. A tall 25-year-old brunette named Joanne Vrouwe was behind the bar.

Her parents, Theodorus and Anna, had three daughters when they left Amsterdam in 1953. None spoke English. They crossed the Atlantic in a ship and landed in Halifax, Nova Scotia, then boarded a train headed west. Theodorus, who worked for an oil company in the Netherlands, had been sponsored by a farmer near Riverhurst, Saskatchewan. The train dropped the family of five in Regina, and Theodorus soon began work as a farmhand.

By 1955, the family had moved into town, assimilating with the help of a burgeoning Dutch community. Theodorus became known as Ted and worked for a Regina shipping company, and Anna gave birth to another daughter, whom they named Joanne.

The family lived in a tiny house on Ninth Avenue, on the far edge of town at the time. They soon moved a few blocks east to Scarth Street, north of downtown Regina, where the main crossroads, a nod to the British Commonwealth, was Albert Street and Victoria Avenue.

Ted found a job with Burns Foods, at a slaughterhouse and feed plant, and embarked on a long career as a butcher that lasted until the plant closed without warning. After working at the bus depot for a spell, he caught on with International Packers, another slaughterhouse in town.

Joanne was a pragmatic, hardworking sort, her singsong voice disguising a feisty toughness. She became pregnant while in high school, and gave birth to a baby boy in 1972, at age 17. She never told the baby's father, and she immediately handed the boy over for adoption.

After high school, she worked days as a dental technician and nights and weekends as a bartender. Her father told Joanne she would make more money working at the packing plant. So she got a job there, quit as a dental technician and kept her bartending gig, saving enough money to buy herself a small house in Regina.

About a month after taking the new job, in 1979, Joanne's 52-

year-old mother died unexpectedly while visiting relatives in Holland. Part of the emotional fallout was the end of a long relationship Joanne had with a boyfriend. That was when a 26-year-old RCMP cadet and Dutch immigrant walked into her bar.

Born in 1954, Len was the oldest of four boys, the first two born in postwar Holland. In 1958, the Boogaards, like the Vrouwes, crossed the Atlantic for the uncertain potential of a better life. The Boogaards settled in Toronto, living in the basement of relatives. Len's father, Pieter, had worked as a load coordinator for a shipping company in Holland. In Toronto, he got a job cleaning car dealerships, making 25 cents an hour. Len's mother, Nieltje, had worked in a bakery in Holland, but stayed home in Canada to raise the boys. She took the name Nancy, because no one could pronounce her Dutch name. Pieter became Peter, and Peter became a school janitor, a job he held until 1991, quitting only after the death of his youngest son—Len's brother—of bone cancer at age 20.

Household rules were strict. The family was part of the Dutch Christian Reformed Church, with twice-a-week catechism classes and two church services on Sundays. While neighborhood children played outside on Sundays, Len was kept indoors, dressed in his church best.

After hopscotching between the homes of relatives—from one family's basement to another family's farm—the Boogaards bought a small house in 1963. Money remained tight. Little was spent on Christmas gifts, and the area rug in the living room, brought from Holland and worn from use, was dyed by Len's mother in a persistent attempt to preserve it.

The Boogaards spoke Dutch at home, and Len did not know English when he arrived for the first day of kindergarten. But he adapted quickly, becoming a good student, if a bit of a troublemaker, with a natural skepticism toward protocol and authority. He was

granted dual citizenship when he was 13, an age when he suffered
from the debilitating pain of scoliosis. When doctors thought Len
had quit growing, at age 17, they performed back surgery. It kept
him in a body cast for months, and left him wearing a back brace
long after that.

An uncle helped get Len into college in the Netherlands. By
then, though, Dutch was Len's second language, and he struggled to
read it well enough to keep up with his studies. He also learned that
he would be required to serve in the Dutch military if he stayed. So
he returned to Canada and graduated from St. Lawrence College
in Cornwall, Ontario, with a mechanical engineering diploma. In
1978, Len's brother Bill joined the Royal Canadian Mounted Police
and was posted in suburban Vancouver. Len moved in with him and
took a job in a mechanical engineering lab, doing research and development for oil-field machinery components. He spent his days in
front of a drafting board.

It was a good job, but his brother had all the interesting stories, the ones about chasing bad guys and investigating crimes. His
curiosity piqued, Len spent nights and weekends with the auxiliary
RCMP. He could not carry a gun, but he could ride along on calls.
It was enough of a taste to get Len excited about a career change.
He applied to the RCMP and was accepted. He reported to Depot
Division in November 1980 for 24 weeks of training, a military-style
form of boot camp. On New Year's Day, granted rare time off, he
headed to Checkers.

Dark and handsome, with a furry mustache and a penchant for
sarcasm and straight-faced jokes, Len made small talk with the young
woman behind the bar. Joanne was coy. She told Len, as she told all
the other RCMP members and recruits who wandered in armed
with bravado and pickup lines, that she would never date a cop.

But she was taken by Len's cool confidence, and they did have a lot in common, including their Dutch roots and strict upbringings. When Len returned another day, carrying flowers, Joanne could not resist.

Theirs was a shotgun romance, ignited by spark and the impending calendar. Len would be out of training by summer and handed a posting—probably in a tiny town far away. Maybe the RCMP would note that Joanne owned a house and had a job in Regina and keep the couple in the big city. They did not know. He could be assigned anywhere across the country.

Len graduated from training in May, and he and Joanne were married on June 27. The ceremony was held in the small, dark chapel at the RCMP Depot. The stained-glass windows behind the pulpit depicted two Mounties. One held a bugle; the other, a musket. Len was dressed in red serge, the formal uniform of the RCMP. Eight others in red serge, holding lances, comprised a color guard. Len's brother Bill was best man, and their other brothers were groomsmen. Joanne was accompanied at the altar by her sisters. About 100 friends and family members sat in the wooden pews and happily congratulated the young couple as they burst into the warm sunshine out front.

Derek Leendert Boogaard was born less than a year later, on June 23, 1982, at Saskatoon City Hospital. The middle name honored his father. The boy was 9 pounds, 5½ ounces, the heftiest of the oncoming wave of Boogaard babies, and he stretched 21½ inches. The family dressed him in a Toronto Maple Leafs onesie, and within weeks, doctors recommended solid baby food from a jar to quell his insatiable hunger.

And here he was, a few years later, an oversized toddler gazing at the faces in the bleachers until his eyes locked on those of his parents. The habit never faded.

"I remember when I would sit in the bench, I would always look

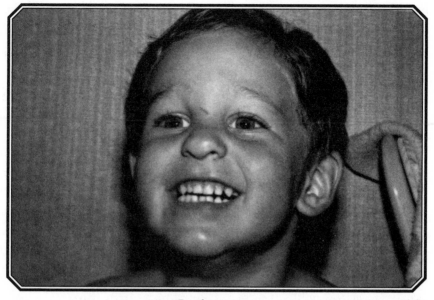

Derek, age two.

for my mom and dad in the stands," Derek wrote 20 years later, in notes he recorded about his childhood.

"And of course I still do it in the NHL," he added in parentheses.

As he grew older, recognition came with a subtle nod. But at five, it came with a giant grin and a wild wave, like someone flagging a passing car. The puck was at the other end of the ice, but it did not matter. Derek saw his father. He saw his mother, pregnant with a little girl, and his two younger brothers, Ryan and Aaron Nicholas, propped onto the bleachers in little bundles.

Derek smiled. He waved. His parents waved back, returning the enthusiasm exponentially, then shooing the boy to turn the other way and chase the puck.

They were all there when Derek scored his first goal, sweeping the puck with his long stick past the goalie burdened by padding. It hardly mattered that the goal came against Derek's own team. The family cheered and laughed.

Hockey was something to do, something that nearly all the little boys and a growing number of little girls did, and Derek, in that respect, was no different than the rest. He was just like everyone else. That is why Derek liked it.

ON A MAP, Saskatchewan is a vertical rectangle, about twice as tall as it is wide, the shape a child might make when asked to draw a big building. It stretches about 750 miles north from the American border and is narrower near the top, along the 60th parallel, because the curve of the Earth bends the longitudinal lines together as they extend toward the poles.

If Saskatchewan were part of the United States, it would be the third-largest state—smaller than Texas, bigger than California. But Saskatchewan's million residents represent only about one thirty-eighth of California's population. The northern half of the province is a wrinkled carpet of forests and large lakes. Its towns are mostly outposts, and paved roads are few. So are people. The center of gravity lies in the southern half, where Saskatoon and Regina, the provincial capital, each have a population around 200,000. The surrounding landscape is smoothed improbably flat by long-receded glaciers and left sprinkled with shallow lakes. In the short summers, dry land is consumed mostly by grain-covered fields—canary-yellow stripes of canola, ocean-blue swatches of flax. Mostly, though, there is wheat.

"The Lord said, 'Let there be wheat,' and Saskatchewan was born," Canadian humorist Stephen Leacock wrote nearly a century ago.

Saskatchewan's southern half is not unlike the Great Plains states of the American Midwest, dotted with small towns connected by two-lane roads that frame, in straight lines, endless stretches of farms and ranches. The difference with Saskatchewan, though, is its scale, as if it were smoothed and stretched with a rolling pin. On a clear day, a familiar joke goes in Saskatchewan, you can see the back of your own head.

The elastic geography is mirrored by a quiet tolerance of extremes. The hottest temperature ever recorded in Canada was in Saskatchewan, yet temperatures throughout the province in winter can be stuck below freezing for weeks at a time. Tornadoes are a summertime concern, and the cold wind blowing eastward off the Canadian Rockies in Alberta, with nothing to slow it for thousands of miles, is a wintertime torment.

Most corners feel like the edge of nowhere. By some accounts, a town has made it when it gets a stoplight or, perhaps more usefully, a Tim Hortons, the ubiquitous coffee-and-donut chain started by and named for a hockey player who died in a car crash during his 24th season in the National Hockey League.

By sheer numbers, Saskatchewan does not produce the most NHL players. That is Ontario, by a large margin. By style, Saskatchewan does not produce the most talented playmakers, the smoothest skaters, or the biggest stars. But it does, with little argument, produce the toughest players—if not more than any other province, certainly the most per capita. Nearly any credible list of the fiercest, scrappiest players in hockey history will include a broad sample of Saskatchewan natives, from Eddie Shore to Dave "The Hammer" Schultz, Clark Gillies to Dave "Tiger" Williams, Joey Kocur to Wendel Clark, Theo Fleury to Dave Manson.

None of them played professionally in Saskatchewan, because the province has never had an NHL team. The closest are hundreds of miles away—in Winnipeg to the east and Calgary and Edmonton to the west. But that does not mean that Saskatchewan culture does not revolve largely around hockey. It simply means that culture revolves largely around children playing hockey—"minor hockey," in Canadian parlance.

That is why Len and Joanne placed young Derek into hockey

programs, why they spent countless hours in chilly rinks sitting on wooden benches or standing on concrete floors, why they spent their money on hand-me-down equipment and registration fees, and why they spent their vacation budgets on long driving trips to attend hockey tournaments. They did everything they could to acclimate their children into the local culture—especially Derek.

"We just wanted him to be happy," Joanne said.

Like youth and high-school football in Texas or Nebraska, minor hockey in Saskatchewan sets the rhythm of the seasons as much as the planting and harvesting of the fields. Civic life in Saskatchewan, as in much of Canada, is not centered on schools or shopping malls, but the local rink. Hockey allows small communities and extended families to convene on pale, cold weekend days and dark, frozen weekday nights.

"The winters of my childhood were long, long seasons," reads a portion of Roch Carrier's short story "The Hockey Sweater," an excerpt of which was included on the back of the Canadian five-dollar bill for many years. "We lived in three places—the school, the church and the skating rink—but our real life was on the skating rink."

It was at one of those rinks, when Derek was five, that Len, his family new to the area, found himself seated in the bleachers behind a few other parents. Two women talked about the team roster and pointed out their sons. One pointed to the unknown boy with the big frame, taller than the rest.

"He's the worst player on the team," she said.

Len's mind, like that of any good cop, captured details and filed them in a mental vault. He never forgot the way the mother said it and the way she pointed at Derek. He always wondered: Whatever happened to her little boy? Whatever happened to all the other little boys on the ice that day?

Hockey was a unit of measurement in Canada, and few grew as big as Derek.

. . .

THE FIRST RCMP assignment was in Hanley, a blip of a farming town bypassed by time and Provincial Highway 11, just to the east. Few cars that traveled the 160 miles between Regina and Saskatoon found time or reason to exit. The Canadian National Railway still made routine stops, though, and empty cars were loaded with wheat and other grains harvested from the surrounding prairie.

The detachment, with six officers, was responsible for a vast area measuring roughly 1,000 square miles. It was the first place that Len saw tumbleweeds, which he thought existed only in John Wayne movies. The patrol cars had no air conditioning, so the summer was spent speeding along the two-lane roads with the windows down—something said to cause hearing loss in the left ears of rural RCMP members.

During his first winter there, Len found the town had no snow-plow, instead using an open-cab tractor that dragged three large tires behind it. Working an overnight shift, Len parked his patrol car along the highway. Nearly an hour went by before he saw another car. Finally, the crystals in the freezing air, like a million tiny, float-ing mirrors, reflected the headlights of a car still on the far side of the horizon. Len waited. The crystals sparkled. Eventually, the car emerged over the edge of the earth and moved almost imperceptibly toward Len. It took several more minutes before it reached him and passed, trailing only darkness.

My god, Len thought, this place is flat.

His first major investigation centered on the death of a university professor. A stolen car had broken down along Highway 11. The thieves used a teenaged girl in their group as a hitchhiking lure for another. The professor picked her up and was jumped by the others. They drove his car into a field, threw him out, and ran him over.

Len was called to the scene to investigate the homicide. He

attended the autopsy and was responsible for the court exhibits. All in the group were convicted. Len was hooked.

Len and Joanne lived in a second-floor apartment above the bank in downtown Hanley. When Joanne went into labor, they rushed to Saskatoon City Hospital.

And on those days and nights when Derek would not stop crying, and an exhausted Joanne was at her wit's end trying to keep him quiet, Len took the infant seat from the family car and strapped it into his police cruiser. He drove up and down the lonesome highway. It never failed to soothe Derek, at any age.

THE ROYAL CANADIAN MOUNTED POLICE was a sprawling government agency, headquartered in Ottawa. It had roughly 30,000 employees across the country, from street cops to white-collar bureaucrats. Its duties included protecting the country from large-scale threats linked to terrorism, organized crime, drugs, and counterfeiting. But the RCMP also was a national police force that provided policing to all of the provinces except Ontario and Quebec, three territories, 200 Aboriginal communities, and all but the largest cities.

Small towns in places like Saskatchewan did not have their own police departments. They had an outpost of ever-changing RCMP members. To Canadians, they were ordinary cops blended into the background of daily life. Americans were more likely to call them "Mounties," and picture them atop horses and looking like Dudley Do-Right, the befuddled and cheerful cartoon character.

Do-Right was usually drawn wearing the RCMP dress uniform, the "red serge," including the heavy wool red coat, knickers-length pants with a yellow vertical stripe, black leather riding boots, and brown, flat-brimmed hat that Americans might compare to one worn by a national-park ranger. That was the ceremonial uniform, and what Len wore to his wedding. RCMP members on duty typically looked more like a standard police officer seen in other countries— hard-brimmed cap, light-blue shirt, shiny black shoes, and the telling yellow-striped pants.

Recruits, after being vetted through an application process (and, beginning in 1974, including women), were assigned to a 32-person troop and spent 24 weeks in basic training at Depot Division. Their rigorous schedule included physical training, classroom study, field exercises, and, at noon every day, marching on the parade ground in front of the chapel.

When they graduated, they were assigned to someplace, any-place, in the country. Typically, they began in a small, rural town and worked their way toward the cities. Postings were temporary, and the RCMP tried to shuffle members every three to five years. The fear was both burnout and familiarity. Too much time in a small town allowed members and their families to grow close to residents. Rela-tionships might taint a critical sense of objectivity and fairness. The side effect was that police officers were perpetual outsiders, especially in the smallest towns, seen as agents of government with little appre-ciation for the machination of a town's unique structure, rhythm, and values. They were a necessary part of civic life, their oversight appreciated by most, but rarely did RCMP members weave them-selves deeply into a community's social fabric.

It could make investigations difficult, as Len found when wit-nesses stonewalled to protect people they knew. Simple traffic stops could be spun into coffee-shop gossip. Conversations sometimes stopped when Len walked in.

Finding close friends proved difficult for the Boogaards, even with a growing brood of children who might otherwise serve as conduits to lasting relationships. Some parents simply did not want their children hanging around the family of the town police officer, whether because they knew that the Boogaards would soon be on the move again or for reasons having to do with distrust and small-town politics.

Len and Joanne quickly recognized the trickle-down effects of nomadic police work. Len liked his job, but did not love what it was doing for his family. And he was never crazy about Saskatchewan, which he considered rural and unrefined compared to places like Toronto and Vancouver.

So before Len could be reassigned to his next posting, and now with two young boys, he again followed the lead of his brother Bill, leaving the RCMP for the York Regional Police in Ontario, north of Toronto. It was close to Len's parents, and one of Joanne's sisters lived in the vicinity, too. Ontario was where Aaron was born in August 1986 and Krysten was born in February 1988. It was where five-year-old Derek played hockey for the first time.

But the move did not bring the Boogaards the serenity they anticipated. Len's 12-hour shifts and hour-long commute in each direction kept him from home. The suburbs of Toronto were more expensive than what the family was used to in Saskatchewan, and Joanne, with four children under the age of six, had no time to work.

Len reconsidered his career after three years in Ontario. He missed the relative independence of the RCMP—the freedom to structure shifts the way he wanted, to investigate cases from start to finish. With the York police department, he felt confined by the regimen. There were uniform inspections. He had to log every action and record all the miles he drove in the car, making note of any scratch to its paint. He was told what area to patrol, which streets not to cross. Even if he was the first responder to a crime, he usually handed his notes to an investigator who took on the case. He felt suffocated by the bureaucracy. The RCMP gave you a car, they gave you a gun, and they trusted you with them.

Besides, Joanne missed home on the prairie. The Boogaards convinced themselves that their children would be better off growing up in western Canada, after all.

Len rejoined the RCMP in the summer of 1988. And just as his oldest child, Derek, was to start first grade, Len's first posting in his second tour was in another tiny town on the plains of southern Saskatchewan.

THE TRANS-CANADA HIGHWAY spans nearly 5,000 miles from St. John's, Newfoundland, in the east to Victoria, British Columbia, in the west, making it the longest national highway in the world. The barren 500-mile stretch across the prairie in southern Saskatchewan and Alberta, between Regina and Calgary, is among the most desolate of all. The windblown road strings together a series of midsized hubs, most more than 100 miles from the next, whose compounded names are synonymous with tough-minded, no-nonsense junior hockey: Moose Jaw; Swift Current; Medicine Hat.

Herbert, Saskatchewan, population 700, sat at a rare bend in the road, on the north side of the highway and across the railroad tracks that loosely paralleled it. Its rectangular grid measured about 10 blocks in one direction and five blocks in the other. There were a few stores, a post office, and a school. On the north side, on a plateau above a string of small lakes, there was a white, aluminum-sided hockey rink, where Derek played for the Herbert Hawks, clad in maroon.

Like many small towns dotting the prairie, Herbert was founded after the Canadian government, in 1903, opened up much of its land to settlement, calling southern Saskatchewan the "World's Choicest Wheat Lands." Many of those who rushed into the Herbert area early in the 20th century were Mennonites, particularly Russian-German

Mennonites who had homesteaded first in Manitoba or the northern United States. Decades later, when the Boogaards arrived, Mennonite roots in Herbert were thinned but deep.

The Boogaards bought a house in the middle of a block on the south side of town. Neighbors took a fondness to Joanne, with her sweet manner and her hands full with four rambunctious children. They did not know what to make of Len, with his brusque temperament. Whether by design or disposition, he rarely socialized, and when neighbors saw him outside of his police work, it was often at the rink, standing silently alone and occasionally shouting orders at his children.

Len soon found something amiss in Herbert. A couple members of the Mennonite congregation came to the police, concerned about a youth minister's relationships with young boys. As the RCMP investigated, immigration officials found that the man was a former American Marine convicted and discharged in a child-molestation case. Immigration officials issued a warrant. Len made the arrest.

Some disbelieving church members objected. A few filed complaints against Len in an attempt to discredit him, saying they had spotted him in his police car not wearing his seat belt or that he illegally towed his kids behind a snowmobile. The RCMP dismissed those complaints. But the harassment extended beyond Len. As the Boogaard children got older, they regularly learned at school that their father had arrested or cited someone in a classmate's family, or had embarked on an investigation that threatened reputations and the local social order. The aggrieved could not reasonably take out their frustration on Len. It was the Boogaard children, particularly Derek, who most often felt the brunt of resentment, manifested in slights from both children and adults.

"It was kind of tough growing up for our family because we moved around, and it was hard I think because my dad was a police officer," Derek wrote as an adult, his notes sprinkled with misspelled words. "Not so much as from the ages of 6–12 because us kids didn't see it yet. Make a long story short, the first year my dad got on a case when we were in Herbert SK. It is a very religious town. Found out something about the prist [sic] and had to deport him back to wherever he came from. The town kinda resented us and this was the first year we were there."

Among the four Boogaard children, assimilation problems were starkest for Derek. He stood out for his size, the biggest student in class. People mistook him for a much older boy, and expected that he act like one, too. But he was easily distracted and occasionally disruptive, and when trouble arose in the classroom or the playground, children were quick to point to big, clumsy Derek, who had few friends to back his side of the story.

Joanne, knowing Derek had few friends, invited every child in Derek's class to his summertime birthday parties, hoping at least some of them would come. The first-grade party had a dinosaur theme and only a couple of children.

Many teachers considered Derek to be a bully, and they were not surprised. His father, after all, was the gruff new RCMP member.

"Do you know who my father is?" a defiant Derek asked his teacher on at least one occasion.

In fourth grade, he was relegated to a closet in the back of the classroom, the walls acting as blinders to keep him focused straight ahead.

Derek's report cards were filled with low grades and comments from teachers who gingerly informed the Boogaards of his classroom troubles. One grade-school teacher called Derek "challenging" and said he "is capable of doing much better." But Derek "is very hard on himself and gives up very quickly."

At times, the teacher wrote, Derek could be a good team player. But "when things don't go well, he can display poor team spirit and sportsmanship."

The Boogaards got Derek a tutor and had him repeat a year in grade school. While it helped Derek catch up academically, it further stigmatized him. His size stood out even more among his younger classmates.

The Boogaards compensated by encouraging Derek to play hockey and join the swim team, where friendships could be formed away from the confining caste system of school.

"My team was called the Herbert Hawks," Derek wrote. "We had maroon jerseys & socks with white lettering saying Herbert across them. I'm pretty sure I started out with the number 42 in Herbert."

Joanne provided an escape by taking the children to a sister's cabin on a lake, where Derek swam and an uncle taught him to hunt. Len took Derek away by letting the boy ride along in the patrol car.

Soon, though, the RCMP said it was time to move again. And the Boogaards, with four children between the ages of five and 11, were happy to go.

IT WAS 1993, the summer that Derek turned 11, that the Boogaards moved 300 miles northeast to a town called Melfort. With about 5,000 residents, it was a metropolis compared to the earlier places that Len was assigned.

The family house was at 316 Churchill Drive, a U-shaped lane off Brunswick Street. It faced south, into the low winter sun, and its blond-brick facade was framed by two tall spruce trees. Len planted a basketball hoop into concrete on one side of the driveway.

The Boogaards filled the space inside with numbers and volume. As the children grew, the square footage of the home seemed to shrink, and the kitchen table got smaller when surrounded by six Boogaards. The basement was a refuge, filled with boys playing video games or wrestling on the floor. More and more, they tumbled out the doors and into the yard.

The neighborhood was filled with split-level houses, most with one-car garages. A hockey goal in the driveway marked where children lived. Across Brunswick Street sat a wide, open park, and in the middle of the park was a massive grass-covered mound, taller than any house. In winter, children sledded down in every direction.

The summit provided views of the strikingly flat surroundings. In all directions, the horizon was a tease. The tallest structures to puncture the landscape were a water tower, a grain silo, and a pair of brick apartment buildings on the north edge of town, not far from the police station where Len worked. Tract houses at Melfort's boundaries seeped into empty fields that stretched to the far edge of the sky.

Melfort had a few traffic lights, mostly along the two-lane highway lined with a jumble of motels, gas stations, and restaurants. At the corner of Manitoba Street and Stovel Avenue was the Main Arena. It was sided with pea-green aluminum and had a painted-white cinderblock facade. The arched roof displayed the year it was built: 1931.

"Again, the same stuff happened as in Herbert," Derek wrote in his notes years later. "They picked on the new kid."

The first nemesis was a boy named Evan Folden. He and Derek met on a soccer field, and Folden, a year older, took an instant dislike to the hulking stranger. There were a few mocking taunts. A crowd gathered. Finally, the intensity led to a wrestling match and a few wild swings. Folden emerged with a bloody nose.

He was cleaning himself off in the school bathroom when Derek walked in. He, too, had a bloody nose, but Folden hadn't caused it. It had come at the fist of an older girl. She had stood up for Folden and repaid Derek's punch with a spot-on punch of her own.

Folden would become a friend and hockey teammate, but not

before more scuffling. A wintertime snowball fight got ugly when Derek drilled Folden in the face from close range. Folden charged. Derek's nose streamed blood into the cold air. He came home with his jacket torn.

Derek was viewed as a litmus test of toughness for other boys, particularly older ones, who saw in him an oversized kid with glasses—a physically imposing, meek-minded target. Some nicknamed him "Stupidgaard." Even the friends of Derek's brother Ryan, sometimes two grades younger, would come over and pile on Derek, as if he were a piece of playground equipment or an oversized family dog.

Derek quietly suffered the indignities of his size. His knees ached as a teenager because of the growth spurts. He was diagnosed with Osgood-Schlatter disease, a condition in which the cartilage at the end of the large leg bones swells to the point of pain. Derek wore braces on his legs during bouts of debilitating discomfort.

In the pool, young children hung from him like a float toy. In the rink, rivets attaching the blades to the boots of his hockey skates constantly gave way under his weight.

Amid a rough-and-tumble childhood, the boys took to "cage raging." They wore hockey equipment and fought, imitating the toughest enforcers of the time—people like Bob Probert, Rob Ray, and Tie Domi.

"It's where you put your gloves and helmet on and just go at it like a hockey fight and the loser is the one on the ground," Derek wrote. "This is where you kinda learn how to punch."

Derek rarely considered repercussions. He once moved a friend's trampoline close to the garage, climbed to the roof, and—encouraged by other teens—belly flopped onto the canvas. The springs broke and the frame collapsed. Derek hit the ground with a thud, bruising his ribs. Another time, he rode a sled down a mound and into the street, in front of a passing police car. The young female officer, Jody Vail, knew that he was the son of another RCMP member, the one who was training her. She lectured Derek about safety and the importance of making sound decisions.

Somewhat inadvertently, Derek found refuge straddling school cliques while not succumbing to any of them. He was goofy enough, crazy enough, to be entertaining. He was mild-mannered enough, self-deprecating enough, to be endearing. It got him by.

He meshed with the jocks because of his hockey stature. Derek was never the best player on his team, but he was always the biggest. For most of his childhood, that was enough to earn him a perennial roster spot on the top-level teams in town. But Derek also glided into the outcast world of the skateboarders, a clique called the "skids."

"The girls were even attracted to the skids," Derek later wrote. "Luckily for me, I was friends with both sides."

Hockey was the constant, and while his parents did not force it upon Derek, they encouraged it. It was good for him, they thought. It provided structure. It instilled discipline. It occupied his free time and surrounded him with friends. It supplied him with coaches who could serve as mentors.

As much as anything, though, it connected him with family. The Boogaards were leery of outside forces on their vulnerable son. And Derek appreciated the cocoon that the combination of hockey and family provided.

"I think the best part of playing hockey from ages 3 until 16 was the little road trips with dad," Derek wrote years later.

AT ABOUT SIX FEET, Len was not a particularly tall man—all four of his children eventually grew taller them him, apparently inheriting height from their mother—but he was sturdy and broad-shouldered. He expected discipline from his children, and the threat of his temper was the concealed weapon that kept them in line. Derek both loved and feared his father.

Len's mustache and steely eyes seemed a disguise for his feelings. The inflection of his voice was as steady as a bass drum, and he was fluent in the languages of inquiry and sarcasm. It all made it difficult to decipher his thoughts. Even the most mundane interactions felt part of a silent, internal investigation.

But Len had a playful side, revealed only to some. And Derek came to appreciate, and emulate, his father's dark sense of humor.

Derek gleefully sat in the front seat of the police cruiser and watched as his father pulled drivers over and wrote traffic tickets. He wanted to hear all of his father's stories. Some of them, like the one about the man whose excuse for not wearing his seat belt was that he had "anal seizures," became family chestnuts, told over and over.

Derek also liked the story of Len coming to the scene of a large deer that had been struck by a car, its hind legs broken, but still alive. Len removed his standard-issue .38 revolver and shot the deer in the back of the head. It dropped instantly. On his next pass down the highway, Len saw the same deer, a stain of blood on its head, standing as if nothing was wrong. Flabbergasted, Len stopped and shot it again, with a different gun. Derek, unable to control his laughter, asked to have the story told again and again.

Those stories of adventure—the pursuit of bad guys, the unpredictable bursts of action—made Derek think he might like to become a cop someday, too, as long as he could bypass all the tedious paperwork. That was too much like school.

As much as Len's vocation threw up hurdles to acceptance for Derek, there was a measure of prestige in having a police officer as a father. Joanne was the prototypical hockey mom, and most of Derek's friends had one like her, too—shuttling children to practices in the Ford Aerostar and making meals and providing heavy doses of hugs and understanding. But none of his friends had a cop for a dad.

Sometimes, Len came straight from work and drove the boys and their friends in a police cruiser, often all the way to Saskatoon,

Len Boogaard with his sons: Aaron (in arms),
Ryan (center), and Derek (right).

about two hours away, or any of the small towns that interrupted the landscape.

"I don't know how many times my dad got in trouble taking us to hockey in the cop cars but I [sic] was awesome and I [sic] so happy and thankful that he cared enough to get yelled at from his boss just to see his kids enjoying a sport," Derek remembered.

When the car was full, Derek sat up front while his teammates sat in back. Usually, he crowded in back with the others. And when the boys grew too wild, Len would get their attention by pointing out something on the broad fields of nothingness.

"Look!" he screamed.

Wide-eyed faces spun forward. Len stomped on the brakes, smashing the smiles into the clear acrylic partition that divided the front seat from the back. The boys collapsed in laughter.

There were plenty of times, though, that it was just Len and Derek in the car. With towns spread across the countryside, quilted together by threads of two-lane roads, driving long distances was as much a part of childhood as family dinners and sibling spats. They stopped for after-school candy bars and Slurpees on the way out of town. They filled their bellies after the game with rink burgers, the cheap staple of Canadian hockey rinks.

"I would eat my food as fast as I could so I couldn't feel the cold right when we got in the car," Derek wrote.

Sometimes, watching from his usual vantage point, standing alone at the end of the rink, Len recognized that Derek needed a postgame boost. Derek had heard the teases of opposing players or fans, or he had received little ice time and been chided by coaches. Maybe Derek was injured or had had the rivets of another skate buckle and pop under his weight. On these occasions, Len would pull into an icy abandoned parking lot and spin the police car into a dizzying series of donuts. Or he would pull alongside a pasture and moo at the cows through the car's loudspeaker.

There was never much talking, because neither Len nor Derek minded long silences, but there was comfort in close company. The radio on the way home would pick up the signal from some radio tower far over the horizon, relaying games of the Toronto Maple Leafs. Or it would be set to the station broadcasting the games of the Melfort Mustangs of the Saskatchewan Junior Hockey League. Inevitably, Derek would doze off to the sound of hockey and the hum of the highway. And he would awaken only when the car turned left into the driveway on Churchill Drive and the glowing light from the garage door opener shone brightly and the car's windshield nudged the fuzzy tennis ball hanging from the ceiling, telling the Boogaards that they had arrived and that a warm house full of family waited inside.

· · ·

IN MINOR HOCKEY, size mattered. Derek usually found himself on the top-level team. The smallest kids had to prove that they belonged. The biggest kids had to show that they did not.

Derek was never the most talented player on his minor hockey teams—if talent was defined by the usual metrics of goals and puck control, shiftiness and speed. While he could build speed with his long strides, he had none of the nimbleness needed in the quick-changing flow of hockey games. His knees sore from growth spurts, he was awkward, like a newborn foal. One coach called him a baby giraffe on skates. Opposing players avoided him because of his size, but opposing coaches often countered his presence with a speedy lineup that could exploit Derek's slower pace.

Derek usually played defense, a big obstacle planted in front of the goal to gum up the opponents' offense. When he was young, he rarely went out of his way to knock down other players on the ice. They usually just skated into him unintentionally and fell, losers in a physics equation.

There were always whispers. Len and Joanne saw the head shakes and the nudges. They overheard the after-practice conversations between concerned parents and youth coaches. They were adept in the art of deciphering what others thought of their son.

"I remember some parents complaining about the way I played," Derek wrote years later. "They would complain about the penelties [sic] I took and said I should have never made any of the 'AA' teams. So it was a struggle mentally hearing that stuff."

Derek idolized Wendel Clark and Doug Gilmour, who spent several seasons in the early 1990s as teammates with the Toronto Maple Leafs. Neither man was six feet tall or weighed 200 pounds, and both were dependable scorers. But they had reputations for fearlessness and—especially so in Clark's case—a willingness to dole out big checks and fight in the name of defending teammates.

Clark grew up in Kelvington, Saskatchewan, a tiny town a couple of hours south of Melfort. He was a provincial hero, chosen by the Maple Leafs with the first-overall choice of the 1985 NHL draft. He spent 13 of his 15 NHL seasons in Toronto, serving as captain in the early 1990s. And while he scored 330 goals in 793 games, he was assessed 1,690 penalty minutes, many of them in five-minute increments for fighting.

Gilmour, from Kingston, Ontario, was drafted in 1982, in the seventh round, by the St. Louis Blues. In 1992–93, when Derek was 10, Gilmour played for Toronto and scored a career-high 127 points. He also had 100 penalty minutes that season, one of the highest totals on the team. For two summers, the Boogaards sent Derek to Toronto for a week to attend Gilmour's youth hockey camp. Derek returned with stories about Gilmour—Doug Gilmour!—skating on the ice with the kids.

In eighth grade, Derek received an assignment asking students how they planned to make a living. He wrote that he wanted to play in the NHL with Wendel Clark and Doug Gilmour. The teacher asked Derek for a backup plan. "I don't have a backup plan," Derek remembered telling the teacher in the notes he later wrote. "And I'm going to play in the NHL one day!"

He spent three days in detention.

Derek had his immediate sights set on the Western Hockey League, the top-level junior hockey league for boys 16 and over, considered the ultimate destination for young players in western Canada. It was one of three major-junior leagues in Canada, along with the Ontario Hockey League and the Quebec Major Junior Hockey League. They were considered the sturdiest stepping-stones to professional hockey, though most never make it that far.

Teams in the WHL could draft players the year that they turned 15. Derek was constantly reminded that size could not be taught, and he thought he might be selected if he had a good season. There might be a team willing to take a chance on a kid with size.

In the fall of 1996, Derek arrived for tryouts for Melfort's bantam-level teams, for boys who turned 14 that year. For the first time, Derek did not make the top-level team. He was relegated to Melfort's "A" team rather than the higher-caliber "AA" squad.

Derek was surprised and upset. He played on the second-tier team, but groused about playing time and complained about treatment from coaches. Interest in the sport ebbed. He was skateboarding and snowboarding and melding into a new circle of non-hockey-playing friends.

Suitably distracted, frustrated by his prospects, Derek quit hockey. His younger brothers, Ryan and Aaron, followed his lead. They, too, would have more free time, that cherished teenage commodity. No hockey practices, no games, no long drives after school and return drives late at night. For Derek, at 14, there was no greater pleasure than freedom from authority and hard work.

Len and Joanne did not try to talk Derek into playing again. They knew hockey was a childhood diversion and would end sometime. There was zero expectation of it becoming a career. And if Derek wasn't good enough to play on Melfort's top team, then it was obvious that the end was coming sooner rather than later.

That spring, in 1997, the Western Hockey League's 18 franchises, from Portland, Oregon, to Brandon, Manitoba, including the Saskatchewan cities of Moose Jaw, Regina, and Saskatoon, took turns stocking their future teams.

Predicting talent at such an early age is a fickle business. Of the 18 boys chosen in the first round, about half eventually played some level of professional hockey. Four reached the NHL. The first player chosen, a boy from Yorkton, Saskatchewan, named Jarrett Stoll, was selected by Edmonton. Five years later, he embarked on an NHL career as a center that would last more than a decade.

A boy from Melfort, Jason Armstrong, was chosen in the third round, 53rd overall. He never reached major-junior hockey and became a farmer.

There were 195 boys chosen in the draft. Derek was not one of them.

THE TIMING OF Floyd Halcro's call was perfect. A small man with a baritone voice and a bushy mustache, Halcro was taking over the Melfort Bantam AA team that fall. He had a son on the team. And he was friends with Len.

By summer, Derek's latest growth spurt pushed the 15-year-old to six feet, four inches and 210 pounds. The tedium of the long days, the thoughts of another school year of struggle, made Derek consider what he wanted to do with his life. With a 65 average in ninth grade, he knew he would not go to college. Maybe he would become a cop, like his father. Maybe join the military. Maybe work the oil fields across the prairie. There was good money in that, Derek had heard.

Halcro, though, thought Derek had long-range hockey potential, given the combination of his size and skating stride. He saw that hockey became more physical the older the boys got, and that someone like Derek might be handy as an on-ice bodyguard. Besides, he liked Derek and knew that the Boogaards worried for him.

Halcro told Derek he could audition for the AA team. He told him that he thought his size was a benefit, not a curse, and that his other skills were underestimated. Derek was rejuvenated with confidence and direction.

Halcro, Len, and Brian Folden, Evan's father, took turns shuttling their sons to Saskatoon for "acceleration" workouts several times a week. At a gym, the boys used treadmill-like machines to improve their leg strength and skating strides.

But Len knew what Derek's role would be on the ice. Almost every teenager in hockey would find himself in a fight, sooner or later. And Derek's size meant he would be expected to do so, to step in to protect his teammates. It also meant that other teams would test his toughness. And if Derek was going to fight, Len was going to be sure he was prepared for it. He found a gym in Saskatoon and registered Derek for boxing lessons, too.

It was a cramped place on the upper floor of an old warehouse near downtown. The trainer was a weathered old man with gold chains around his neck and gold rings on his fingers. He told Derek he could turn him into a boxer.

"I'm not here to be a boxer," Derek said. "I just wanna learn how to punch on skates."

There was more money in boxing than in hockey, the man said.

"I want to try the hockey thing first," Derek told him.

Between skating workouts and boxing lessons, the 100-mile trips to and from Saskatoon became a metronome to daily life. Derek lifted weights. He ran down gravel roads outside Melfort while Len trailed behind him in the car. Some days, Derek rode his bike alone toward Saskatoon. Len gave him a 30-minute head start to see how far Derek got.

"My dad was pretty much my trainer that summer," Derek wrote.

Like taffy, Derek grew taller and thinner, and the chubbiness that he carried with him as a child melted away. In pictures, his head still popped high above those of classmates and teammates, but the roundness of his face was gone.

After training camp, Halcro put Derek on the season roster. He dismissed the calls from other parents saying that Derek, that son of a cop, did not deserve a spot on the town's top team, that he was not only a danger to others but an obstacle to the success and promising future of boys of their own.

"I'll take who I want on the team," Halcro told the naysayers. "If somebody is going to go somewhere, this kid will do it."

Until boys reached junior at age 16, fighting was met with stiff penalties, usually suspensions. But body-to-body checking was part of the game at the bantam level, and Derek could serve as a deterrent to opponents wanting to charge the star players. Checks escalated into skirmishes. Teams, imitating those from major junior on up to the professional ranks, stocked themselves with a bruiser or two.

Derek's size often worked against him. When boys collided, the bigger one was usually whistled, and opponents learned to coax Derek into penalties to gain a man advantage. Halcro heard the taunts from other players, coaches, and fans. He heard the laughs when Derek fell clumsily. He heard the jeers when Derek knocked someone down. If only they knew the boy, he thought to himself. A meek, quiet boy, without a malicious bone in his body. A boy who wanted to protect his friends, not hurt others, who liked to fend off trouble before it started.

Derek occasionally came to Halcro with confidential news: some teammates were drinking or using drugs. Halcro, wanting both to keep his team intact and steer the teenaged boys from trouble, intervened. He never revealed that Derek was his source.

During a game at a tournament in Prince Albert, Halcro became upset with officials, and his caustic tongue got him ejected. He was still steaming when the tournament ended late that night and he, his son, Len, and Derek headed to the rink parking lot for the drive home. Halcro started the engine and began clearing snow from his red four-door Ford truck. Nearby, two officials, lacking a brush, cleaned the snow off their car with their hands. Halcro offered his brush. The officials sensed sarcasm, and an argument ensued over the best place to stick the brush.

Len stepped out of the truck and stopped one of the officials headed toward Halcro. Halcro was willing to take on the other. But Derek unfolded himself from the back seat and emerged to slide between them.

"Floyd, he's not worth it," Derek said as he tugged Halcro back to the car.

AMONG THE ARMY of scouts who crossed the prairies in the dead of winter, looking for teenaged hockey talent in forlorn rinks in small towns linked by snow-swept highways, Melfort was never a favorite stop. There were only a couple of passable restaurants, one of them the Italian place in the strip mall. There wasn't even a Tim Hortons back then. The Travelodge, where the CanAm Highway from Regina makes a hard left on its way to Prince Albert, was the only decent place to stay.

Old Main Arena was an outdated barn, not a great place to see a game. The ceiling, about 20 feet up, was lined by fluorescent lights. Electric heaters, with coils that turned a fiery orange when hot, hung from the ceiling and pointed toward the three rows of wooden bleachers. There was a small foyer where people milled about or bought hot cocoa from the snack stand. The dressing rooms were nothing but painted concrete-block walls embedded with steel hooks to hang gear.

By then, Main Arena was Melfort's secondary rink. The Northern Lights Palace, with seating for 1,800 and an indoor swimming pool, with individual stalls in the dressing rooms and seat backs in the stands, had been built a block away, on the other side of Melfort's curling club.

The new arena was home to the Melfort Mustangs, part of the Saskatchewan Junior Hockey League, a tier below the major-junior Western Hockey League. The Mustangs had won the league championship in 1992 and 1996. They sometimes played in front of more than 1,000 fans. Their games were broadcast on the local radio station, its signal uninterrupted for miles and miles across the plains.

Derek's team, the bantam-level Mustangs, sometimes practiced and played at Northern Lights. But on this particular night, an especially cold one in southern Saskatchewan, the team was at Main Arena. The heaters glowed orange. A few dozen people huddled beneath them. Len, in his police uniform, stood alone behind the boards at one end of the rink.

About a dozen WHL scouts sat in a loose cluster on one side. Among them were two men representing the Regina Pats: Brent Parker and Todd Ripplinger.

Parker was the team's general manager, a measured man who had grown up around minor-league sports. Parker's father had owned and operated teams for years, including a AAA baseball team in Calgary and a minor-league hockey team in Kansas City. When the Regina Pats, founded in 1917 and considered the oldest major-junior team in the world, were for sale in 1995, the WHL asked the Parkers to buy them. Brent was named general manager.

Ripplinger was the director of scouting. A Regina native, he had been a WHL scout for years for the Kamloops Blazers before Parker hired him to stock the hometown team. Ripplinger—"Ripper"— was a bundle of fast-talking energy who spent winters cruising the vast frozen spaces of the Prairie provinces chasing rumors of teenaged hockey players among the dim rinks in desolate towns. No matter the season, his ruddy complexion gave Ripplinger the look of someone who had just come in from the cold.

Parker and Ripplinger had been at a tournament in Prince Albert, about 90 minutes away. Ripplinger wanted to detour through Melfort to see a couple of young players on his list. The other scouts, he could be sure, were there to watch the same boys. None of them were there to watch Derek.

Things did not go well for the home team. North Battleford built a 7–2 lead in the third period, and the game's tenor straddled the faint line between aggressive and cheap.

Parker, Ripplinger, and the other scouts could not help but notice a tall, gangly defenseman on the Melfort team. His hockey shorts were noticeably short and his arms seemed to hang to his knees. He spent shifts knocking down opposing players with his combination of momentum and menace.

At one point, the Melfort goalie, Brett Condy, dropped and controlled a loose puck. A North Battleford player poked under Condy with his stick. The whistle blew. Derek, coming to Condy's defense, roughly grabbed the opponent and shoved him hard. Other players converged in a familiar post-whistle hockey scrum of grabs and insults.

But this one was different. Nudges turned to shoves, which turned into punches. It quickly got out of control, like a bar fight. The boys began pounding on one another, their sticks and gloves littering the ice in front of the goal. Officials were overmatched. Fans stood.

"So I pulled a guy outta the pile and kicked the shit outta him," Derek recalled years later.

He pummeled one boy and was ready to take on others. Officials scrambled to restore order, but it was like helplessly stomping out a spreading brush fire. They peeled boys from the tempest, but there were more boys than officials. They were only a few years older and certainly smaller than Derek, at the center of the chaos.

Eventually, the fire burned itself out, and officials pulled Derek away and escorted him toward the penalty box. An opposing player barked something from the bench that caught Derek's attention and relit his fuse. He broke free of the clutches of officials and rushed the visitors' bench. He clambered inside, his arms swinging wildly. Like spooked cats, players escaped over the wall and through the gates at each end of the bench. Even the opposing coach backed away from the one-man siege.

"It felt like I had a force feild [sic] on me cause that team just scurried as far back as they could," Derek remembered.

In the stands, the scouts stood dumbstruck, jaws unhinged. Opposing parents shouted at the teenaged monster. A group of older boys from the high school cheered wildly. Joanne Boogaard, surrounded by her three younger children, sat in stunned silence. She had never seen Derek lash out so uncontrollably.

Finally corralled again by officials and ejected from the game, Derek was guided toward the large open gate at the end of the ice. Awaiting him was a uniformed member of the Royal Canadian Mounted Police.

"Oh my God, they called the cops," Parker said. It was Derek's father.

Derek stomped past Len and into an empty locker room. He threw equipment bags and kicked benches with his skates. He sat until the adrenaline waned and reality sunk in. He showered and dressed in time to watch the end of the game.

Derek silently sidled close to his father. Len said nothing to his son. Smoldering, he shot Derek a glance of disappointment and anger. The boy knew he was in trouble. He knew he had blown an opportunity.

Len eventually nodded to the stands. He pointed out the scouts clustered on one side, wearing colorful shirts and jackets with logos that broadcast their affiliations.

"Are you happy with what you did?" Len asked his son. It was a rhetorical question. Derek knew there was only one answer, and he did not have to say it.

Neither deciphered the buzz of excitement from the scouts. None of them had come to see a boy named Boogaard, but they knew who he was now. They nonchalantly whispered to one another and tried to mask their giddiness from their competitors.

Parker and Ripplinger nudged one another. They slipped out of the old rink and into the cold night. There was a long drive ahead of them, back to Regina. But first, they drove just a few blocks, to the Hi-Lo Motor Inn along the highway. They asked the clerk at the front desk to use the fax machine.

On a piece of blank paper, they wrote, "Regina Pats would like to add D. Boogaard, Melfort." In a small office 500 miles west, at the headquarters of the Western Hockey League in Calgary, the machine beeped and buzzed and printed out the message. It would be discovered early the next morning, but the time stamp would show that it was sent before midnight—the day before.

Several teams sent similar notes to the league office the following morning, making their claims on Derek Boogaard. It was too late. Derek had already been added to the 50-man protected list of the Regina Pats. They had first rights on him. He would be invited to their training camp the following fall.

Through the dark on the three-hour drive home, Parker and Ripplinger could not get over what they had seen. They talked about Derek all the way.

"We just couldn't get him out of our head," Ripplinger recalled. "It was . . . you know what? If you like that kind of stuff, it was impressive, really impressive what he did, how strong he was. And you thought, 'Maybe this guy could be an animal one day.'"

They even conjured up a nickname. "The Boogeyman," they called him.

Ripplinger called the Boogaards with the news. He told Len and Joanne that their son had been added to their list, but warned that there were no guarantees he would remain on the roster. He could be dropped just as quickly as he was signed. Derek needed to keep doing what he was doing—intimidating the other boys, protecting his teammates, knocking bodies to the ice. Ripplinger said he would be back in Melfort in a few days to talk to the family about what it all meant and where it could all lead.

Not long afterward, Len called Ripplinger. Derek was too shy to make the call himself, but Len handed the phone to him.

"Do you think you might be able to bring some hockey shorts with you when you come?" the boy asked sheepishly.

Derek had outgrown his.

2

THE FIRST REPORT OF organized hockey played indoors came in 1875, according to the Society for International Hockey Research. That game was noted in two Montreal papers, and took place between two teams of nine players each at the Victoria Skating Rink.

It concluded with a fight.

"The game is generally played with a large rubber ball, each side striving to knock it through the bounds of the other's field," the Montreal *Daily Witness* reported on page 2 of its March 4, 1875, edition. "In order to spare the heads and nerves of the spectators, last evening, a flat piece of board was used instead of a ball; it slid about between the players with great velocity; the result being that the Creighton team won two games to one for the Torrance. Owing to some boys skating about during the play, an unfortunate disagreement arose; one little boy was struck across the head, and the man who did so was afterwards called to account, a regular fight taking place in which a bench was broken and other damage caused. It was the intention of the players to have another game, but this disgraceful affair put a stopper on it."

There was no mention of a referee, and the sport's self-policing origins gave root to fighting as a means of justice. Early games were often sticky affairs with little passing, turning rushes toward the goal into a clog of clutches, holds, punches, and stick whacks. Without strong rules to forbid such nefarious impediments, players often settled disputes by punching or swinging back.

In 1905, Allan Loney, an amateur player in Ontario, became the first hockey player charged with murder for an on-ice attack. Alcide Laurin died on the ice after Loney clubbed him with a stick. Charges against Loney were reduced to manslaughter and he was ultimately acquitted, the jury apparently persuaded that Loney acted in self-defense.

In March 1907, Owen "Bud" McCourt, star player for Cornwall of the Federal Amateur Hockey League, died hours after being hit in the head with a stick by Charles Masson of the Ottawa Victorias.

"The game was becoming rather rough and full of cross checking, tripping and slashing as a result of the referee's leniency," the lead story of the *Evening Citizen* in Ottawa reported the day after the fight.

McCourt had traded blows with a Victorias player named Arthur Throop when Masson surged forward, raised his stick, and hit McCourt over the head. Retaliation was immediate; Throop was dropped with a five-inch gash on his head by one of McCourt's teammates. He and McCourt were helped off the ice by doctors.

McCourt returned to the game, but later fell unconscious in the locker room and was found to have a cracked skull. He died hours later. By morning, Masson was charged with manslaughter. "I'm very sorry," he said upon learning of the death.

Masson was found not guilty. There was not enough evidence to demonstrate that, amid all the violence, Masson delivered the fatal blow.

The referee that night was a man named Emmett Quinn. From 1910 to 1916, Quinn was president of the National Hockey Association, which reorganized and became the foundation of the new National Hockey League in 1917.

The NHL was heavy with vigilante justice in its early years. The blue lines, roughly dividing the ice into thirds, were introduced in 1918. Forward passing was allowed only in the middle section of the rink, the "neutral" zone, meaning any player rushing toward the net with the puck was ambushed by defenders. Elbows turned to fists, and game-stopping fights became part of the show.

Owners were quick to recognize the excitement such violence stirred in hockey crowds. But knowing that on-ice deaths could threaten the sport's future—scores of fatalities in American football in the early 1900s nearly led to the sport's banishment, fueled in part by President Theodore Roosevelt's frustration with its unmitigated violence—they worked to find a balance amid the orchestrated chaos. The ultimate result was Rule 56, instituted in 1922. It said that fighting was against the rules. But the penalty assessed—five minutes in the penalty box—was hardly a deterrent. It not-so-delicately forced players and coaches to determine whether overly rough play was worth the threat of getting beat up, or whether beating someone up was worth the price of a five-minute penalty.

It proved the perfect middle ground. Like the initial dictum of placing a basketball hoop 10 feet off the ground, or of setting baseball bases 90 feet apart, five minutes for fighting was an early guideline that endured. The NHL guideline was virtually unchanged nearly a century later, labeled as Rule 46.14.

"A major penalty shall be imposed on any player who fights," the rulebook read. A "major penalty," compared to a "minor penalty," was deemed worthy of extended time in the penalty box.

"For the first major penalty in any one game, the offender, except the goalkeeper, shall be ruled off the ice for five (5) minutes during which time no substitute shall be permitted," the rule said.

Of course, a fight involves at least two participants, meaning that each team typically lost a man to the penalty box. Such offsetting penalties left teams at equal strength, diluting the punitive notion of the penalty itself.

All that made hockey unique among major team sports. In soccer, football, basketball, and baseball, for example, simply swinging a fist at an opponent was usually grounds for immediate expulsion from the game. Subsequent fines and suspensions were common for any such momentary lapses of self-control. Adding to hockey's peculiarity, it was typically not the aggrieved parties who sought retribution. When a star player was perceived to have been mistreated or handled too roughly by an opponent—to be the victim of a player "taking liberties," in the euphemistic parlance of the game—the team might turn to the enforcer.

The term "enforcer" was a bit of a euphemism, too, an obtuse and honorable title of respect that grew alongside the role itself. Enforcer was not an official position on the team, but a title unofficially applied to those whose jobs as fighters overshadowed their play. Referees enforced the black-and-white rules. Enforcers, as if deputized, operated in the gray areas. In the glossiest version of the job description, enforcers kept the peace.

When the NHL adopted the fighting rule in 1922, there was a sense, one that persisted and percolated through the highest levels of hockey leadership through the league's first century, that fighting acted as a safety valve—a "thermostat," in the words of NHL commissioner Gary Bettman—against more dangerous, spontaneous violence. Allow two willing combatants to fight, the theory went, and the frequency of cheap shots, from elbows to sticks over the head, would dissipate.

In other words, fighting was necessary to control violence.

The philosophy became a sporting version of nuclear armament: the best way to protect players from violent onslaughts was the threat of more violence, even if the missiles were kept in the silo.

But, in hockey, they never were.

. . .

DEREK KNEW NO ONE when he arrived for the Regina Pats' training camp in 1998. The other boys, some as old as 20, eyed the tall, quiet 16-year-old with a mix of derision and anxiety. Some knew that they would be fighting him, and that their roster spot in the Western Hockey League might depend on whether they could beat him up.

Derek was given practice gear in the team's red, white, and blue colors. He got to choose a Sher-Wood stick, the nicest he had ever held. But he really wanted to know about the competition. He asked the trainer: Who do I need to watch out for?

Todd Fedoruk, the trainer said. "The Fridge." He was a 19-year-old from Redwater, Alberta, fearless and sharp-tongued, a seventh-round draft choice of the NHL's Philadelphia Flyers the year before. He was a WHL veteran, having played parts of three seasons for the Kelowna Rockets before being traded to the Pats. The season before, he had seven goals, eight assists, and 200 penalty minutes, many of them in exchange for 17 fights. At six foot two and 230 pounds, he was built like a kitchen appliance.

Also, steer clear of Kyle Freadrich, the trainer said. Derek had noticed Freadrich on the roster. Nearly 20, he was listed at six feet, six inches and 254 pounds. In 112 games for the Pats the previous two seasons, he had just seven goals and eight assists, but 411 penalty minutes. He had had a team-high 25 fights the season before.

On-ice workouts did not begin until the next morning, but Len wanted Derek to absorb the atmosphere. Len and Derek, now several inches taller than his father, stood in the lobby of the arena. Boys came and went.

"I kept asking Dad if we could go but he said, 'No, just wait,'" Derek wrote years later. "I think he did it to see how I would react."

Derek pointed out Fedoruk. I have to watch out for that guy, he said. Then Freadrich walked by.

"He looked like the Grim Reaper," Derek wrote. "His eyes pushed back in his head. His forehead hung over his eyes, so you could almost not see his eyes. His nose was a bit crooked and he had no front teeth."

Derek knew he was being sized up, too.

"My body wasn't showing any signs of fear but I was definetly [sic] scared in my head," he wrote.

Len secured rooms at the RCMP Depot barracks, a few miles away. They ate fast food, getting five Arby's sandwiches for five dollars.

"That night it felt like I only slept 20 minutes," Derek wrote. "I was anxious, excited, scared and I wanted to hit anything that touched the puck."

Derek arrived two hours early for the 10 o'clock start. He quietly got himself dressed and walked into the hallway. He saw another player, as tall as Derek, with "some weird Elvis-looking hair," putting tape on his hockey sticks.

"He walks up to me," Derek recalled in his notes, "gets in my face and says, 'You're fucking dead! I'm going to fucking kill you and you will regret coming here!'"

His name was Travis Churchman. An 18-year-old from Calgary, with a doo-wop haircut and a steel-wool patch of a beard on his chin, he was six foot four and 235 pounds. And when Derek took the ice that morning, Churchman was there, repeating the threats he had made in the hallway. The two were placed on opposite teams.

The scrimmage began. Derek was tapped by the coach to take a shift. He chased opposing players and tried to crush them with checks. He felt a tug on the back of his jersey.

"I turn around and Churchy is there, squared up and ready to go," Derek wrote.

Derek had never been in a "staged" hockey fight, the kind that did not come from a spontaneous combustion of emotion during the course of intense play. They were fights without spark, meant to attract attention or send messages. Derek had seen them countless times on highlight reels and during National Hockey League games. He knew what to do. He flicked his gloves from his hands and took off his helmet—part of the protocol at the time, meant to reduce the pain absorbed by hands pounding plastic. He raised his fists and glided slowly in time with Churchman. Derek swung with a looping arm. His right fist crashed against Churchman's face.

It was over. Churchman skulked away, holding his hands to his face. His nose was broken. Derek left the ice exhausted, relieved, and happy. Pats coaches and scouts laughed and congratulated him, patting him on the back for doing a good job on his first day.

IN THE 1970s, comedian Rodney Dangerfield famously said that he went to a boxing match and a hockey game broke out, a joke that needed no explanation to a mainstream audience. Paul Newman starred in *Slap Shot*, a 1977 film about a struggling minor-league team that used over-the-top violence, mostly at the hands of a motley threesome called the Hanson Brothers, to attract crowds in a dying town. For decades, clips from that movie remained a staple of NHL arenas, an effort to get the fans excited during lulls in the action.

A caricatured archetype of the hockey enforcer took hold—a big, dumb, lovable lug, a "goon," portrayed with a black eye, a knot on his skull, a bandage on his chin, and a smile of missing teeth. They were underdogs, of a sort—men who might otherwise have no business being in the NHL, men who clung to the bottom edge of the roster, whose next fight might be their last. Some barely played and rarely scored. But they were seen as a sort of outed superhero—blue-collar, understated types with selfless alter egos and a devotion to helping those in need. It was work that most of their own teammates would not consider themselves.

"I hate the word 'goon,'" Fedoruk, who went on from Regina to become an NHL enforcer, said after his playing career. "It should almost be changed to 'the guardian.' There's no better feeling then when you're in the penalty box after a good tilt, both teams are jacked up. You get to rest, you're resting for five minutes, and there's no better feeling than when the boys get a rise from you showing up, putting yourself out there. I'm getting chills right now from talking about it.

"We want to play that game so bad, and we're willing to do that part of it to play," Fedoruk added. "The appreciation we get from our teammates is everything to us."

Fans, too, saw something noble and human in the enforcer—a good-guy counterweight to some of hockey's darkest episodes.

The sport's history could be marked by violent milestones. At the end of Game 4 of the 1927 Stanley Cup final, Boston Bruins defenseman Billy Coutu, a vicious player known for wielding sharp elbows and a dangerous stick, attacked two referees, knocking one down with a punch and tackling the other. He received a lifetime ban from the game.

About the same time, boxing promoter Tex Rickard's new NHL franchise, the New York Rangers, parked ambulances outside Madison Square Garden. More ambulances brought more fans, apparently lured by the prospect of violence.

The Rangers also used "Dead or Alive" posters, featuring the likes of notorious Boston brawler Eddie Shore, from Saskatchewan, to drum up business. In 1933, Shore chased and tripped Toronto's Ace Bailey, who fell to the ice and was knocked unconscious with a brain hemorrhage. Shore was knocked out by one retaliatory punch from Toronto's Red Horner.

Bailey was read his last rites. Shore, reawakened, was told he would be charged with manslaughter if and when Bailey died. But Bailey made a surprise recovery, though he never resumed his hockey career. Shore did, and was inducted into the Hockey Hall of Fame in 1947.

In March 1955, Montreal Canadiens star Maurice "Rocket" Richard was suspended for the rest of the season and the playoffs after punching a referee who was trying to prevent him from retaliating against a Boston player. The incident led to the "Richard Riot," in which angry fans at the Montreal Forum threw debris at NHL president Clarence Campbell, forcing the forfeiture of a game against the Detroit Red Wings. The disturbance moved outside, where 60 were arrested during a night of vandalism and looting. The Canadiens, without the best scorer of the era, lost in the Stanley Cup final.

In 1968, Philadelphia's Larry Zeidel and Boston's Eddie Shack pummeled one another with their sticks, taking long, deliberate swings. During the next preseason, St. Louis's Wayne Maki clubbed Boston's Ted Green, fracturing his skull. He was later acquitted of assault charges.

The allowance of fighting as an outlet for aggression—or the thin five-minute penalty associated with it—did not deter those assaults. Such incidents merely slowed over the years as a reflection of society's changing views toward violence. But fighting—a more controlled form of hockey violence—was on the rise. In 1960–61, the NHL averaged 0.2 fights per game, or one for every five contests. The rate rose rapidly until 1987–88, when the average game had 1.3 fights.

That period included the rise of the Boston Bruins, who resurrected the art of intimidation and mixed it with uncommon skill, winning the Stanley Cup in 1970 and 1972. Led by future Hall of

Famers Bobby Orr and Phil Esposito, the Bruins showed that grace and intimidation were not mutually exclusive. They led the league in penalty minutes in 1970 and were third in 1972.

In 1970, the team with the most fights—as measured by fighting penalties—was the Philadelphia Flyers, with 37. An NHL expansion franchise in 1967, the Flyers quickly built a fan base and a championship team with muscle. The Broad Street Bullies, as they were called, won the Stanley Cup in 1974 and 1975.

Dave "The Hammer" Schultz, from Saskatchewan, had 472 penalty minutes during the second championship season, a record that still stands. He helped give rise to the narrowly defined role of the enforcer in both hockey and popular culture.

Fighting grew exponentially. When the Flyers won the Stanley Cup in 1975, they had 77 fights. By 1980, the top-fighting team, the Vancouver Canucks, had 92. In 1988, the Bruins led the NHL with 132. By then, some team owners in the NHL wondered aloud if it was too much. Their concerns had nothing to do with protecting the health of players. It had to do with marketing.

In 1986, *Sports Illustrated* wrote extensively about fighting in hockey. "Oh, dear," the story read. "Just when you thought it was safe to take the kids to an NHL game again—goon hockey is back."

"The NHL has got to decide," the story concluded, "whether to continue presenting itself as a carnival show or to rejoin the ranks of major-league sport."

The NHL was increasingly ambivalent about the role of the enforcer. The league's board of governors, composed of owners, took occasional stabs at reducing fights, but the push of anti-fighting pacifists was routinely checked by compromise.

By 1992, a minority faction of team owners proposed that fighting players be ejected, the type of rule common not only in other sports, but in most hockey leagues around the world and in North American colleges, where fighting was rare. The idea was debated and dismissed in lieu of stricter rules targeting "instigators," those deemed to have started the fight. "NHL Settles for a Jab in Confrontation with Goons," read the headline in the *New York Times*.

The battle was between traditionalists and progressives, and, to some extent, Canadians and non-Canadians. European players had begun to flood the NHL, and the league was expanding deep into the United States. Traditionalists wanted to cling tightly to the game's roots, to protect the physical brand of hockey made in Canada. Progressives saw fighting as an obstacle to the mainstream growth of the sport.

"I think fighting will suffer an evolutionary death," Pittsburgh Penguins owner Howard Baldwin said at the time. "But it will be helped by mortal stab wounds like this."

Gary Bettman became NHL commissioner in 1993. He often cited statistics indicating fighting's slowly shrinking role in the league during his tenure. That raised uncomfortable questions about why the league was averse to nudging it further from the game. If less fighting was good, wouldn't no fighting be better?

DEREK BARELY PLAYED most of the preseason for the Regina Pats, despite his knockout debut at training camp. The Pats moved him from defenseman to left wing, mostly because a fourth-line forward plays far fewer minutes than a defenseman, limiting Derek's time on the ice. Beyond fighting, Derek was a liability.

But coach Parry Shockey told Derek one day that he would play the next night against the Moose Jaw Warriors. Derek called his parents and told them.

Moose Jaw was an hour's drive west of Regina down the Trans-Canada Highway, and the Warriors and Pats were bitter rivals. Around the Western Hockey League, teams often did not warm up on the ice at the same time because pregame fights were common, and that was particularly true in Moose Jaw. The Moose Jaw Civic Centre, the squat, 3,000-seat arena nicknamed the "Crushed Can," was packed.

The Pats did their warmups first. Derek scanned the faces in the crowd as he circled the ice. He found his mom and dad, as well as Ryan, Aaron, and Krysten. He smiled and gave them a nod.

After last-minute preparations and speeches in the locker room, the Pats headed back to the ice for introductions.

"The place was really loud, and it felt as if the fans were on top of you," Derek wrote. "You obviously got the boos as we were walking threw [sic] the tunnel. I think that's the worst I have ever heard people yelling and screaming at the tunnel."

Fourteen-year-old Ryan took on the role of Derek's advance scout for fighting. He scanned web sites and online bulletin boards for information on players Derek might face. Against Moose Jaw, one potential foe was a 20-year-old named Kevin Lapp. He was six foot seven and 250 pounds, and was the league's No. 2-rated fighter, according to at least one site, behind Regina's Kyle Freadrich.

Derek was the last of the Regina players to get a shift. "You're up," Shockey finally said. Derek clambered over the boards.

"Not even 5 seconds on the ice I get a tug," Derek wrote. "So I turn around and there was Kevin Lapp. Just standing there waiting for the gloves to drop. He said, 'Ready to go?' I said, 'Yep.' "

The fight was nothing more than a quick flurry of punches. "He absolutely destroyed me," Derek wrote.

The Boogaards had come to watch Derek play and saw only a few seconds of him getting beat up. He went to the dressing room to check his wounds. After the game, after spending a few minutes with his family, he boarded the bus and sat near the front.

"The vets were obviously in the back of the bus," Derek wrote. "But I knew those guys were making fun of me."

Shockey called Derek into his office the next day. The Pats were demoting Derek, sending him to the Regina Pat Canadians, the city's top midget team, a classification for 16- and 17-year-olds, a big step down from the WHL.

Len waited for his son outside the Agridome, the Pats' arena in Regina.

"He didn't have much to say," Derek wrote. "But later on in the car ride he said he was proud of me making it this far, when all the people in Melfort said that I wasn't any good. He said I shoved it up there [sic] asses already."

THE PEAK OF FIGHTING in the late 1980s gave way to another NHL trend: that of the one-trick enforcer, a player who provided little value to the team beyond the threat of revenge and the occasional use of it. It coincided with a league-wide scoring boom, propelled by the likes of Wayne Gretzky and the Edmonton Oilers.

Gretzky, from Brantford, Ontario, may be the world's most famous Canadian. A suave, swift, and slight six-foot, 185-pound center, he won seven straight scoring titles in the 1980s and ultimately shattered NHL career records for goals and assists. The high-scoring Oilers dazzled fans on their way to five Stanley Cup championships in seven seasons, starting in 1984.

Gretzky gave much of the credit to players who scored little— on-ice bodyguards like Dave Semenko, Kevin McClelland, and Marty McSorley, each of whom had nearly 10 times as many penalty minutes as points during their NHL careers. McSorley followed Gretzky to the Los Angeles Kings in 1988 to serve as his personal protector.

Teams imitated the strategy. High-scoring, highly paid stars needed security. The golden age of the hockey enforcer was born, stretching through McSorley and Bob Probert, Tie Domi, Georges

Laraque, Rob Ray, and Donald Brashear. They increasingly settled their teammates' scores by fighting each other. Imagine in American football, if a linebacker hit a quarterback with what the quarterback's team believed was too much force. Or if a baseball pitcher plunked a star batter with a ball, or a basketball player committed a hard foul on a top scorer. The equivalent to hockey's brand of justice would find those teams sending a specific player from their bench—someone hardly valued for his skill as a player, perhaps rarely used—and having them fight one another.

Their bouts combined the brutality of boxing and the showmanship of professional wrestling. The men sometimes fought for no purpose other than to satisfy the expectation of fans or the chance to be relevant. Coaches used them to stem the opposing team's momentum or change the tenor of the game—maybe "send a message" for the next time the teams played. It felt like a sideshow. But the punches were real.

When the enforcers fought, the game clock stopped. Other players, restricted by stricter rules barring entry into a fight, backed away and watched. Fans, invariably, stood and cheered, often more vociferously than when a goal was scored.

Television cameras zoomed in, and a graphic providing each fighter's height and weight often appeared on the screen. Play-by-play men took on the role of boxing announcers, their hyper-charged voices rising and falling with every blow. Punches produced a reflexive chorus of oooohs from the crowd. The volume ratcheted with the sight of blood, flying equipment, maybe a dislodged tooth. The fight ended only when one of the players fell to the ice or when the violence slowed, like the dwindling energy of popcorn when nearly every kernel has popped. That was the sign to officials to step in and nudge the combatants toward the penalty box.

Sometimes fights ended unceremoniously with a clumsy slip and fall. Sometimes they ended with two men, like exhausted heavy-

weights, clinging to one another. A knockout punch by the hometown enforcer usually brought the loudest cheer of the night.

When officials declared an end to the combat, fans gave standing
ovations. Teammates banged their sticks on the boards in appreciation. Replays of the fight, usually in slow motion, filled the giant
video screens in the arenas and the television screens at home. Fights
were staples of the nightly sports highlight packages.

In the mid-1990s, a hockey fan from Long Island, New York,
named David Singer began to archive fights in the NHL and, eventually, leagues around the world, including the major-junior leagues
of Canada and the minor leagues of the United States. What began
as an unheralded blog turned into HockeyFights.com, a full-fledged,
up-to-date repository, in 1999. It had links to video clips of recent
fights. Users voted on winners, and some described the blow-by-
blow action in detailed accounts.

The site, like its growing posse of imitators, had pages for each
enforcer that included career fight logs dating to junior hockey. It
had statistical analysis, showing trends in fighting, and tracked fights
from about a dozen leagues around the world. Enforcers themselves
used it to replay their own fights and scout opponents for the next,
some of the tens of millions of page views the site received each
NHL season.

Without sites like HockeyFights.com and DropYourGloves.com,
it might be difficult to find that the Medicine Hat Tigers led the
WHL in 1997–98 with 211 fights—far more than teams in the NHL.
Or that the Regina Pats had 183, or that Kyle Freadrich and Barret
Jackman, each on his way to the NHL, would lead the team with 25
each. Or that Travis Churchman had 14.

Each of those boys had ambitions for professional hockey, and
the NHL of the late 1990s still had plenty of appetite for enforcers.
Most would prefer to have reached the NHL on the merit of their
other hockey skills, but were glad to have found a well-traveled back

entrance to a world where they were respected by teammates and revered by fans.

Into this era entered a gangly 16-year-old named Derek.

DEREK THOUGHT HE was too good to play for the Pat Canadians. He had been playing with and fighting 20-year-old boys working toward the NHL. Now he was on a second-tier team with boys his own age. And he was not getting much playing time.

"I was playing cocky and thought I didn't deserve to be there," Derek wrote. "I look back on it now and I do regret acting like that."

Coach Leo MacDonald played Derek a few shifts a game. Derek used his infrequent ice time to show how he could intimidate with his energy and hammer opposing players with big checks. MacDonald was not impressed. The Pat Canadians were winning—on their way, in fact, to capturing the Air Canada Cup, awarded to the national midget-level champions. They did not need Derek's brand of hockey.

In December, the Pat Canadians headed to the Mac's tournament in Calgary, a prestigious event for top midget teams from across Canada. Game after game, Derek sat on the bench. He was embarrassed and annoyed. As he watched his teammates take turns on the ice, Derek stewed. He finally turned to MacDonald during the middle of the game.

"I'm good. I can play," Derek said. "I'm right here in front of you."

MacDonald told Derek to keep quiet. Derek exploded in anger. On the way to the dressing room, he corralled the coach in the hallway.

"I lit into him again and we got into the room and I said he was an awful coach and didn't know how to coach," Derek wrote later.

Derek carried his belongings into the hallway and found a pay phone. He called his mother. Joanne was in Swift Current, visiting family, and drove five hours to Calgary to retrieve Derek.

For much of the way back across the flat Saskatchewan prairie, he cried.

JUST WHEN DEREK'S hockey aspirations had stalled, Todd Ripplinger was there again. The Regina Pats' head scout had had a feeling Derek would clash with MacDonald, the coach of the Pat Canadians. He was not surprised to learn that Derek was no longer on the team. By then, Ripplinger had already called another Regina coach named Don Pankewich.

The Regina Capitals were a Junior B team—a group of 16- to 20-year-olds a couple of cuts below the Western Hockey League. It was hardly a stepping-stone to a hockey career, but it was a timely teenage diversion.

Derek's parents were having marital problems, sparked by Len's relationship with Jody Vail, the newest RCMP member assigned to Melfort. She was blond and petite, about 10 years younger than Len. A friend of Derek's told him that Len's car was constantly parked at her house. Derek kept the revelation to himself, but Joanne soon caught on. One argument between his parents ended with a phone being pulled from a wall and Derek playing peacemaker.

The Boogaards had been in Melfort about five years, and it was about time for the RCMP to move the family again. Len negotiated a transfer to Regina, well timed for Derek's move there for hockey. Joanne hoped that the move to Regina, her hometown, could keep the family together.

Len, Derek, and Ryan settled in Regina first, into an apartment. Joanne stayed in Melfort with Aaron and Krysten, the two younger children, to sell the house. The Boogaards found a tri-level home on the north side of Regina, on a shady section of Woodward Avenue. They renovated the house before they moved in, with three bedrooms upstairs and a couple more on the lowest level, so that there were bedrooms for each of the children.

The house was near Archbishop O'Neill High, a Catholic school that Pats players attended. But Derek found few friends. He had been cut from the 1998–99 Pats team, and he had been kicked off the Pat Canadians, too.

Derek immediately fit in with the Capitals. He liked the coach. He made several good friends. The pressure in the South Saskatchewan Junior Hockey League was several degrees below that of the WHL, and the Capitals were one of the better teams, making it to that season's final. Derek's love for hockey, so often ignited and extinguished, was ignited again.

The Pats were still intrigued by Derek's size, and invited him to skate with them on days when the Capitals did not practice. They stoked his ambition. He stoked their interest with a growth spurt. If he made the Pats, he might be the biggest player in the WHL.

Derek turned 17 in June and spent the summer lifting weights, preparing for his second training camp with the Pats. The older Pats whom Derek had found intimidating—boys like Todd Fedoruk and Kyle Freadrich—were gone to professional training camps. But other willing fighters remained, including Travis Churchman and future NHL defenseman Barret Jackman. They found a burgeoning rival whom they barely recognized from a year before. Derek had grown three inches, to six foot seven, and the camp roster listed him at 255 pounds, 45 more than he had weighed a year earlier.

Trying to make an impression, Derek fought 12 times in the first four scrimmages.

"Derek Boogaard, a 17-year-old man-child, was in four or five fights, depending on who is doing the counting, during one scrimmage at the Regina Pats' training camp yesterday," the *Leader-Post*, Regina's daily newspaper, reported on September 1, 1999.

The headline read "Beware of the Boogeyman." The article said that the first fight, on the first shift, ended with Derek "bodyslamming" Churchman to the ice. Another fight with Churchman ended the same way, and the two then stood up and boxed.

"This one was pretty much a sawoff," the story said.

Derek was big, but his fighting skills were unrefined. He tried to knock every opponent out with one punch. He had no strategy, no moves. He fell down easily.

Aside from the fighting, Derek had little usefulness on the ice. He could build up good speed but had little agility. He was not a great puck handler. He did not have innate hockey sense, the ability to see plays forming before they happened, to know where the puck needed to go without pausing for consideration. He was clumsy. He often botched drills in practices, interrupting the flow and frustrating coaches.

Mainly, he was raw, and there was no time for raw at this level. Coaches were paid to win and to fill seats. Derek, as enticing a prospect as he was, was not good enough to do either.

The Pats won four of their first five games. Derek barely played. But in the one loss, a 3–0 defeat at Swift Current on September 29, Derek got into his first regular-season major-junior hockey fight.

Mat Sommerfeld was not a big kid, but he was a sturdy one, a farm boy willing to dish it out and take it in equal doses. He grew up in Shellbrook, Saskatchewan, a town not unlike Melfort and about 90 minutes away. A few years earlier, as 14-year-olds on competing teams, Derek and Sommerfeld tussled during a game in Shellbrook. Afterward, Sommerfeld was in the arena lobby with friends when Boogaard approached. He introduced himself and thanked Sommerfeld for the fight. They shook hands.

But now they were 17, and the stakes were far higher. Late in the second period, awaiting a face-off, the boys began to scuffle. The referee told them to wait for the puck to drop. They did. Then they flipped their gloves off and flung their sticks to the side. They casually removed their helmets and tossed them aside as they circled clockwise. Derek closed the gap and jousted with his right hand. He grabbed Sommerfeld with his left hand, and Sommerfeld grabbed back, slipping to his knees momentarily. They wrangled and tried to punch one another. Sommerfeld pulled the back of Derek's jersey onto Derek's head. They fell in a heap and continued to jab and pull. Two officials jumped on top to separate the boys.

Sommerfeld rose first, holding Derek's uniform nameplate— BOOGAARD—in his hands. As he skated to the penalty box, he held the fabric trophy overhead, like a boxer displaying a championship belt. The crowd on its feet, Sommerfeld tossed it dismissively aside.

On October 11, at Red Deer, Derek fought again, this time against Steve MacIntyre, a burly, six-foot, six-inch 19-year-old from a blip of a Saskatchewan town called Brock. MacIntyre won with little effort, but Derek was rewarded with another chance two nights later, at home against the Kelowna Rockets.

Ryan Boogaard had scouted the Rockets. Ryan, two years younger than Derek, played hockey, too. He was not built like an enforcer the way Derek was. And he was not as smooth with the puck as Aaron, the third of the Boogaard boys. But Ryan followed the WHL closely. He scoured statistics and tracked the online bulletin boards for information on players. Before the Pats hosted the Rockets at Regina's Agridome, Ryan told Derek about Mitch Fritz. He was two years older than Derek and stood six foot seven. Ryan told his brother that Fritz had a strange style, an overhand, club-like punch that he compared to Donkey Kong, the video-game villain.

"I was never nervous before my fights," Derek wrote. "I think I just excepted [sic] the fact that I could get hurt."

Fritz took the ice during Derek's first shift and asked for a fight. The boys dropped their gloves and removed their helmets. Derek swung a wild right hand that punctured only air. Fritz used his own long reach to pull Derek in close. Fritz tied Derek in knots and pounded him with a series of jabs and overhand "Donkey Kong punches," Derek wrote, until officials interrupted.

"After the fight, he was waving his finger in the air like he was the champ," Derek wrote. "I never did like that when guys show-boated. It just pissed me off even more, and in junior hockey, you saw a lot of it."

Fritz saw reason to gloat. On a hockey fight web site, someone reported that Fritz landed 10 of his 26 punches. Derek threw five punches and did not land any of them.

The Regina Pats had seen enough. Before Derek played again, he was traded. There is little in hockey more useless than an enforcer who loses fights.

3

PRINCE GEORGE, BRITISH COLUMBIA, was a mill town. Spreading mostly west from the confluence of the Fraser and Nechako Rivers, it sprawled over a pine-covered landscape shaped like a rumpled blanket. It began as a fur-trading post two centuries ago and became a vital stop on the way to other places—the Yukon or the coast or the latest gold rush. It was connected to the national railroad in the early 1900s, and by the middle of the 20th century its lumber business was booming. Paper mills followed.

By the time Derek arrived in a trade, Prince George was a photogenic city of 70,000 people, seemingly quarantined from the country's major population centers. But the Western Hockey League moved the Victoria Cougars to Prince George in 1994, attracted by the promise of a 6,000-seat arena, called the Multiplex, that opened in 1995.

Derek said goodbye to his dad, his mom, his sister and brothers, a family breaking apart. When he stepped off the plane and onto the tarmac at the airport in Prince George in late October 1999, he was 17 and far from home for the first time.

A man wearing a black Prince George Cougars jacket greeted him. It was Ed Dempsey, the team's head coach. He drove Derek the 20 minutes through the curvy, tree-lined roads from the airport into town.

"I wasn't feeling too good because I wasn't used to the trees and the hills," Derek wrote years later. "I was always used to the flat feilds [sic] of SK."

He had to get used to it. WHL teams traveled by bus, and franchises were flung as far as 1,000 miles apart. Prince George was about nine hours west of Edmonton and 10 hours north of Vancouver. No place on the schedule was more remote. The nearest road game was in Kamloops, a six-hour drive.

A few times a season, the Cougars embarked on multi-game road trips that lasted a week or more, swinging as far south as Portland, Oregon, and as far east as Brandon, Manitoba. It was not unusual for the team bus to roll back into Prince George in broad daylight, 12 hours or more after playing a game far away.

The bus traveled about 40,000 miles each winter. While Derek was in Prince George, the Cougars replaced a three-year-old bus that had been purchased for $400,000 with a new one costing $530,000. The buses were specially designed with 12 bunks in the back and reclining seats in the front. The veteran players, ranked by games played, got to sleep in bunks on long trips. Players like Derek, when he first arrived, were relegated to sleeping while sitting.

The buses often drove through the middle of the night. To the east, the roads were often icy and windswept as they crossed great, dark prairies. In the west, many roads curled around and over snow-covered mountains. Tragedy was just one impassable sheet of ice away, and junior hockey was haunted by the memory and worry of fatal accidents.

The Pats had traded Derek to Prince George for a 17-year-old forward named Jonathan Parker. Two years earlier, Parker had been the fifth-overall choice in the WHL Bantam Draft, a swift prospect from Winnipeg expected to be a high scorer for Prince George. In his first season, Parker scored only four goals. Derek, by contrast, had not been among the 195 boys chosen in that same bantam draft, just an invitee to training camp. If nothing else, their trade was a stark reminder of the fickleness of potential and the short amount of time the boys were given to realize it.

The Cougars were a middling team with a fervent following and what might seem a geographic disadvantage. But teams had to travel all the way to Prince George to play, too, and the Cougars were always a tough opponent at home. They wanted to get tougher. The season before Derek arrived, Prince George had the fewest fights of any team in the 18-team WHL—84 in 72 games. Regina, which had signed Derek but demoted him in favor of other enforcers, led the league with 164.

It was a strange contradiction in a place like Prince George.

"Prince George is not a place where you're going to get a majority to vote on getting hockey to stop the fighting," said Jim Swanson, the sports editor of the *Prince George Citizen* for 14 years. "It's not going to happen. It's not a rough town, but it's an honest town, and it's a town that likes its hard-nosed players."

Derek's first meeting was with the equipment manager. Nothing fit. A ring of cloth was sewn to the bottom of the largest jersey to make it longer. Two smaller rings were added to the cuffs to lengthen Derek's sleeves. Larger shin pads and hockey pants were ordered.

Derek stood out from the beginning. At his first practice, less than 24 hours after arriving from Regina, coaches were pleased with his loping skating stride. His skills were better than they imagined.

Reporters gawked at his height. The newspaper featured Derek in a Halloween-inspired layout, introducing him as "The Boogeyman."

The Cougars wanted muscle. They wanted someone to get fans excited. Derek's confidence soared.

After that first practice, Derek was called into the office of general manager Daryl Lubiniecki.

"If you win a few fights in this town," Lubiniecki told Derek, "you could run for mayor."

. . .

THE FIRST PUNCH that 17-year-old Derek threw for the Cougars came on November 3, 1999. It was an overhand right that struck Eric Godard of the Lethbridge Hurricanes in the jaw.

There were 5,552 fans in the arena that night. It was late in the third period. A tight game had been broken open with two quick goals, giving Prince George a 4–1 lead. So the Lethbridge coach sent Godard onto the ice. Godard was 19, stood six foot four, and weighed 215 pounds. He had been in 15 fights in the season's first 15 games, on his way to leading the Western Hockey League in fights and penalty minutes that season.

Dempsey, the Prince George coach, responded by tapping Derek's shoulder. Fans cheered as the boys began the familiar ritual. Derek landed the first punch. Godard hit back with a couple of quick jabs to the face, and Derek moved in closer. The boys clutched each other by the jerseys and got their arms tangled, as if caught in the same straitjacket. They scooted one another around the ice. Three officials circled and watched, casually tossing obstacles out of the way—sticks, helmets, and gloves that the boys had dropped to the ice before the fight.

The duel passed in front of the Prince George bench, then the Lethbridge one. Teammates of both boys watched the fight with expressionless faces. But the fans wanted to see their new enforcer take down one of the league's top fighters. They stood.

Godard was able to free himself just enough to hit Derek with a few short punches. After a minute of stand-up wrestling and fighting, the officials stepped between the exhausted boys and pulled them apart.

Both boys, given the requisite five-minute matching penalties, headed to the dressing rooms because there were only 72 seconds left in the game. But it was not the end of the fighting. With two seconds remaining, six players—three from each side—fought, too. Such was the WHL, where teenaged boxing matches were a routine part of the hockey entertainment.

For Derek, it was not a memorable debut. It blended into what became a miserable season.

"I don't remember my first fight in P.G. actually," he later wrote. "But they never turned out good for me. I was getting beat up a lot. My confidence was shot to shit. I was fighting with the coaches, and I would hear the snickers from the guys that I was a pussy and I didn't know how to fight. It was a very long year for me. I struggled with everything it seemed like. No matter what I did."

As much as anything, he was homesick. Letting Derek move 1,000 miles away was the hardest thing the Boogaards did. Joanne, especially, could not fathom sending him alone into this strange, unknown world to play a game in which he had so little future. The risks seemed to far outweigh the rewards. And Derek had been handed over to another family, strangers, at what might be the most trying point in his life.

In the tumultuous world of junior hockey, billet families were meant to provide stability—a home away from home, a sanctuary from the pressures and anxieties of playing top-level hockey, going to new schools, and simply growing up. Each team cultivated a list of trusted billets. Some were couples with no children, or couples whose children had grown and moved on. Others were large families who welcomed an older-brother figure, or two or three, into their lives for most of the school year. The families received game tickets and a monthly stipend of a few hundred dollars to cover the extra groceries and the cost of time and gas ferrying the boys to practices and games.

Benefits were largely intangible—an inside relationship with the local team (and the prestige that came with it), plus the satisfaction of steering boys through a time in life that can be difficult enough without the unique pressures of junior hockey. The costs were mostly intangible, too. There were meals to make, clothes to wash, school assignments to monitor. For top-level hockey players in their late teens, the problems magnified. There were concerns over curfews, drinking, and girls.

During Derek's second season with the Cougars, an extensive story by Swanson in the *Prince George Citizen* highlighted Derek's difficulties—the marital problems of his parents, the teasing of teammates, the carousel of four billet families that he rotated through in his first year.

"Mr. Swanson has no right bringing these boys' personal lives into the attention of the public eye," one woman wrote in a letter to the editor published by the newspaper. "These fellows are continually looked at under a microscope by the Cougars administration, agents, scouts, and other hockey officials. These teenagers are a long way from their real homes. We billet families do the best we can to pick up the pieces when our boys come home from a bad game. We don't always know what to say or do, but a hearty attempt is made to get them to grin at least once before they go to sleep."

There were countless reasons why a relationship between the player and his billet family did not work. They ranged from simple personality clashes to religious differences to sexual relationships that developed between players and family members, including the billet mothers.

Derek usually found billet families unbearably constricting. In turn, they found him unusually aloof. He had a habit of unintentional discourtesies, ranging from quiet brooding to post-curfew calls for a ride home. His shyness could be construed by strangers as rudeness. Struggles at school built pressure on billet families, and Derek's size and style of play only fostered stereotypes of the doltish goon. He was not part of the clique of popular hockey players with whom families wanted to associate themselves. Most were willing to pass him along to another family.

Gone were the comforts of home, far removed by time and distance. By the time Derek had been traded from Regina to Prince George, the Cougars had already taken a road swing through Saskatchewan. The Cougars did not return until mid-February. For the first time, when Derek scanned the crowd for familiar faces, he did not see any. The distance to Prince George made it a difficult and expensive place for his family to visit. Even talking to his parents was difficult, in the days before Skype and cell-phone texting, Facebook and constant e-mail access.

But Derek's parents would listen to radio broadcasts streamed live through their computers. Sometimes, they would call the station and ask to be placed on hold so that they could listen to the Cougars' games. Derek did not play many minutes, and his arrival on the ice often prefaced a fight. His parents would hear the blow-by-blow of

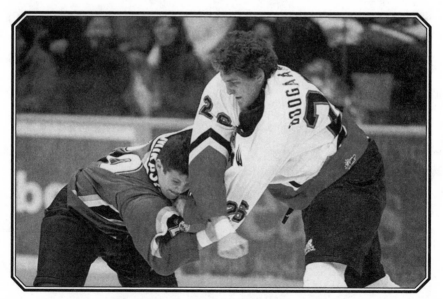

Derek fights for the Prince George Cougars.

the excited play-by-play announcer—the gloves coming off, the boys swinging their fists, the groans and cheers of the crowd. Then they would hear that Derek had gone to the penalty box or, sometimes, to the dressing room. And that might be the last they heard until the phone rang hours later.

"Mom, I'm okay," Derek would say. "What did it sound like?"

TO APPEASE PARENTS, the Western Hockey League billed itself as a place where education was a priority. It touted a program in which each season spent in the league earned a full-year college scholarship, covering tuition, books, and fees. Dozens of players took advantage every year, and Canadian college teams were filled with former WHL players whose professional prospects had dimmed.

But for those with no college ambitions, attending high school was little more than an annoyance, a daily obstacle on the way to afternoon practice. The older boys, aged 19 and 20, were usually the stars of the team, and they had finished high school or were too old to be required to attend. The younger boys simply needed to stay enrolled to be eligible to play. The only educational expectation the Cougars placed on their players was to maintain grades in line with those they had when they arrived.

Derek played three-plus seasons in the WHL, and left at age 20 without completing the 10th grade. Once he was too old to be required to attend high school—but was more than welcome to continue playing junior hockey—Derek called home to say that he was taking a law class at a community college. His parents were excited. When asked a few weeks later how the class was going, Derek hesitantly admitted that he had dropped the class, trading it for one that taught country-and-western line dancing. A teammate was taking the course, Derek said, and it was filled with lots of cute girls.

Most players were not from Prince George, so they had few friends at Prince George Secondary School beyond their own teammates. The hockey team was its own clique, a group of ever-changing outsiders made momentarily famous by their spot on the team. They were, by turns, both revered and reviled, and sometimes those feelings ebbed with wins and losses.

Most boys at the major-junior level had been the best players on their team for many years, stars at every level. Not Derek. He was an unproven entity, prized for his size but not his talent. He was shy, and could sometimes make people laugh with his quirky sense of humor, but those were not traits that endeared testosterone-filled teenagers to one another. To teammates, Derek was a one-dimensional player, brought in to perform a task he was failing to do well.

In practice, coaches chided him for botching drills and worried that he would accidentally injure star players with a clumsy collision. One older teammate, in particular, routinely threatened to beat up Derek.

He instead found friends in some of the fringes of high-school culture, not unlike the skateboarders and snowboarders Derek had come to know in Melfort.

One of Derek's best friends was Eric Hoarau, who had moved with his family from Nairobi at the age of seven. Eric was black, five foot seven, and did not play hockey, and his father ran an auto-repair shop on the edge of downtown called Simba Motors. Somehow, he was assigned to sit behind Derek, a foot taller, in English class. Derek spent hours at the shop and was a frequent guest at the Hoarau house. He peppered the family with questions about where they came from, why they moved to Canada, how they ended up in Prince George.

Derek had a natural curiosity about others, and about their cultures, a healthy appetite to learn more that rarely translated to his schoolwork. He didn't find his life all that interesting, and most hockey players came from a similar background. Strangers from different cultures, with stories Derek had never heard before, were far more intriguing to him. He asked more questions than he answered, mostly out of inquisitiveness, partly to deflect attention.

Still, like most of his teammates, Derek drank, at school parties outside of town and, eventually, at bars in Prince George. Drinking was a long-standing rite of passage in junior hockey. The drinking age was 19, which meant about half of the roster was of legal age. But bars were lax, even for the underaged, especially when it came to Cougars players, who carried an air of celebrity.

"There were no drugs, but there was booze," said Lubiniecki, the veteran general manager. "I used to have a standard in the Western Hockey League: My rule will be that if a kid is worse than I was when I was when I grew up, then he's out of here. And I never found a kid as bad as I was."

While in Prince George, Derek also became introduced to another enduring staple of junior hockey: the puck bunny.

It was a term, used somewhat derisively and often abbreviated to "pucks," for the young women who hung around the team hoping to attract the affection of a player. They were the sirens of junior hockey. They scouted from the stands, mingled near the locker rooms, and found their way to the bars where players congregated. Most relationships were as fleeting as a winter storm, but the NHL is filled with players married to pucks.

Derek had never had a girlfriend. His lifelong shyness was magnified around girls. He could recite Eddie Murphy comedy routines in front of close friends, but he was painfully reticent around girls. But they were noticing him.

Derek was miserable for much of his time in Prince George. He did not like the coach, Ed Dempsey, for the same reason he struggled with so many authority figures. Derek felt untrusted and underestimated. He did not like the assistant coach, Dallas Thompson, who was also in charge of coordinating the school and billet programs for

the Cougars. Thompson had plenty of issues with Derek away from
the ice.

"He was a boy in a man's body," Thompson said of Derek.
"Everything was in a hurry. He knew what he wanted to do: he
wanted to play in the NHL. A lot of things, like school and growing
up, got accelerated a bit, and I think it overwhelmed him at times."

THE COUGARS WERE a good team that season, on their way to
reaching the league semifinals in the playoffs. And they were popular. Of the 18 teams in the Western Hockey League, Prince George
was fourth in attendance, averaging 5,801 fans per home game, trailing only teams in the larger cities of Spokane, Portland, and Calgary.

Six players from the 1999–2000 Prince George team ultimately
reached the National Hockey League, at least for a few games. It was
hard to imagine that Derek would be one of them. Twenty-seven
players scored points for the Cougars, but Derek had no goals and no
assists in 33 games. He led the Cougars in fights, with 16 (plus three
with Regina before the trade), but the team had plenty of others who
were willing to do the dirty work, too. In all, the Cougars had 107
game-stopping fights, a big increase from the season before, and 21
players engaged in at least one.

The users of one web site determined Derek's fighting record
to be 6–9–1, with three bouts not judged. One victory came three
nights after Derek's Prince George debut brawl with Eric Godard.
During a game with four fights, Derek drilled a player from the
Kamloops Blazers named Jason Bone with two hard rights, knocking
the boy to his knees and spilling blood on the ice.

At home in November against Kelowna, Derek was matched
again with Mitch Fritz, with his Donkey Kong punches and finger-
wagging bravado. In an uncommonly short bout, Derek lunged with
a right hand that missed, and Fritz responded with a flurry of right

hands that tagged Derek several times in the face. Derek fell to the ice. Fritz headed to the penalty box. Derek left immediately for the dressing room—a humbled enforcer's sign of injury and defeat.

Fritz beat Derek again in January, surprising him with a quick barrage that knocked Derek down. In February, prompted by Derek's beating of one of Fritz's teammates earlier in the game, they met again during the first of a seven-game, 12-day road trip east. By now, Derek was well schooled in the choreography of hockey fights. Waiting for a face-off near one goal, Fritz asked Derek if he wanted to fight. Derek nodded casually. Once the puck dropped, the two swerved their way to the middle of the rink, shedding equipment and building anticipation.

The crowd rose as the boys slid toward center ice, the circus's center ring. Fritz skated toward Derek and struck him with his right fist as Derek moved backward. The blow dropped Derek to the ice, a signal for officials to intervene. But Derek quickly jumped to his feet. With an official draped on each boy, each player bigger than the men trying to contain them, Derek fired a right hand that knocked Fritz off balance.

Fritz, angered, tried to duck and wrangle out of the official's hold, but could not get close enough to continue the fight. The boys shouted at one another, like boxers held back by their handlers. The Kelowna crowd cheered.

The Cougars headed to Swift Current. Mat Sommerfeld, Derek's old nemesis, cracked Derek's chin with a series of left-hand jabs. The boys fell to their knees and sprung up. Sommerfeld hit Derek with a right, knocking him to his knees momentarily again. Sommerfeld landed more punches until Derek wrestled his opponent to the ice in a pile.

Derek called Len late that night. In the pile, he said, Sommerfeld bit him on the hand. In the hours since, it had swelled grotesquely and kept Derek awake with pain.

Len drove two hours from Regina to Swift Current and took Derek to the hospital in the middle of the night. Doctors diagnosed an infection and gave Derek shots. Len, frustrated at being called to intervene in his son's care, began to wonder whether teams had the best interests of the boys in mind.

"Then came the night that was good and kind of a bad thing for me," Derek wrote.

It was March 3, 2000. The Cougars were home, in front of another sold-out crowd of 5,970, playing the Tri-City Americans. In the second period, Derek faced a 19-year-old named Mike Lee, a six-foot, 230-pounder from Alaska.

The fight ended almost as soon as it started. Lee smacked Derek with a punch. The boys were escorted to the penalty box. Derek, without revealing that he was hurt, sat trying to coordinate his jaw and get it back into place.

"I couldn't close my mouth," Derek wrote later. "My teeth wouldn't line up."

His jaw was broken. X-rays at the hospital proved it, and doctors said the jaw required surgical repair. Derek awoke to find his mouth wired shut. Doctors placed him on a liquid diet. His season over, the Cougars sent him home to Regina.

Derek had been missing teeth from previous fights and a stick he took to the mouth. Now, between the wires, he had a hole where he could insert a straw during the six weeks his jaw was wired shut. The hole in his teeth, he found, was the perfect size for French fries.

DEREK TURNED 18 in June, and he privately wondered if he might get selected in that month's National Hockey League draft. The notion was ridiculous enough that he kept it to himself.

"I was still kinda hoping that somebody would take a chance on me," he wrote as an adult.

No one did. But several of Derek's teammates and opponents were drafted. Sommerfeld, Derek's rival, was selected in the eighth round, 253rd overall, by the Florida Panthers. (He played two more seasons of junior hockey before leaving the game with complications from concussions, and became a farmer near his hometown.)

The broken jaw and wired mouth gave Derek plenty of time to ponder where he wanted his life to go. He was not going to graduate from high school. He likely was headed toward a career of labor, working the oil fields or in a manufacturing plant somewhere, and if he did not play hockey, that future would start sooner rather than later. His family was little solace.

The house in Regina was remodeled and ready, and the Boogaards moved in at about the time Derek completed his first season in Prince George. A month later, the day after Mother's Day, Joanne returned home to find that Len had moved out. Their marriage, approaching its 20th anniversary, was headed for divorce.

Derek escaped by burying himself in his hockey pursuits. Another season like the last, and opportunity would expire. He spent much of the summer at a gym called Level 10 Fitness, with a trainer named Dan Farthing. Derek now had a leanness that was evident everywhere from his thinning cheeks to his broadening chest and flattening stomach.

He boxed. He ran. He spent hours with his brother Ryan, reviewing videos of his fights and scouting his opponents. Derek never felt more prepared and more anxious to start a season. Yet he nearly quit before it began.

Derek wanted to choose his billet family, but the Cougars were not going to let Derek dictate his living arrangements. Derek had not been unhappy with his primary first-year billets, but he had made a connection with another family. Mike and Caren Tobin owned a jewelry store in a well-tended strip mall in Prince George, and they lived in a neatly landscaped, remodeled two-story house on a quiet street outside of town. They had toddler-aged twin daughters. They had been billets for a few years and were hosting one of Derek's teammates. The boy told the Tobins about Derek.

"Mike, you should see this guy," the boy said. "He's so big, he won't even fit in my car."

The Tobins said to invite him over.

"Here's this giant, pimple-faced galoot walking in the door," Mike Tobin recalled. "And he was shy. Oh, my God, was he shy."

Derek sat quietly on the couch, watching television. Caren asked if he wanted something to drink. No, thank you, Derek mumbled. Something to eat? No, thank you, he said.

"He kept to himself," Caren Tobin said. "But once he became your friend, he would always be there for you."

Mike Tobin had had a difficult childhood and quit school after the eighth grade. A family connection led to an apprenticeship as a goldsmith, which led to his own jewelry business, built into a success. Mike had just purchased a Porsche, and the Tobin residence might have been the nicest home Derek had ever been inside.

Derek soon fell for Caren's roast beef, and Mike was soon taking him to movies and sparking an interest in high-performance cars. Derek opened up. At a time when Derek's own family was breaking apart, the Tobins offered reliable comfort. Mike became the sort of big-brother figure that Derek had not had—part friend, part role model.

It was part of a lifelong pattern for Derek. He usually painted adults, particularly those with some authority over his life, in one of two stark shades. Either you were for Derek or against him; there was little in between. He did not like most of his teachers, who put demands on him that he never fully understood. He adored about half of the coaches he had and detested the others. Whether authority figures fell on one side or the other was usually a reflection of the amount of faith they showed in Derek—or, conversely, the amount of pressure and discipline they exerted on him.

More than anyone, Mike Tobin boosted Derek's confidence, listened to his problems, and offered a worry-free place to unwind. There was no harping about hockey or school or anything else. A neighbor of the Tobins worked at the high school. She warned them that Derek was not worth the trouble—a bad student, a bad kid. The Tobins never saw it.

There were several hockey players living with billets in the neighborhood, and the Tobin home became a hub. When the boys gathered, either to watch television on the big screen in the basement or to have a big dinner, the Tobins usually told them to bring Derek.

But the Cougars denied Derek's request to live with the Tobins. When Derek arrived at the airport for his second season in Prince George, he was driven to the home of another family. Nice people, Derek recalled, but they were smokers, and Derek wanted no part of that. He sulked. He moved through another billet family before settling with still another. Derek liked them, but the husband was a statistician for the Cougars. Derek felt as if he was being monitored by the team.

His frustration boiled over following a run-in with Thompson, the assistant coach and the one in charge of billeting. Thompson, persistently frustrated by Derek on and off the ice, was not happy with the way Derek casually greeted Thompson's wife, the daughter of the owner. Thompson berated Derek for the disrespectful slight.

That was it. Derek decided to quit. He bought a plane ticket to Regina and called his father to say he was coming home. He went into the dressing room and told teammates he was leaving. A couple of them tried to talk him out of it.

Derek went to tell Mike Tobin.

"Don't be a quitter," Tobin said. "That's what they want you to do."

Tobin had seen firsthand how players were treated as disposable goods. He had come home from work several times over the years to find boys in tears, packing their bags, told they had been shipped somewhere else.

Derek said he would demand a trade. Tobin laughed. He knew Derek had no standing to make demands. He didn't even have enough standing to request billets. They would dismiss him as a cancer and sit him. They've got you, Derek, Tobin told him. You can sulk or prove them wrong.

Derek met with the Prince George coaches the next day. As if his mouth were still wired shut, he mostly stayed quiet, swallowing his frustration. He never used the plane ticket.

DEREK FOUGHT 31 TIMES in 2000–01, more than any other season of his life. The first was on September 27, at home against the Kootenay Ice. He beat up Trevor Johnson, who was nine inches shorter and more than 50 pounds lighter than Derek, who weighed himself daily and usually hovered between 240 and 250 pounds.

On October 8 against Regina, Derek and David Kaczowka fought twice, giving Derek a chance to show his former team what it had traded away a year before. Kaczowka was on his way to a league-high 50 fights that season. But Derek stood strong, edging him in the first fight with a quick rash of punches thrown despite having his jersey pulled over his head. The second fight, part of a five-on-five line brawl, was quickly strangled by officials.

The next night, Prince George hosted the Tri-City Americans. Derek was nervous. It was time to repay Mike Lee, the fighter who had broken Derek's jaw seven months earlier. The coaches put their pugilists out on the ice early in the first period.

Derek sidled up to Lee. "Wanna go?" he asked.

Derek wasted little time in delivering several big blows, exacting his revenge.

Later in the game, the Americans sent another player out to fight Derek. He dispatched him, too.

The Boogeyman's payback tour was in full force. On October 11, Prince George played at Swift Current. Midway through the second period, Derek found himself on the ice with Sommerfeld, his nemesis, recently drafted. Derek surprised Sommerfeld with a left hand, then followed with a right. Another right hand smashed into Sommerfeld's face, bloodying his nose.

Suddenly, during home games in Prince George, the Multiplex would fill with the sound of Derek's name, a call and answer that echoed through the sold-out arena. One side shouted, "Boo!" The other responded, "Gaard!"

The coaches found that Derek, finally, could do what the best fighters could do: strike fear into opposing teams, change the way they treated the star players, shift the momentum with a crowd-pleasing beating. Other WHL teams began inquiring about trades for him.

It was all about the fighting. Derek didn't register a point until his 54th WHL game, an assist again Kamloops.

"It's nice to have something other than penalty minutes beside my name," Boogaard told the *Prince George Citizen* that night. "When I get a goal, I'll grab the puck myself and no one will stop me."

It happened on January 3, 2001. Derek, now playing meaningful shifts alongside top players, found a puck in the slot and jammed it through the legs of the Kamloops goalie. He never saw it go in, but the reaction of the crowd told him. A chant bounced through the arena—*Boo-gey, Boo-gey, Boo-gey* . . .

Derek wanted to be famous for the glory of goals, not the fury of his fists. Now, at 18, he dreamed of being an all-around player, someone like Bob Probert or his boyhood hero, Wendel Clark—men with scoring punch to go with their punches, respected players who could be trusted to be on the ice while the clock was ticking, not just when it stopped for a fight.

"I have to work harder, and not always look for the fights," Derek said after he scored his first goal.

But Derek did not score again during the regular season. His reputation was cemented and his future ordained. Internet fight fans gave Derek an 18–4–4 record that season. Five other fights were not reviewed. He had 245 penalty minutes, eighth highest in the league. He was voted "toughest player" in the Western Hockey League's Western Conference.

GAME 4 OF Prince George's playoff series with the Portland Winter Hawks took place on April 4, 2001, at the sold-out Multiplex. Portland led the series, two games to one, and the teams headed to overtime.

And there was Derek, playing left wing in sudden-death of a game that Prince George was desperate to win, the score tied, 4–4, the seats filled with 6,000 anxious Cougars fans, Prince George coach Ed Dempsey looking for someone to be the star.

"All of a sudden, Ed said our line was up," Derek later wrote.

Teammate Devin Wilson dumped the puck into a corner. Derek chased it down. He tried to center it to Dan Baum, but the puck bounced around before Baum was able to stab it. His shot trickled behind the Portland goalie.

"I turned around and the puck was just sitting there," Derek recalled.

He swiped it in.

The crowd erupted.

"I don't think I ever saw our rink, or Derek, that happy," Thompson, then the assistant coach, said a decade later.

Teammates ambushed Derek, burying him in a pile. One rushed to grab the puck so that Derek would have the memento.

"It was an unbelievable feeling," Derek wrote. "The guys came out of the bench and the place was going nuts. It was the best feeling I had the last 2 years."

The giddiness of the goal trailed the Cougars out of town. The series now even, the Cougars boarded their bus for Portland, 700 miles and more than 14 hours away. But the boost that Derek provided evaporated. The Winter Hawks beat Prince George handily in Game 5, shutting them out 6–0.

The teams returned to Prince George—14 hours back north—for Game 6. Before another raucous sold-out crowd, the Cougars held a 3–1 lead midway through the second period. But the bottom dropped out in mere moments. Portland scored four unanswered goals, one of them on a power play after a Derek penalty, and the season ticked to a disappointing close.

In the final seconds, with the score 5–3, Dempsey again sent Derek onto the ice. Just as the Portland goalie bent over to pick up the puck as a souvenir, Derek barreled into him.

Portland coach Mike Williamson was incensed. He accused Dempsey of sending Derek out to try to hurt his players, and the coaches had a shouting match under the stands 30 minutes after the game.

The Western Hockey League suspended Dempsey for three games and fined him $5,000. But Derek took the brunt of the punishment. He was suspended for seven games, to be served at the start of the following season.

"It's very unfortunate, because the talk around the league had been how much improvement Boogaard has shown recently," WHL vice president Rick Doerksen told the *Prince George Citizen*. "But what he did was an unprovoked act that has no place in our league."

Derek never revealed Dempsey's instructions to him. Part of the enforcer's code was to quietly accept responsibility.

THE NATIONAL HOCKEY LEAGUE Entry Draft was scheduled for two days beginning June 23, Derek's 19th birthday. Derek again wondered if he might be selected. Joanne Boogaard thought that such hope was ridiculous. She wanted Derek to quit hockey.

In early May, 14-year-old Aaron Boogaard was chosen in the first round, 14th overall, of the WHL Bantam Draft, by the Calgary Hitmen. Aaron was already six foot one and 200 pounds, and he was a much faster, far niftier puck handler than Derek. The combination of his own abilities and his brother's reputation made him a treasured recruit. Derek was never drafted by the WHL. He only gained notice with his size and with an out-of-character tirade in a small-town rink. Four years later, after his second year in the WHL, he was one of the better enforcers in the rough-and-tumble league, but hardly a star.

Joanne demanded that Derek get an off-season job. She had little patience for laziness. After all, Joanne had two jobs after high school, all the way until she married Len years later. Now she was a single mother of four children. She was not going to allow Derek to sit around all summer. Hockey had become a tool of procrastination. It was time to move on—if not school, then work.

Len Boogaard lived in a nearby apartment. He was in a full-fledged relationship with Jody Vail, the Royal Canadian Mounted Police member he had helped train in Melfort beginning in 1997. Joanne had tried to ensure that Jody would not be transferred to Regina when the Boogaards moved there, but Jody was transferred to a small town about 30 minutes away. The Boogaards divorced, after several years of tumultuous separations, and Len and Jody would marry a year later, in 2002.

Len trod the middle ground when it came to Derek's hockey career. Pick what you are going to do, and do it all the way, he told his son. If you want to play hockey, prepare for the next season. If you are finished, get a job.

Derek did both. He found work at a golf course near the RCMP Depot. He hated it from the first day. He was up at 5, at work by 6, and spent eight hours on a lawn mower. After work, he went home to eat, and then to the gym.

"At the time I was so shocked and pissed that Mom thought I wasn't going anywhere with hockey," Derek wrote years later. "My Dad said I could move in with him, but I was pissed right off that I didn't want to be in the same city as the family. Now I know that times were tough for Mom because of them divorceing [sic] and my dad re-marrying. It was kind of tough for me as well but in the end the constint [sic] fighting and always arguing was and is never good."

Derek soon had enough. He abruptly left Regina and returned to Prince George. He moved in with Mike and Caren Tobin, taking the guest bedroom at the front of the house, overlooking the driveway. Unlike his own family, the Tobins did not disappoint. There was no fighting, no nagging, and no doubt. And because it was the off-season, the Cougars had no say in the living arrangement.

Derek made himself at home, fixing three poached eggs and toast for himself every morning, always cleaning his own dishes. Mike Tobin let Derek drive his black GMC Sierra Denali, with the black leather interior and the Quadrasteer system. Derek helped with yard work, but not much before finding a shady spot on a chaise longue. At the birthday party for the twin girls, Derek spent hours happily shoveling children in and out of a giant bounce house in the front yard.

Derek was at the Tobins' when he received a call from a Minnesota Wild scout named Paul Charles. Derek felt as if he was applying for a job, and he nervously answered the questions. The thought of getting drafted suddenly consumed him.

Derek watched the start of the draft on his birthday. Atlanta chose a Russian named Ilya Kovalchuk with the first pick. With the sixth choice, Minnesota selected Mikko Koivu of Finland. With the 12th pick, Nashville chose one of Derek's Prince George teammates, Dan Hamhuis. Seven WHL players were chosen in the first round. Another 10 were chosen in the second, and six more in the third. Derek was not among them.

Caren Tobin made dinner and a birthday cake. A couple of friends came over, and Derek blew out the candles. Then he and his friends headed to the Iron Horse bar. With Derek of legal drinking age, his friends made sure he celebrated his birthday with an over-indulgence of beers and shots. He arrived back to the Tobins' well after midnight.

In Regina early the next morning, a phone rang inside the house on Woodward Avenue. Joanne answered. A man introduced himself as Tommy Thompson, the chief scout of the Minnesota Wild. He told Joanne that the Wild had drafted her son Derek.

Joanne was confused.

"But he's already on a team, in Prince George," she replied.

"No, this is the National Hockey League," Thompson said.

"The NHL?" Joanne said, incredulously. "You've got to be kidding."

Moments later, a phone rang in Prince George. Caren Tobin answered. She called up to Derek's room, but he was asleep and did not respond. She went upstairs and knocked on the door. Then she banged on it.

"Take a message," Derek moaned.

She ordered him to the phone. She and Mike knew what was happening, and Derek came downstairs, groggy.

"Hello?" he said. "Uh-huh. Uh-huh. Yeah. Okay. Yeah. Okay. Thanks."

He hung up, expressionless.

"Well?" Caren said.

"I got drafted by Minnesota," Derek said. He was chosen in the seventh round, 202nd overall.

The Tobins wrapped Derek in hugs.

"I was very excited as well," Derek wrote later. "With a huge headache."

THE WILD HELD a four-week camp for prospects in Breezy Point, Minnesota, a few weeks later, but Derek first had to stop in Saint Paul, the team's headquarters. In his hotel room, he found a package of forms to fill out and information to read. It explained that teams had two years to sign a player after they drafted him, a sort of tryout period as boys move through the ranks of junior and the minor leagues.

Derek walked to the Xcel Energy Center, the Wild's downtown arena. The team had only played one season, and the arena still felt brand new. The dressing room was the biggest Derek had seen. An equipment manager fitted him for gear. For the first time, everything Derek tried on was new, as if made exclusively for him. He pulled a Wild jersey over his head. There was no need to sew an extra ring of material to the bottom, or at the ends of the sleeves. It fit perfectly.

While Derek was in Breezy Point, the Cougars, far away, openly discussed trading him. They knew that Derek would miss the first seven games of the 72-game schedule because of the suspension. He had been through several billet families and now had requested to stay with the Tobins. The Cougars were weary of handling Derek. Junior hockey was an assembly line, and replacements were ready.

"He's got one goal, he's drafted now, and now he probably thinks he's going to be on the power play and on the second line," Lubiniecki, the team's general manager, told the *Prince George Citizen*.

Derek brimmed with confidence. He returned to Prince George in tremendous shape, weighing 245 pounds. His long hair had been cut short again. He was no longer an outcast, but an NHL draft pick with a future. He was wanted.

Derek's family noticed the change. During a visit to Prince George, Len asked to speak privately to Mike Tobin.

"I just can't believe the change in Derek," Len said. "We went to Earls the other day, and a girl walked up to our table. Six months ago, if a girl would have walked up to our table and starting talking to him, he would have crawled under the table. I can't believe the difference."

Derek was gone again, back with the Wild for training camp and a rookie camp for several NHL teams in Traverse City, Michigan. During one scrimmage, Derek thought he had a player lined up for a big hit. He took several long strides and turned his shoulder to smash the opponent into the side boards. The other player ducked at the last moment.

Derek crashed through the glass, shattering it into thousands of tiny pieces. His body folded over the boards and flipped out of the rink. The arena went silent as coaches and scouts rose with worry and awe.

Derek stood and, with a sheepish grin, climbed back over the boards, onto the ice. Pebbles of broken glass encrusted his jersey. When Derek came to the rink the next day, he found a taped outline of a large player on the new pane of glass, as if it were the sidewalk of a crime scene.

Derek was with the Wild for training camp in Saint Paul during the September 11, 2001, terrorist attacks on New York and Washington, D.C. Two days later, during a scrimmage, he exchanged punches with the Wild's veteran enforcer, Matt Johnson.

Wild head coach Jacques Lemaire was not a fan of players beating up teammates. He shouted down from his seat in the stands, asking another player to break up the fight. A day later, Derek was sent, as expected, back to Prince George for the WHL season.

Derek did not want to be there, and the Cougars were not excited to have him. He sat out the first seven games because of his suspension, but other players combined to take on Derek's role, fighting 13 times in the seven games. The Cougars had won three of their last four games when they, along with Derek, embarked on a long, eastward road trip.

At the first stop, in Red Deer, Alberta, Derek twice fought Jeff Smith, a sturdy 20-year-old enforcer from Regina. Derek looked stronger and more fearless than ever.

But he snapped the next night in Calgary. On Derek's first shift, 80 seconds into the first period against the Hitmen, he was penalized for roughing. Later, the teams had two bloody brawls while Derek was penned in the bench. Prince George led, 5–3, early in the third period, when Derek was called for roughing again. This time, he did not quietly skate toward the penalty box. He could not be constrained.

It was unlike anything Derek's family had seen since his rampage into the opponents' bench as a 14-year-old in Melfort. A linesman tried to pry Derek away and escort him off the ice. Derek shoved him—a huge breach of rules and protocol. He threw his helmet toward opposing players. He flashed his middle finger to the referee.

Derek was immediately ejected from the game, and the WHL quickly suspended him indefinitely. The Cougars were furious. They had been trying to trade him.

"He's got to get smarter," Lubiniecki told the *Prince George Citizen*. "The bottom line is, right now Derek Boogaard just can't keep it together. He's becoming a liability from the fact that he can't play the games because the league won't let him. He won't use the thought process he needs to, to keep himself in games. If anyone has tried to make this guy a responsible player, it's our organization."

The league ultimately handed Derek a four-game suspension, but the Cougars were finished with him. Before he could play again for Prince George, Derek was traded to the Medicine Hat Tigers. In return, Prince George received a 19-year-old third-line center named Denny Johnston and a fourth-round pick in the next year's bantam draft.

"I painted my own picture," Derek told the *Prince George Citizen*. "It was me who caused this trade to happen."

Only Derek and his mother knew what truly had made Derek snap in Calgary. Joanne had driven from Regina to Calgary, eight hours away, because there was something she wanted to tell her son. And she did not want to do it over the phone.

Months earlier, the same week that Len had moved out, Joanne received a letter from social services. Joanne had become pregnant when she was in high school, years before she met Len, a decade before she had Derek. She had the baby, a healthy boy, and then gave him up for adoption. She'd kept it a secret, even from the birth father, a boy she barely knew. It was still a secret nearly three decades later. But the baby boy had grown into a man and had come looking for his birth mother, the way Joanne always wondered if he might. His name was Curtis Heide.

Curtis had grown up in the family of an RCMP member, too, and the coincidences did not end there. His adoptive father had been posted across Saskatchewan, just like Len. At times, they were posted in nearby detachments. The men and their families never crossed paths.

Of course, Joanne wanted to meet the son she never knew. Curtis was tall and strong, like the Boogaard kids. He was quiet and humble, too, though never much of a hockey player. He had a good job in the oil-and-gas exploration industry that fueled much of the economy in the Prairie provinces.

Joanne told her three youngest children, all of whom were supportive of the news and the addition of another family member. Then she came to Calgary to tell Derek, at a restaurant before Prince George's game against the Hitmen.

He did not take the news well. He was devastated to know that his mother had kept a secret from him all his life. He was hurt to learn that he was not the oldest of her children. For most of his life, family was the one reliable thing that Derek had. It had collapsed like a thin facade, first through divorce, now through another kind of betrayal.

"I don't want to know about this," he said, pushing the photograph of his half-brother back across the table. "I don't want to hear about this."

Derek carried the emotion silently to that night's game at Calgary's Saddledome. And with his mother in the stands watching, Derek did just what he was growing accustomed to doing whenever he needed an outlet from the hurt and pain, whenever he felt someone he could trust had disappointed him.

He brought it to the ice. And he took it out on someone else.

THE FIRST TIME Derek laid eyes on his girlfriend was when he flew her to Minnesota to sneak her into the Wild's summer camp in 2002.

Janella D'Amore. You couldn't make up a name like that. And when she walked toward him inside the terminal of the tiny airport, Derek tried his best to play it cool. He leaned against a post and watched her walk his way. In those few heart-fluttering moments, he saw everything he hoped to see. She was petite and pretty and perky, the kind of girl Derek always liked but rarely captured, with big brown eyes and wavy brown hair. And it wasn't just how she looked. She had come all that way just for him.

Derek was 20. He was still shy and insecure around women, a trait he never could shake, the meek alter ego behind his on-ice invincibility. But in junior hockey, many young women knew who he was, especially once he was drafted.

One such woman discovered Derek when the Medicine Hat Tigers came to Portland, Oregon, in the winter of 2001 and 2002. She talked about him with her friends, including Janella, a figure skater who worked at the ice rink. Janella had not met Derek, but she was always a willing matchmaker. To gauge Derek's interest in her friend, Janella sent him instant messages on the computer, the era's version of passing notes. Derek responded with a dismissive remark about the other woman.

What a jerk, Janella thought. Communication stopped.

But then, from nowhere, Derek sent an instant message to Janella a few weeks later.

"Hi," he wrote. Oh, no, Janella thought. This guy.

She thought about not answering. But she did. And she slowly found Derek to be nothing like what she imagined. His words were self-effacing and sweet. The ogre she had conjured in her mind was surprisingly kind and gentle. Janella tried to make sense of it. She asked him why he had been so rude to her friend.

"Are you kidding me?" Derek replied. "I couldn't stand her. That girl was a total puck bunny."

The long-distance relationship between Derek and Janella grew for weeks, through instant messages and late-night talks. Since Janella had a job, she paid the phone bills—several hundred dollars those first months.

Janella was intrigued by Derek. Hockey players usually struck her as brash, fueled by testosterone and a sense of entitlement. They

worked hard and partied hard, she found. Pretty girls were an adorn-
ment that they came to expect. Derek, though, did not talk much
about hockey, and never much about himself. He wanted to know
about her. He made her feel important, but he also seemed nervous.
Sincere. Fragile.

Amid their phone and online conversations, Derek was headed
again to the Wild's summer camp at Breezy Point, Minnesota, held
at a sprawling lakeside resort. Derek had seen other players sneak
girlfriends in the year before. They hatched a plan. Derek arranged
for Janella to fly to Minnesota. She agreed. She paid for it.

He had no car, but he borrowed a friend's Jeep and waited inside
the tiny airport's terminal. She got off the plane and ducked into a
bathroom to check her appearance and take a deep breath.

She saw him from a distance. He was huge. She pretended not to
notice him and walked past.

"Janella," Derek finally called out. "You didn't recognize me?"

They laughed and hugged. He thought she was beautiful. She
thought he was handsome. Derek never thought of himself that way.
He would always say that Janella was too pretty for him.

He carried her bag and they walked to the car.

"Don't drive me into the woods and chop me into little pieces,"
Janella said.

Derek's room had two single beds, but they pushed them together
to make one big one. They talked and took pictures. When Derek
left for practice, Janella walked around the resort, bought things for
him in the gift shop, went to the bar for a drink. When he returned,
they took a boat ride on the lake.

But after one workout, Derek returned with bad news. The
team had found out, he said. Janella was moved to another room,
and her return flight home was moved up a day. The secret tryst
was over.

If Derek got in trouble from the team, Janella never heard about it.

. . .

MEDICINE HAT SITS in southeastern Alberta, about a 30-minute
drive to the Saskatchewan border. A sunny prairie city of 60,000,
supposedly named for the lost headdress of a Cree medicine man,
Medicine Hat provided Derek a fresh start, closer to home, only
a four-and-a-half-hour drive east on the Trans-Canada Highway
to Regina.

But the Minnesota Wild was worried about its seventh-round
draft pick. Derek had gone ballistic in Calgary and been traded to the
Tigers, a team on its way to a last-place finish in the Western Hockey
League's Central Division. Derek thought he should play more, con-
sidering his breakout season in Prince George and that he had been
drafted by an NHL team.

Medicine Hat coach Bob Loucks, however, had another 19-year-
old enforcer, a smaller scrapper from Saskatoon named Ryan Olynyk,
a holdover for the Tigers from the previous season. Derek and Olynyk
fought once in Prince George, but it was not much of a bout. A
few minutes after beating up one of Olynyk's teammates, Derek had
checked Olynyk hard with a clean hit. When Derek skated away,
Olynyk attacked from behind. Derek drilled Olynyk with a right
hand. The fight ended.

Now they were teammates, but Olynyk handled most of the fighting. He led the WHL with 41 fights that season. Derek had 16. Derek
dismissed Loucks as just another coach who underestimated him.

Doris Sullivan saw it unfold from her unique vantage point as a
billet mother. She and her husband, Kelly, had housed a dozen players over many years, and they had another Tigers player staying with
them that season. Derek walked into their lives, trailing a teammate.

As in Prince George, Derek found a home where he'd rather stay.
Unlike in Prince George, there was little argument from the team.
Derek moved in with the Sullivans after Christmas. They laughed at

how he had to duck through doorways and how he rested his elbow on top of the refrigerator, and how he consumed entire batches of cookies at once, before they had cooled.

It was no coincidence that the billets Derek clung to were those who wanted to spend time with Derek, and not just give him a place to live. When Derek sulked, the mood was usually tinged with disappointment, not anger. More often than not, somebody he trusted had disappointed him, or expressed disappointment in him. While Derek was adept at hiding his physical pain, he did a poor job of disguising hurt feelings. Size disguised fragility.

The Sullivans had hosted a dozen or more boys over the years, but Derek stood out—and not because of his size. He must have been burned somewhere along the line, to put up those guards at such a young age, Doris Sullivan thought.

The Sullivans found Derek to be much as the Tobins in Prince George had found him. He was quiet and unassuming, content to let the conversations lull. What they all did together—watch television, play video games, go on errands—was not the important thing. He just wanted company, to be part of something, even if it felt to others like nothing at all.

Derek considered Medicine Hat a stopover between the NHL draft and a professional career. He fought when opponents dared to fight him, and the home fans still showered him with "Boo-gey, Boo-gey" chants. He had 178 penalty minutes with Medicine Hat in 2001–02, and was suspended for a total of 14 games for various rough-play infractions. He scored once. It came in February, at Regina's Agridome, against his original WHL team. In goal for the Pats was Josh Harding, a Regina native who would be selected by the Minnesota Wild in the second round of the NHL draft four months later.

Derek's family was in the crowd. When Derek took the ice, he scanned the stands and found their faces. And when he scored, his mother thought, once again, that maybe he could be more than an enforcer, if only someone would give him that chance.

Why don't you stand in front of the goal, where you have a better chance of scoring, she asked him again and again. She hated the fighting—all the blows that Derek took, but, too, all the ones he delivered with increasing ferocity and effect. She thought about the other boys' mothers, too.

"I'm not here to score goals," Derek told the Regina newspaper, the *Leader-Post*. "I'm here to regulate, to enforce; don't let other people push around our smaller players. It's what I do."

A man called the Sullivan house. He introduced himself to Doris as Barry MacKenzie, recently hired as the coordinator of player development for the Wild. After a player got drafted, it was Mac-Kenzie's job to track his progress.

Derek was his first assignment. MacKenzie had talked to other billets that Derek had been through in Prince George and Medicine Hat, and he wanted Doris Sullivan's opinion. She gave Derek a glowing endorsement—fun to have, polite and helpful, never a problem.

MacKenzie was surprised. Others told a different story, about an aloof young man who did not like to follow rules. Sullivan suggested that others probably had not taken the time to get to know Derek well.

MacKenzie came to Medicine Hat. Before a game, he took Derek to Earls, part of an upscale restaurant chain. Derek ordered a steak.

"The coach isn't giving me a chance," MacKenzie recalled Derek telling him. "I don't think they like me here. I'm not getting enough ice time."

MacKenzie listened attentively and kept his thoughts to himself. He watched that night's game, and then the next day's practice. He was not impressed by Derek's work ethic and enthusiasm. He thought Derek was going through the motions. He invited Derek out again. This time, he took him to McDonald's.

"With what I've seen in the last 24 hours," MacKenzie told Derek, "you want to eat at Earls, but you're going to have to get used to eating at McDonald's."

THAT SUMMER, about the time that Derek met Janella, the Medicine Hat Tigers made a coaching change. Bob Loucks was gone. Medicine Hat hired a 45-year-old from tiny Climax, Saskatchewan, named Willie Desjardins.

When training camp opened in 2002, the Tigers had some players, like Derek, who were born in 1982 and had already turned 20. They had other players born in late 1986, yet to turn 16. Derek was more than a foot taller than some boys, and almost twice their weight.

Derek was a team leader, by virtue of his age, size, and NHL draft status, and Desjardins liked him from the start. He was surprised that Derek could skate so well for a player his size, and he noticed he had a powerful shot. Desjardins found Derek different than many young enforcers bent on building reputations with brash talk and punkish behavior. Derek was a surprisingly meek soul. Desjardins wondered if he was nasty enough to do his job.

In November, late in a lopsided loss at Swift Current, Derek took part in a 10-player brawl. The fights began slowly, and Derek stood aside, casually talking to an opposing player as others paired off to fight. He slowly turned to another Swift Current player, Mitch Love. After a few words were exchanged, Derek shoved the six-foot Love in the chest.

The boys were soon swinging fists, and two of the four on-ice officials rushed in to break them apart. Derek shook them off and hammered Love with a few right-hand uppercuts. The officials kept tugging, and the four-person scrum slid from one face-off circle to the front of the net. Derek threw haymakers until Love and one official fell to the ice. When Derek jabbed his fallen opponent with his left fist, the other official jumped and slid off Derek's back.

Finally, the boys were escorted to the penalty box, Derek pointing at Love, while four other players continued to fight. The crowd cheered and whistled.

Desjardins had his answer. Derek—big, gentle Derek—showed he could flip the switch. He did not have to be mean. He just had to show he could be, when it mattered.

In October, just weeks into the season, Western Hockey League teams had to rid their rosters of all but three 20-year-olds. Two boys were released. Derek stayed.

It was a strange but happy fall for Derek. He lived with the Sullivans. He had a girlfriend. He felt grown up, respected, and upwardly mobile, and it showed. A former teammate from Melfort, Brett Condy, once saw Derek in a Medicine Hat bar, dancing with a "really good-looking girl," Condy said. "You never saw that in Melfort."

On October 20, Medicine Hat played in Calgary, at the Saddledome. For the first and only time, Derek played against his 16-year-old brother Aaron, a first-year right wing with the Calgary Hitmen. He had been drafted 15th overall in the bantam draft 18 months earlier.

"People had the perception that he was going to be the same player as me," Derek wrote years later.

But Aaron was a smaller, quicker version of Derek. He showed no predisposition to fighting. He would do it if asked, however, and already had, in a game about a week earlier.

"Leave Nick alone," Joanne Boogaard told Derek before their game, calling Aaron by his middle name, as family and close friends did. "Don't you dare go after him."

It was Aaron who tried to goad Derek, slashing him across the legs with his stick. Derek, never one to back down in the basement in Melfort or anywhere else his brothers prodded him, would not retaliate. He would not flip the switch.

The hometown Hitmen won easily, 4–1. Medicine Hat's lone goal was scored by Derek. He ended Calgary's shutout bid in the game's final minutes, poking the puck past goalie Brent Krahn. It would stand as the second and final goal in Derek's 73-game career in Medicine Hat.

Among those who cheered from the stands were Len and Joanne. Between them sat 18-year-old Ryan and 13-year-old Krysten. Also there, next to Joanne, was Curtis Heide, Derek's half-brother, now a married man of 30 who had recently set out to find his birth mother.

Over the past year, Curtis had come to know the rest of the family. He had come to Regina and met Ryan, Aaron, and Krysten. Everyone liked Curtis. He had introduced his wife, Gladys, and Gladys's five-year-old son, Curtis's stepson.

Now it was Derek's turn. He was nervous about meeting Curtis, but not as nervous as Curtis was to meet him. When the game ended, the Boogaards and Curtis moved to the front row of the Saddledome in Calgary. Derek and Curtis met. The group posed for photographs—Derek in his Medicine Hat jersey, Aaron in his Calgary Hitmen jersey, everyone wearing a brave smile. It was hard to imagine that night, but Curtis and Derek, with little more than size and a birth mother in common, were on their way to a budding relationship.

In late November, Medicine Hat embarked on a long road trip to the American Northwest. Janella met Derek in Seattle, and then introduced him to her family before the next game in Portland. She had given him a ring on an earlier trip to Medicine Hat. The guys in the locker room teased him, unaware that she was his first serious girlfriend.

Derek's world was upended before the road trip was over. The Tigers released him.

There was irony in the shuffle. Medicine Hat dropped Derek because it wanted to shore up its defense and had signed defenseman Ryan Stempfle to take his place.

Stempfle had been released by his team, the Saskatoon Blades, when they called up Denny Johnston from a lower level. Derek and Johnston had been traded for one another just over a year earlier.

"It came as a surprise," Boogaard told the local newspaper. "I'm disappointed, but the team needs a defenseman and you can't do anything about the situation."

His Western Hockey League career was over.

The final tally: three-plus seasons, three teams, three goals.

And 670 penalty minutes, mostly from his 70 fights.

4

D EREK WAS SUDDENLY WITHOUT a team, and the Wild
searched for a place to put him. They opted for their affiliate
in the East Coast Hockey League: the Louisiana IceGators of Lafayette, Louisiana.

"We've got a guy to send you who has been treated as kind of a
circus act in juniors," Tom Lynn, the assistant general manager of the
Wild, told IceGators coach Dave Farrish.

Derek made his professional debut with the IceGators on December 20, 2002, in a game in Biloxi, Mississippi. He was 20 and had a
contract to pay him $35,000 for the season. There was no mistaking
Derek when he took the ice, wearing number 30—an oversized jersey usually reserved for goalies and their bulky pads, but the only one
the IceGators had that was big enough to fit.

The IceGators were completing a 6–2 victory over the Mississippi Sea Wolves, and much of the announced crowd of 2,565 had
headed out of the Mississippi Coast Coliseum. Derek fired a wrist
shot that looked to be headed into the net, only to have it gloved
by the goalie at the last moment. In the waning seconds, Derek
approached a Mississippi enforcer, testing his appetite for a fight. The
other player skated away.

Farrish took great satisfaction in that. The coach had seen Derek in two rookie camps in Minnesota with the Wild, and knew what he could mean to a game.

"People know he's out there, because if he ever hits you you're going to be Wile E. Coyote on the asphalt," Farrish told the Lafayette newspaper, the *Advertiser*, after the game. "It's great to have him on the ice. As you've seen tonight, nobody took any physical liberties towards us, and I think that was another big factor in the game."

But Derek would have to prove himself to be more than a theoretical intimidator the next night, in his home debut. It was a Saturday, and the Cajundome in Lafayette was filled with 5,090 fans. Surprisingly, Derek picked up his first professional point—an assist—before he got into his first professional fight.

The IceGators were on their way to another 6–2 victory, this one over the Arkansas RiverBlades. Early in the third period, Derek awaited a face-off next to Arkansas's Mark Scott, a six-foot-four, 215-pound enforcer from Manitoba. The gloves dropped in sync with the puck. Scott, 25 years old, landed the first punch, a right-hand jab to Derek's chin. Derek swung wildly with his right hand and missed. Scott hit Derek squarely with a right hand, then managed to wrestle Derek's jersey over his head. Holding tight, Scott hit Derek with a left hand before Derek freed himself from the constraints of his opponent and his own jersey.

Derek swung his dangerous right hand and struck Scott in the back of the head, on the helmet. Unlike in the Western Hockey League, the professional players kept their helmets on. That meant many bare-knuckled punches struck a hard shell of plastic, not the relative squishiness of a human skull or jaw.

Derek was growing accustomed to the annual damage. Early each season, after a couple of fights, Derek's hands were grossly misshapen and swollen. The backs of them looked inflated and were marked by red and blue smudges, and sometimes the tooth marks of opponents. The fingers were thick, like sausages, and so crooked that

Derek had trouble extending them. The knuckles, taking the brunt of each blow they delivered, rarely had time to scab and heal until the off-season. If the next fight came within a week or two—and they usually did—the skin of the knuckles would flap open again, pouring blood or oozing pus. First aid came in the form of towels and a bucket of icy water in the penalty box.

"The thing that worried me wasn't the concussions," Len Boogaard said years later. "It never really was an issue. It was never brought to the forefront. It was never deemed to be problematic. You got your bell rung? Well, here's a Tylenol or whatever. The only thing that bothered me was his hands. He would fight and his knuckles would be pushed back into the wrist. And then he'd have to have it manipulated and have his knuckles put back in place. His hands were a mess. My concern was always, okay, he's going to suffer with this later on in life, in terms of arthritis. It was his hands that I was more worried about."

Derek bashed his fist against Scott's helmet once. Twice. Three times. Four times. Scott finally fell to the ice. The intoxicated crowd blared its endorsement.

The night's work was not over. With about three minutes left in the game, Louisiana firmly in control, Derek checked a much smaller opponent named Damon Whitten into the boards. Derek flung off his gloves and punched Whitten in the head with a right hand. A linesman quickly jumped between the two players. Derek pushed past the official and hit Whitten again. Around them, the eight other skaters on the ice dropped their gloves, too.

Long a staple of junior and minor-league hockey, though increasingly rare in the NHL, line brawls were a peculiar sight. Sometimes staged to coincide with a face-off, sometimes sparked more spontaneously, the players paired off into one-on-one duels, like gangs in a dark alley. Even goalies sometimes skated to the middle of the rink to fight one another.

"Right now, there is an abundance of toughness on this club," Farrish said after the victory, happy to have Derek's presence. "I think that will stop teams from being as aggressive as they were against us at the start of the season."

Derek wanted to build his reputation fast, and he was just getting started. In Louisiana's next game, against the Jackson Bandits in Mississippi, he fought 5-foot, 11-inch Dave Stewart, a 28-year-old minor-league antagonist. The men grabbed each other and spun around. Stewart could not reach Derek with most of his punches. Derek landed one to the back of Stewart's head, but missed wildly on others, a narrow victory.

Derek fought twice two nights later in Baton Rouge, Louisiana. Jason Norrie was a 25-year-old vagabond, a six-foot, three-inch bundle of bad intentions. In a 12-year career that began in the Western Hockey League and wound through the American minor leagues, he played for 18 franchises. Derek beat him up midway through the first period. Norrie wanted more, and the two fought off of a face-off late in the third period. Derek hit Norrie in the head with a couple of right hands. Norrie retaliated with fists filled with Derek's own jersey. Amid the clutching, Derek managed to pull Norrie's helmet loose and toss it aside. He embarked on what had become his preferred strategy—holding the opponent's shoulder with the left hand and firing well-cocked punches with the right.

Like a panicked moth caught in a spider's web, the smaller man fluttered wildly to break free. Derek tried his full repertoire—an uppercut here, a roundhouse there, a quick jab with the clutching left hand. He and Norrie switched hands, quickly grabbing the other with their rights. Derek tried to punch with his left, his weaker arm, and connected twice. Two officials circled with no intention to break it up. One had his arms crossed, as if unimpressed by the spectacle. Finally, as the energy of the fight fizzled and the players nodded a silent signal, the officials stepped in. The fight lasted 90 seconds, the same as a heavyweight boxing round. Fans cheered the effort.

Four games. Four fights. All victories.

"He got into some pretty good scraps initially," Farrish recalled of Derek later. "And word gets around fast."

THE AMERICAN DEEP SOUTH was hardly a hockey hotbed. But in the 1990s, the sport saw a vast opportunity for growth there. To the chagrin of Canadians, especially, hockey migrated south, fueled in large part by Canadian imports—teams and players.

Derek was one of them. By the time he arrived in Louisiana, the roots planted in the Sunbelt were in full bloom, led by the NHL, which had placed expansion teams or moved existing franchises to places such as Dallas, Phoenix, Nashville, Raleigh, Tampa, and Miami.

The East Coast Hockey League was founded in 1988. Among the five original teams, stretching from Erie, Pennsylvania, to Knoxville, Tennessee, were the Johnstown (Pennsylvania) Chiefs, named for the fictitious hard-fighting Chiefs of the movie *Slap Shot*. Much of the film had been shot in Johnstown's Cambria County War Memorial Arena.

The ECHL grew quickly. By the start of the 1995 season, there were 21 teams, including the Louisiana IceGators, planted in mid-sized cities not unlike those of the Western Hockey League. But the culture could not have been more different. Fans of the WHL followed their teams with religious fervor and tracked the progress of the teenaged players from years before they arrived until well into the pros. Most fans in the ECHL were simply looking for something to do on a Saturday night. Hockey was a curiosity, and hardly a passion. Plenty of potential fans had never seen ice other than the kind that filled a glass of sweet tea. The ECHL was "AA" professional hockey, two deep levels below the NHL, and the rosters were filled mostly with unknown players from Canada or the northern climes of the United States.

A few players were on their way up. A few were on the way down. Most were in a holding pattern, stuck in their mid-20s in the middle level of pro hockey, unable to climb upward with any momentum, waiting for something—an injury, a relationship, an honest coach—to nudge them out of the game. Of the 33 teammates who played for the 2002–03 IceGators alongside Derek, only three ever played in the NHL—and for a grand total of 67 games. By comparison, seven teammates from the Medicine Hat team that Derek left behind in December went on to play in the NHL, combining for more than 1,400 career games.

Franchises needed to find ways to get fans to pay money to watch these strangers play this strange game. The key to success was getting people to fall quickly for the sport, like a crush. To do that, teams used a full arsenal of flirtations. ECHL hockey meant cheap tickets. It meant colorful nicknames. (The league was part of a trend toward nonsensical, unique team names. In 1995, the IceGators became the third team with "Ice" in its name, as if to remind people what sport they played. Their competition included teams called the Lizard Kings, RiverFrogs, and Mysticks.) It meant goofy promotions and contests during games. It meant costumed mascots and community outreach, particularly toward children.

And it meant fighting.

The Louisiana IceGators had 101 fights in 72 games in 2002–03, substantially higher than the league average. Fans willing to buy tickets knew that at least one fight was likely. A line brawl was possible. And when the opponent was the rival Mississippi Sea Wolves, violence was practically assured.

A season-high 7,726 fans were at the Cajundome on March 22,

2003, as the IceGators and Sea Wolves chased a division title. Louisiana's 5–3 victory was punctuated by a game-ending bench-clearing brawl. It took a posse of coaches, officials, and the Lafayette sheriff's department to clear the rink of 36 players. As the players fought, the arena cast the players in bright spotlights, like performers on a stage. Derek grabbed Jeff Hutchins, a 24-year-old forward who never shied from a fight, and pounded him with several blows to the head.

Breaking both the unwritten code of fighting and the written rule making it illegal to join a fight, a Mississippi goalie arrived to try to save Hutchins from Derek. He clumsily knocked the two fighters down, but they continued to punch one another. A linesman arrived to intervene, but the combatants stood and shrugged him off, sending the official looking for an easier fight to stop. Another Mississippi player charged Derek, suddenly a matador avoiding charging bulls. Derek was tackled from behind, and Hutchins climbed on top. The fight died. Others started.

Derek was one of five players suspended, but he received the harshest penalty: six games. He missed the last four regular-season games, and played in only two playoff games as the IceGators were upset in the second round.

Derek finished his first professional season with one goal and 240 penalty minutes, almost identical to the 245 penalty minutes he had in Prince George during his breakout season two years before. But he did it in roughly half as many games—33, compared with 61 in Prince George. Most important for Derek's career: according to online judges, he won all 13 of his fights.

His family tried to track his progress from afar, but the ECHL elicited little coverage. All the Boogaards knew was that when Derek returned to Regina for the summer, he had a girlfriend and a fist full of swollen knuckles.

. . .

BEFORE HE WAS SENT to Louisiana, Derek had wanted to surprise Janella at Christmas by visiting her at home in Vancouver, Washington, just across the Columbia River from Portland. He wrote a Christmas card to her mother, asking if she would pick him up at the airport and keep his plan a secret.

"So make sure her other boyfriend isn't over there!" he wrote. "(It's a joke.) Just bug her about it.

"I want to tell you how much your daughter has made such an impact on my life, in such a short period of time that we have been together," Derek continued. "She keeps me outta so much trouble this year and most guys wouldn't like that. She is helping get to where I want to go one day, and that is the National Hockey League. I am going to play there, but now I am going to get there faster because of her."

Near the end of his handwritten note, neatly scrawled on the inside flap of the card, Derek wrote: "Everybody that I know have come up to me and have asked me this year what has happened to me? It's great. I love it that people have come up to me, and I've told them that it is your daughter that's changed me."

The surprise Christmas trip never happened, because Derek was sent to play in Louisiana. But Janella soon joined him, and they lived together in a Lafayette apartment with rented furniture. They had a little bit of money and a lot of spare time. They spent it at a nearby alligator farm. They found a breeder of bulldogs, and spent afternoons playing with the puppies, daydreaming of someday raising their own. They went to amusement parks, such as Six Flags New Orleans. On roller coasters, Derek, terrified, held the bar in front of him with clenched fists.

They filled their nights at beer joints and with quiet dinners at home. Derek collected cookbooks and experimented with barbecue recipes. He created extravagant dinners at the holidays, even when it was just two of them eating. They once got into a food fight, flinging food and squirting ketchup, mustard, and chocolate syrup across the kitchen. They ended up in the shower, fully dressed.

Derek's height stalled just short of six foot eight, and weight became a consistent issue. He sometimes ballooned to 300 pounds in the off-season, and then spent the season slowly shedding it. At the end of the season in Louisiana, he stepped onto a coin-operated scale at a store and weighed 269 pounds—12 more than his listed weight. To help shed pounds, Derek and Janella together went on a cabbage-soup diet.

Derek wore glasses, jeans, and whatever clean T-shirt was in the drawer. But he spent money on shoes. It was important to have a good pair of shoes. Someone had told him that once.

ECHL players were rarely stars, beyond the small communities of fans who bought season tickets and showed up at promotional events. Derek was less of a star than others—a midseason addition, much younger than most of his teammates, a player who created occasional and quick bursts of adrenaline but did not dazzle with any semblance of an all-around game.

Still, among hockey executives, his was the future with the most promise.

In May, the Wild offered Derek his first NHL contract. He had shown enough for a minimal payout, and the Wild gave Derek a three-year deal that would pay him an annual NHL salary of $350,000, if and when he reached the top rung of professional hockey. If he continued to play in the ECHL, he would earn $35,000. If he played in the American Hockey League, one level below the NHL and one above the ECHL, he would be paid $45,000.

Derek signed his name to it, in a space next to the signature of Wild general manager Doug Risebrough.

The contract came with a $50,000 signing bonus, worth about $66,500 Canadian at the time. The day before he deposited the check into his Regina account, he had $29.94 in the bank.

One of his first purchases, on his 21st birthday, was for $47.21 at a liquor store. But most of his bonus check went toward a truck: Mike Tobin's black 2002 GMC Sierra Denali, which Derek had driven when it was brand new in Prince George.

Len Boogaard asked his son why he couldn't buy something cheaper, maybe an older truck without all the expensive, flashy options.

"How would that look at the rink?" Derek said.

Derek was headed to the Houston Aeros of the American Hockey League, the top minor-league affiliate of the Wild. He knew that a number of their players had bounced between the NHL and the AHL. A look in the players' parking lot usually could tell you which ones. Derek wanted to belong.

TURN HIM INTO an NHL player. That was the order. Get Derek Boogaard to the Minnesota Wild.

Doug Risebrough had been hired by the Wild in 1999 to build its newly granted expansion franchise. He was an Ontario native, a first-round draft pick of the Montreal Canadiens in 1974, an all-purpose forward who helped them win four consecutive Stanley Cups from 1976 to 1979.

Traded to Calgary in 1982, Risebrough played five seasons for the Flames. He was a pugnacious sort, an upright bed of nails, unafraid to pester bigger players out of their comfort zone. While he scored 185 goals and had 286 assists in 13 NHL seasons, he also had 1,542 penalty minutes. He was only 5 foot 11 and about 180 pounds, but he fought roughly 60 times, including 14 times as a rookie.

Most famously, on January 2, 1986, in Calgary, Risebrough took on Edmonton enforcer Marty McSorley, the longtime protector of Wayne Gretzky and the Oilers' other high-scoring forwards.

Their fight sparked an extended, full-scale brawl between the hated rivals, and McSorley, not surprisingly, pounded the much-smaller Risebrough until the two were separated and steered toward the penalty box.

Somehow, though, Risebrough had McSorley's Edmonton jersey. And while other fights continued on the ice, Risebrough sat in the penalty box and used his sharp skates to slice the jersey into shreds. He tossed the tattered remains of McSorley's jersey onto the ice, eliciting a lusty cheer from the home crowd. The sweater was retrieved and returned to the Oilers. Glen Sather, the coach, hung it in the team's dressing room as a reminder of Edmonton's nastiest rivalry.

Risebrough embarked on a coaching career that eventually led him to become general manager of the Flames, then vice president of hockey operations for the Oilers. Both franchises made perennial trips to the playoffs under his direction. Risebrough's career spanned the arc of the enforcer, from the goon's rise in popular culture in the 1970s to fighting's apex in the late 1980s to the one-dimensional behemoth who took hold in the 1990s.

The early Wild teams had a six-foot, five-inch, 230-pound enforcer named Matt Johnson. He was a perfunctory fighter on a team without much talent to protect. At the end of the 2000–01 season, the Wild's first in the NHL, Risebrough spent a seventh-round draft pick on an even larger player: 19-year-old Derek Boogaard.

Risebrough encouraged Derek to continue boxing lessons, but also sent him to private lessons with a professional figure skater to improve Derek's movement. Risebrough knew the Wild would transition to a new enforcer, from Johnson to Boogaard. In the summer of 2003, he made the mandate clear to the coaches of the Houston Aeros: turn Derek Boogaard, from last season's Louisiana IceGators, into an NHL enforcer.

To Todd McLellan and Matt Shaw, it was a test of imagination. The head coach and assistant coach of the Aeros knew what NHL players looked like. Derek was not one. But it was not their decision. Derek had been foisted upon them.

"Under no uncertain terms, he was going to be in Houston," Shaw, the assistant coach, said of the edict. "And he was going to play."

Derek showed up weeks early for the Aeros' training camp. For a time, amid the heat and humidity of Houston in August, he was the only player there. Derek worked out fiendishly in the weight room and did solo drills on the ice, practicing his skating, shooting, and puck handling. And when he finished, he enthusiastically returned to Shaw, like a puppy playing fetch, to ask what else he could do.

Why don't you go run those hills out there, Shaw suggested, not sure what else to say. The practice facility in suburban Sugar Land, Texas, near a large high-school football stadium, was surrounded by grassy berms. Derek ran up and down the hills. He ran up and down the stadium steps. When he was exhausted, he did it some more. Shaw could not wear him out.

During the season, when practices ended and teammates scattered to the dressing room, Derek was usually the last one to leave the ice. He stood at the coaches' sides, wide-eyed and ready, wondering what he could do next.

The contract Derek signed in May made him see, in stark terms, the difference between a minor-league player and an NHL one: 10 times the salary. Elevated from the ECHL to the AHL, one step removed from the Wild, Derek recognized his upward momentum and did not want to squander it. He was motivated by Risebrough's unbending belief in him, Janella's unwavering support, and the naysayers back in places like Melfort and Regina and Prince George who never imagined Derek Boogaard reaching the NHL.

The Aeros coaches liked Derek. He was eager to do as instructed and had a gentle way about him. McLellan's two young sons adored

Derek, and McLellan appreciated how he always knelt down to the height of children and spoke softly to them.

McLellan, too, had been raised in small-town eastern Saskatchewan and played in the Western Hockey League, for the Saskatoon Blades. He was a late-round draft choice, by the New York Islanders in 1986, and played five career NHL games. And he'd coached in North Battleford, Saskatchewan, part of the Saskatchewan Junior Hockey League that included Melfort.

"Once he entered the program in Houston and you could start to see the heart that this guy had, and the work he was committed to putting in, then there was hope," McLellan said. "And every day the hope grew greater and greater. We became almost father figures to him. Every month he'd take steps and you'd be proud of him, and we'd give him a little bit of a report card. It wasn't about his ability to fight. That was always there. It was about his work ethic and his commitment level to all the other skills that would eventually make him an NHLer that was most impressive to me."

Derek's hit-and-miss relationships with coaches found a sweet spot in Houston. He could sense how close he was to the NHL. He had coaches who believed in him, and who saw that he not only belonged, but that he could outgrow them. Few had viewed Derek that way before—as a player with potential for something bigger than what he already had.

DEREK DREAMED OF building a house one day. He bought software with blueprints and floor plans and read architectural and design magazines. He visited open houses to gather ideas. He searched for land in Kelowna, British Columbia, envisioning a time when he would build several houses—one for him and Janella, surrounded by smaller homes built for his mother, his father, his brothers, and his sister. They would all live close together.

In the fall of 2003, though, the life that Derek and Janella con-
structed in Louisiana simply moved west to suburban Houston, to
an apartment complex in Stafford with the aspirational name of The
Preserve at Colony Lakes. Unlike most players, who filled their
apartments with little more than the necessities of a bed, a couch,
and a large television, Derek wanted a home. He and Janella filled it
with rented furniture they chose together.

In little more than two years, Derek had gone from a throwaway
goon to an NHL draft pick, from the Western Hockey League to the
top step of the minor leagues. If Janella had seen in Derek a chance to
latch onto a future hockey star, as some "puck bunnies" were known
to do, she had both incredible foresight and a willingness to detach
herself from her own ambitions. She followed Derek from Medicine
Hat to Lafayette to Houston, trading part-time jobs and placing college plans on hold. She paid at least as many bills as he did. When
he totaled her car in an accident, they shared Derek's new truck. She
humored Derek's idiosyncrasies, his quixotic quests, and his constant
daydreaming. He went through a phase when he thought he would
open a fast-food franchise when his hockey career ended. During
one spell, he went to Chipotle, day after day, watching the employees and studying the process of efficiently making burritos and tacos
to order.

His fixations ranged from trucks (he scoured car lots until he
bought the one from Mike Tobin) to hammocks, which he wanted
for the porch of the apartment. He went through a phase when he
searched for chopper-style motorcycles. He collected movie DVDs
by the hundreds. Later, he collected high-end liquor bottles (the contents of which he did not drink), then Buddha statues of all shapes
and sizes.

But his greatest infatuation was with bulldogs. In Louisiana,
he and Janella found a breeder out in the country. They visited
often, looking at dogs, frolicking with the puppies. It was one of

their favorite ways to spend an afternoon. They returned again and again, waiting for the right dog at the right time. Finally, after moving to Houston, they returned to the breeder and bought one. Its name was Trinity, with a white coat splotched with charcoal gray, a scrunched-up face, and a protruding lower jaw.

Derek was only 21, but he had re-created some semblance of family. He had a home, a car, a job, a girlfriend, and a dog. Janella, who was 23, wanted more security. Like a lot of girlfriends of young hockey players, she worried about her lack of health insurance and being single without steady employment. They spoke to Derek's agent. He gave them a form that lots of other players used. It provided Janella benefits through Derek's hockey. It implied, but never stated, that the two were married. They filed taxes as a married couple, but never described themselves as such to friends and family.

It was an innocent time. On Janella's birthday, Derek made a birthday card, three feet tall, and filled the living room with balloons. Late one night after a long rain, Derek took Janella to a vacant field next to a strip mall. In the Denali, they zoomed and slid and spun, Derek showing Janella the way his father used to spin donuts in icy Canadian parking lots.

On their way to dry pavement, the truck got stuck. A teammate was summoned to provide a tow. Once rescued, Derek found that one tire had been stripped from the rim. He spent an hour pulling it off and replacing it with the spare tire. Janella took pictures. Derek smiled from ear to ear.

Among the friends that Derek and Janella made in Houston, none were as close as Rick and Heather Bronwell. Rick was an equipment manager for the Aeros. It was Bronwell who assigned Derek the oversized goalie's jersey. It was Bronwell who repaired and replaced Derek's skates when they broke under his weight, the rivets of the blade pulling apart from the boot, time and time again.

But it was Bronwell who saw the quiet side of Derek, too. When the Bronwells had a baby, Derek was there—the first non-family member to hold it, comfortably nuzzling the tiny infant softly in his enormous, bruised hands.

WHEN DEREK'S FIGHTS were shown on the video replay board at the Toyota Center, the downtown arena where the Aeros played their games, they were framed with a title, initially misspelled: BOOGYMAN CAM. Midway through Derek's second season, the Aeros honored him by handing out 3,000 of his likenesses on "Derek Boogaard Bobble-head Night." Not only did his head bobble, but his fists did, too.

Derek fought more for the Houston Aeros than he did during any two-year stretch of his career. When he fought, as was the custom through much of the minor leagues, spotlights shone on him and his opponent. In some cases, music over the arena's sound system—the theme from *Rocky*, for example—provided a soundtrack to the bout. Sometimes a bell rang, as if marking the start of a boxing match. He became one of the team's most popular players, despite not scoring a goal for Houston until his 106th game.

On January 1, 2004, months into the first of Derek's two seasons in Houston, a weekly newspaper called the *Houston Press* devoted a lengthy story to Derek and teammate Chris Bala. Titled "Harvard and the Boogeyman," it offset two seemingly opposite prospects, pondering which had the brighter long-range future, "the brawler or the brainiac."

"He's disconcertingly mellow off the ice, and his most eloquent defense of his play seldom goes beyond a shrug of the shoulders and an acceptance that outsiders will never understand," reporter Richard Connelly wrote of Derek.

"Boogaard lives with his girlfriend, likes watching a lot of movies and *The Simpsons*, but he *loooves* hockey," Connelly explained. "He hopes to coach after his playing days."

Derek made no proclamations about his abilities.

"It's no big secret that I'm not a big goal scorer," he said in the piece. "I just love to hit guys. Some guys have it and some don't."

The story noted that Derek was the only minor-league player regularly featured on the web site WildEnforcers.com, which chronicled the actions of Minnesota's pugilistic players. But it also quoted a skeptic: Kevin Oklobzija of the *Hockey News*, "who's covered the AHL for 19 years."

"I don't think he's a prospect," Oklobzija said. "He's just a guy to fight and to protect the team's other players on this level."

Reaching the NHL was far from a certainty. Derek's 22 regular-season fights in 2003–04 ranked him only 12th in the AHL. Brandon Sugden of the Syracuse Crunch led the league with 41—including six against Rochester's Sean McMorrow. Sugden was far more of a self-promoting brute than Derek. He made no secret that his primary mission was to lead the league in fighting majors. He explained one rivalry with pride.

"I knocked him out cold this year," Sugden said in a 2004 story widely distributed by the Canadian Press. "First game this year, we knew we would fight each other, we nearly went in warmup. But we went during the game and I caught him with a nice right hand to the jaw. He dropped like a sack of potatoes. It took him 10 seconds to get up and then he skated to the wrong box."

The minor leagues were filled with young men like Sugden— older than Derek, a bundle of braggadocio wrapped in menace. He was drafted by the Toronto Maple Leafs in the fifth round of the 1996 draft, but never reached the NHL. In 13 professional seasons, including several early ones in which he later admitted struggling with alcohol and drug use, and despite a lifetime ban from the East Coast Hockey League (later rescinded) for throwing a stick that struck a fan, Sugden played for 12 teams in eight minor leagues. The only time he fought Derek, early in the 2004–05 season, Derek beat him. It was considered Sugden's only loss in more than 30 fights that season.

But things in Houston started slowly for Derek. His first American Hockey League fight was on October 17, 2003, against Milwaukee's Raitis Ivanans, a six-foot-four Latvian who had worked his way up from the lowest levels of minor-league hockey. For Derek, it was, at best, a draw. The two traded blows before Derek fell and Ivanans landed on top of him.

It got worse. In Utah three weeks later, Derek lost twice to the Grizzlies' Mike Sgroi. The first came early in the game, a bout at center ice with an extended preamble of tough talk. Sgroi slipped when throwing a punch, but he recovered to throw another, knocking Derek off balance and to the ice. Sgroi landed three more lefts to Derek's head before skating away to the cheers of the crowd.

The men later traded ankle-high slashes and agreed to a rematch. With efficiency and a high percentage of successful punches, the two took turns with momentum—Sgroi first, Derek second, Sgroi third. Just as Derek hit Sgroi in the head, Sgroi latched on to Derek's helmet and dragged the scrum to the ice.

Sgroi, six foot five and 230 pounds, was 25 that season. He had played in the ECHL and the AHL, just like Derek, and won most of his fights. He even scored a few goals every season, occasionally reaching double digits. But he was not drafted by any NHL teams and never made an NHL regular-season roster. He was a minor-league vagabond who, in the decade after beating up Derek twice in one night, played for nearly 20 teams.

In 2005, he was runner-up in a pay-per-view event called *Battle of the Hockey Enforcers*. The premise was simple: pit hockey enforcers against one another in an on-ice, on-skates boxing tournament— hockey fights without the interruption of an actual hockey game. The event made national news and elicited widespread commentary on the state of hockey, fans, and violence.

Only one city would agree to host the event: Prince George. About 2,000 fans showed up in the 6,000-seat arena. The winner, Dean Mayrand, reportedly made $62,000, more than the going rate for a full season in the AHL.

Mayrand, too, never reached the NHL. He spent years in the Ligue Nord-Américaine de Hockey, a low-level professional circuit in Quebec where the typical game in the mid-2000s had four fights—about six times the rate of fighting in the NHL.

Derek didn't need the constant reminders, but they were there, almost every fight. For every enforcer like Derek within reach of the NHL, there were dozens, maybe hundreds, of others enticed to punch their way to hockey stardom, with almost no chance of getting there.

DEREK FOUND THE schedule of a professional hockey player to be both erratic and mundane. Flares of activity—early-morning skates, afternoon practices, evening games—were divided by hours of mandated lethargy. Games ended late at night, and adrenaline prevented sleep until hours later.

Travel disrupted attempts at normalcy. Games sometimes fell on back-to-back nights in distant cities across different time zones. Stretches like the one that Derek and the Aeros had early in his first season in Houston were not unusual: at Grand Rapids one night, at Milwaukee the next, home for a game in Houston two nights later, a game the next night in San Antonio, a game in Syracuse three nights later, one the next night in Hartford, home for a game, then at Utah two nights later. Planes and buses might depart at midnight or 5 A.M., and arrive at dawn or noon. Checkout times in hotels could be 6 A.M. or 5 P.M.

In the hours before games, players rested in their rooms, which they shared with a teammate, watching television or playing video games. Sometimes they wandered a nearby mall or sat through a movie, killing hours until pre-game meals and bus rides to the arena.

Rare were long stretches of idle time in the dark of night. Rest came in the odd corners of the schedule—on the plane, in the afternoon, maybe a rare day off. Combine the inconsistent schedule with the consistency of pain, which all players endured with little complaint, and sleep was a luxury not always afforded.

By then, Derek had been introduced to Ambien, also known by its generic name, zolpidem. It was never hard to get in professional hockey. It was a prescription sleeping pill, a short-term antidote to insomnia, but it was rarely prescribed; it was merely handed out in training rooms and locker rooms, and often traded among players, like aspirin or Tic Tacs. There were few paper trails of prescriptions or formal dosages tracked. There was little worry of overdoses or abuse, no matter what the fine print on the label might say. If a player thought he needed help sleeping, he received sleeping pills—often Ambien.

It certainly helped Derek sleep, through the pain and in the odd hours, but he did not like the way it made him feel—groggy and off-kilter during the morning skates. With Janella's help, he searched for other sleep aids. He occasionally took melatonin supplements and over-the-counter medicines that made him drowsy. But Ambien was easy to get. All he had to do was ask around.

It was in Derek's first season in Houston that injuries started to mount. In January 2004, having just missed a couple of games because of a sore hip, Derek sprained his wrist during a fight with Cincinnati's Sheldon Brookbank. In the course of a minute, Derek hit Brookbank more than 20 times with his right hand, another five or so with the left. He pulled Brookbanks's helmet off and pounded him with blows to his ribs. Derek's wrist was not examined until the period ended, and he sat on the bench the entire third period. An x-ray taken the next day was negative. It was a sprain.

Ten days later, Derek cut his right hand open with a knockdown blow against the helmet of Chicago's Libor Ustrnul. The team injury report said that Derek "opened up an old laceration on his hand that had been very minor but is now opened up a lot more. Had hand treated at period break—continued play OK."

It was signed *JM*, for Aeros trainer Jerry Meins. He wrote that the injury would be monitored "for infection and healing."

Derek reopened the wound in a fight a week later. A week after that, on February 21, Derek beat up Chicago's Brendan Yarema with several shots to head. When Yarema dropped, Derek helped pull him to his feet and hit him more. As the officials closed in, Derek jabbed Yarema with a left hand. Persuaded the fight was still going, the officials backed away to watch the conclusion of one of Derek's most dominating and violent victories.

Yet Derek, the clear winner, missed the next two games. Upon his return, he immediately opened the wound again in a fight. Medical reports showed that it was swollen for another week and that Derek was prescribed pain relievers. When he played again, he got into a fight against Grand Rapids. He quickly pulled off the opponent's helmet, then pounded him with jackhammer right hands. The trainer later reported that Derek's hand experienced "no increased swelling."

A more debilitating injury came a week later, on March 12, 2004, before the game started. Derek was stretching on the ice when he felt a pop in his back. He was given Vioxx, a widely used anti-inflammatory and pain reliever that was barred in the United States months later because of growing concerns that it could cause cardiovascular problems, such as heart attacks and strokes. For days, Derek received other prescriptions, too, including various muscle relaxants and pain relievers. Finally, tests revealed the extent of the injury: a ruptured disk. On March 17, in an injury log that Derek was asked to keep to monitor his own rehabilitation, he wrote: "Jerry said my hockey season is done for this year and I need surgery. Also said the rupture is 8mm. Doctor told Jerry that doctors start talking surgery when people rupture their discs 4 mm. Said we have to wait and see what doctors in Minnesota have to say about surgery."

He did not skate again for 10 days and missed the rest of the regular season. In his log, Derek wrote that, when the Aeros were on the road, he stayed home and was treated by "Janella D'Amore girlfriend." He managed to play two games in the playoffs as the Aeros were dispatched in the first round.

Back surgery never took place. In a postseason physical exam performed by team doctor Eddie Matsu on April 15, several of Derek's ailments were listed. It was noted that Derek—the doctor's form called him "Eric"—had a bulging disk in his back. It also said he had sustained, during the season, a "fractured" right hand, which was completely healed, an apparent reference to the January sprain. It noted a broken collarbone that Derek sustained as a 13-year-old. It made no mention of concussions, other head injuries, his sore shoulder, or anything else.

"Is presently playing and may continue to play ice hockey," Matsu wrote in his conclusion.

DEREK PLAYED 53 of 80 regular-season games in his first season in Houston. He had no goals, four assists, and 207 penalty minutes. He added an assist and 16 penalty minutes in two playoff games. It was all considered a stirring success. Derek's two-loss night to Sgroi early in the season became a faded memory. He did not lose a fight once the calendar turned to January.

In June, the Wild doubled the number of Boogaards in the organization. Risebrough, the general manager, drafted Aaron Boogaard, four years younger than Derek, in the sixth round, 175th overall, of the NHL Entry Draft. That was one round—27 elections—earlier than the Wild had picked Derek three years before. It was a surprise. Aaron had been steered into an enforcer's role in the Western Hockey League by the Calgary Hitmen, who, disappointed in his progress, traded him to the Tri-City Americans in Washington. In 23 games, Aaron fought just once and scored three times. But the selection of a second Boogaard by the Wild set in motion a unique, tightening bond between Derek and Aaron, linking them on parallel career paths. Suddenly, Derek and Aaron had the same goal: to reach the NHL. That shared ambition was strengthened by the possibility of doing it with the same team. They spent the summer together, working out in Regina, building their strength through long workouts and improving their boxing skills against one another in the ring.

But Derek's competition was about to get tougher. The NHL owners, trying to wrangle a more favorable salary structure with players after the expiration of the collective bargaining agreement, locked out the players. Negotiations stalled. The entire NHL season was canceled. Players scattered to other leagues, looking for a paycheck and a place to play. More than anywhere, the migration beefed up the American Hockey League. Of the 25 regular-season fights that Derek had in his second season in Houston, 16 came against men with NHL experience. Another three were against players who would make the NHL someday, too.

Kip Brennan was Derek's primary nemesis. He played most of the previous season in the NHL, with the Los Angeles Kings and Atlanta Thrashers. Now representing the AHL's Chicago Wolves, Brennan was 24, stood six foot four, and weighed 220 pounds. He and Derek fought in Houston's third game of the season. Brennan ended an otherwise even fight with a big right hand to the side of Derek's head and a wrestling-style takedown. They fought again in late January, then on back-to-back nights in February. And they ended the season, in the playoffs, fighting again. After the first fight, Derek fought Brennan to a draw or beat him every time.

Derek knew that NHL coaches and officials, idled by the lockout, were paying more attention to the AHL than usual. Some minor-league teams visited the big-league arenas to satiate the hunger of starving hockey fans. When the Aeros played a game at the Wild's in Saint Paul, 12,204 saw Derek get an assist, one of four he had that season.

The game against Utah on February 8, 2005, was held in the afternoon, a rare weekday matinee. The crowd at Houston's Toyota Center was announced as 9,062. About 7,000 of those were school children, many watching their first hockey game as part of a team promotion sponsored by the *Houston Chronicle* called "Chronicle Education Field Trip Day."

The lasting memory of a 5–2 home-team victory was forged with 1:44 left in the third period. A Utah player clobbered one of the Aeros. All 10 players on the ice, including the goalies, converged in one corner of the rink and fought. Derek bloodied at least one opponent during a rambling scrum of fits and starts that delayed the game for 15 minutes.

After the game, officials needed another hour to sort out the penalties. It was ruled that the teams combined for 164 penalty minutes. Derek established a team record with 44 of them.

In a March game at Utah, Derek outwrestled an antagonist named Ryan Barnes, but skated away with a bloody nose. More memorably, Derek was granted a penalty shot after being hauled down from behind on a breakaway. Derek's backhanded penalty shot was stopped by the goalie.

"I thought it was good that I actually got a good shot off, instead of fumbling it off into the corner," Derek, a master of self-deprecation, said after the game.

His season's personal highlight, though, came on March 27.

"Aeros forward Derek Boogaard is cheered on a regular basis at Toyota Center," the *Houston Chronicle* wrote. "The 6-7 fan favorite leads the team with 247 penalty minutes and is often on the winning side of his fights. But Sunday night, in one of the biggest games for the Aeros this AHL season, Boogaard was lauded for being more than just his usual intimidating self.'"

Derek scored the game-winning goal. He had captured a rebound and shoveled the puck into the net as he fell. It was his first goal in more than two years, stretching back to his lone season in the East Coast Hockey League. Derek was named the game's No. 1 star. It was such an honor, such an unusual proclamation for him, that Derek saved a copy of the official score sheet.

Still, it was hard to gauge Derek's development over two seasons in Houston. He won fights and was a crowd favorite, but his contributions were rarely tangible. Improvement was not obvious to those who saw him every day.

After the Aeros lost a playoff series to the Chicago Wolves, McLellan and Shaw, Houston's head coach and assistant, met with Chicago coach John Anderson. Shaw and Anderson had known each other for years, and it was common for opposing coaches to chat casually about the series that just ended.

"Boogaard was your best player," Anderson said.

"Seriously?" Shaw replied. Derek had played in all five games, scored no points, and had 38 penalty minutes.

"Yeah, our team was so concerned, so frightened when he was on the ice, it changed their game," Anderson said.

That was when it hit McLellan and Shaw, two full seasons after Derek arrived with explicit instructions from Doug Risebrough to get him to the NHL.

"Good God, maybe this guy is going to play," Shaw thought to himself. "Maybe Doug was right."

· · ·

DEREK'S NAME WAS on the list, and the list was inside Tom Lynn's pocket. Derek was going to be cut from the training camp roster of the Minnesota Wild, again, and sent back to the minor leagues for another season.

Lynn, the Wild's assistant general manager, was responsible for carrying out the cuts—usually three rounds of them, spaced over a couple of weeks during training camp. It was a delicate process. Coaches and executives privately agreed on the names. Lynn secretly made travel arrangements. Players were discreetly retrieved from the dressing room, usually by an equipment manager or trainer to keep suspicions down. Players stopped talking and their backs stiffened whenever Lynn or someone else from management walked in.

It was the first round of cuts in September 2005. The NHL, given a chance to remarket itself after the lockout, returned with a vow to reduce the stickiness of play and add a fan-friendly dose of fluidity. That led teams to believe that the game's pace and scoring would increase. Speed would be prized over strength. Fighting would drop.

But the Wild had bought out the contract over the summer of its veteran enforcer, Matt Johnson. He had struggled with lingering injuries, including concussions. The 28-year-old said he planned to take some time off, get to feeling better and return to the game. He never did.

Lynn carried five names in his pocket to a meeting to confirm the cuts with other team officials before he notified the players. He read the names aloud. Everyone in the room, from general manager Doug Risebrough to head coach Jacques Lemaire, nodded their approval.

Lynn broke the lingering silence. He did not want Derek Boogaard to go without discussion.

"Do we have to let him go on the first cut?" he said. "He's worked so hard. He's been through a couple of summers, he's been a good guy. Maybe we should keep him around. Not to make the team, maybe, but for a few more days, to reward him for his hard work."

Assistant coach Mike Ramsey spoke up.

"I was thinking the same thing," he said. "Boogey's worked hard, he can skate, he's not holding us up in practice or anything. Let's keep him around."

Derek's name was crossed off the list. Someone else was cut instead.

The next night, Derek played against the Buffalo Sabres in a preseason game at the Xcel Energy Center in Saint Paul. In the game's first few minutes, he got into a fight with Andrew Peters, a six-foot-four, 240-pound behemoth, one of the NHL's top enforcers. He had fought 23 times the season before the lockout, more than all but three others in the league.

With the Minnesota crowd on its feet, cheering for the unfamiliar giant wearing the unfamiliar No. 46, Derek absorbed a couple of small shots to his head before the men clasped onto one another's shoulders. Derek squirmed loose and belted Peters with an overhand right fist, sending Peters's helmet flying and dropping his body to the ice.

Two days later, the Wild cut 10 more players. Derek stayed.

At home against the Chicago Blackhawks, he fought Shawn Thornton, an emerging scrapper. Derek lost his helmet, but bombed Thornton with three right hands to the head before tugging Thornton's helmet off. It was a narrow victory for Derek, but he was rewarded with a standing ovation.

"The token appearances are over for Derek Boogaard, the hulking Clydesdale who has become the dark horse of Wild training camp," the Saint Paul *Pioneer Press* reported.

Lynn told the newspaper that Derek was the hardest-working player he had ever seen. Teammates agreed.

"Few expected Boogaard, whom the Wild drafted in the seventh round (202nd overall) in 2001, to survive long with Houston of the American Hockey League let alone compete for an NHL job," the story said.

Lemaire was convinced that Derek changed games—not just through fighting, but by intimidation. When Derek was on the ice, Lemaire could sense the discomfort of opponents, worried about a crushing hit. When Derek was on the bench, they knew a cheap shot could mean his deployment.

"I saw him last year, I never thought he could be at this point," Lemaire told reporters. "And I saw him quite a few times. But he grew through the camp and did things that made me say, 'Hey, maybe he's got a chance to play.' We worked with him on positioning. He seems to understand the game. He's improved his skating. Now it's up to him to keep improving."

Derek made the final team. He got to choose his number. He picked No. 24, in honor of Bob Probert, the longtime enforcer of the Detroit Red Wings and Chicago Blackhawks, widely considered the best of all time.

"A lot of people thought I would never make it, but I always had confidence in myself that if I went out and practiced hard, I'd eventually make it," Derek told the *StarTribune* on the morning of the season opener. "And today's the day. Hopefully I don't get hurt in warmup."

Derek had phoned his parents a couple of days earlier to share the news that he had made the NHL. Joanne was surprised and excited, still wary that her son was a fighter.

"Mom, it's what I do now," Derek told her.

PART II

MINNESOTA

5

DEREK BOOGAARD'S FIRST NHL fight ended with a knockout and a roar of approval.

It was October 16, 2005, the Wild hosting the Anaheim Ducks, the game still in the first period. First-year Ducks coach Randy Carlyle sent Kip Brennan to the ice for a face-off. The Wild tapped Derek. The two had fought five times the season before in the American Hockey League. Brennan had gouged Derek in the eye back in April, enough to temporarily blur his vision, and Derek wanted revenge.

The players lined up along the outer edges of the circle, and Derek nuzzled close. Brennan tapped him on the foot with his stick, a silent invitation. The puck dropped. Brennan backed up, and Derek chased him with two long strides, both men flicking their gloves away.

Brennan quickly managed to remove Derek's helmet as they clutched for position. Derek jabbed with a couple of rights, then a couple of lefts, then held Brennan's jersey by the shoulder with his left hand. Brennan's helmet slipped back on his head, straining the chin strap.

Boom.

Derek hit him flush in the face with his closed right hand. Brennan's legs gave way and he fell to the ice.

"Wow," the television announcer said.

"That's what you call 'decisive,'" his partner added. "You know what? That kind of fight keeps you on the team."

The announcers shared a hearty laugh. The crowd cheered.

Later in the period, after Derek had served his five-minute penalty and been given another shift, he fought again. This time, it was Anaheim's Todd Fedoruk, a six-foot, two-inch puncher from Redwater, Alberta, who had played parts of four seasons with the Philadelphia Flyers. Derek had first come across him at training camp for the Regina Pats, seven years earlier, when Derek was 16 and he'd spied "The Fridge" nervously in the lobby of the Agridome.

"I wasn't surprised when I heard the name 'Boogaard,'" Fedoruk said several years later. "It's kind of a name that sticks out, anyways—'The Boogeyman.' They were talking about him in the NHL when he was still in juniors. 'They got this guy down in western Canada, the Boogeyman, they call him. A name like that, he's gotta definitely have our type of role. We'll be waiting for him when he gets here.' It wasn't a surprise: Boogaard's in the NHL."

Now Fedoruk crouched with his fists up, a left-hander leading with his right shoulder. Derek, five inches taller and 40 pounds heavier, managed two fully cocked punches to the head. The second dislodged Fedoruk's helmet. But Fedoruk grabbed hold of Derek's right sleeve, managing to tangle Derek inside his own jersey—the move of a wily veteran. Derek pulled his right arm out, leaving the empty sleeve dangling. With half of Derek's upper body bare and his head caught awkwardly in his jersey, Fedoruk pounded Derek with punches until both men leaned, exhausted, into the side boards. They coasted off the ice, serenaded with a standing ovation.

Three nights later, in his fifth NHL game, Derek charged to the front of the net, a bull in a china shop, and poked the puck past San Jose Sharks goalie Evgeni Nabokov to give the Wild a 2–1 lead in the third period. Minnesota erupted for four more goals and a 6–1 victory. But the ovation Derek got for scoring a goal was smaller than the one he had received earlier, when he beat up San Jose's Rob Davison. With the puck stopped, Davison rushed in to collide with Derek. Derek responded by coolly battering Davison to the ice. He slid casually toward the penalty box with the ease and expression of a man walking a dog.

In his first five NHL games, all at home, Derek had a goal, an assist, and three fights. Replicas of his No. 24 Boogaard jersey were rushed to stores. Newspaper stories were written about how much Derek had improved his all-around skill to reach the NHL, how he was much more than the goon he had been presumed to be in junior hockey.

"An absolute gimmick," was how Risebrough described Derek's role in junior to the StarTribune. "Like he wasn't even a human being."

Within weeks, Derek's jersey became the fastest-selling of all the players on the Wild. Two months and seven fights into the season, the Pioneer Press carried a column titled "Wild Realize It's Finally Boogey Time." Derek was a rookie, making more money than he imagined but far less than most of his teammates, and he had shown himself to be a sincere, self-deprecating presence off the ice and an energy-inducing hulk on it. The Wild could not have expected more. Risebrough's draft-day bet from four years earlier had paid off.

Len Boogaard expressed a mix of pride and worry over Derek's future.

"He's encountered a number of injuries with his hands, and he's going to have repercussions years down the road," Len told reporter Michael Russo of the StarTribune early in Derek's rookie season. "But what he's accomplished to get here, the obstacles and hurdles he's overcome, I'm very proud. I'm mostly proud that he has a different persona off the ice than what you see on the ice."

. . .

WHENEVER HE WAS asked if he liked to fight, Derek would say some version of the same thing: It has always been part of hockey, and it always will be. If I didn't like it, I wouldn't do it.

But he was not fearless.

"If I think about it, I get nervous sometimes," Derek said in early December of his rookie season. "There are guys here who can put fists through your face."

The worry was always that an opponent would get a clean shot, a one-punch knockout that removed more than a couple of teeth or did more damage than merely crushing the air passages inside the nose. The fear was of the one punch that indelibly rearranged a face, and maybe a career. There was little attention paid to the flurry of blows that the men absorbed, or to the cumulative effect of soon-

Derek bloodied after a fight for the Wild.

forgotten punches that blurred together through fights and games. If nothing got broken, and nothing bled, then there was little reason for concern.

Most players had only vague notions of what a concussion was. Their frames of reference probably began with childhood cartoons, the victims portrayed comically with stars in the eyes and a tweeting bird circling overhead. They might have felt one, or a dozen, and tried to "shake it off," tried to "clear the cobwebs," as if it were no different than slamming a finger in a door.

Concussions occur when the brain bounces against the inside walls of the skull. The damage can include bruising of the brain tissue and tearing of blood vessels and nerve fibers. Microscopic cell damage is possible, which can impact cognitive processing, even motor skills. Severe bruising can lead to swelling, which can cut off oxygen and glucose to the brain, leading to strokes or permanent disabilities.

Concussions do not always involve blows directly to the head. In car accidents, for example, the skull may go untouched, but a sudden stop forces the brain, floating inside in fluid, to bang against it. In sports, however, most concussions come from direct impact—everything from helmet-to-helmet collisions in football to a headfirst fall in skiing, heading the ball in soccer, or fists in boxing or hockey.

Concussions can cause a loss of consciousness, but most do not. Symptoms vary widely, but can include immediate dizziness, confusion, headaches, vision problems, memory loss, even a diminished sense of smell and taste. The treatment usually involves rest, until the symptoms subside. Sometimes, they never fully do. In the case of professional athletes, including countless hockey players, post-concussion syndrome can force early retirements.

Occasionally, the likelihood of a concussion was obvious—a big mid-ice collision, or replays showing a player falling and smacking his head on the ice. But that was not how most concussions happened. They happened during seemingly benign checks against the boards, the accidental stick to the jaw or knee to the head, the short uppercut in a hockey fight that was overshadowed by the flailing, jaw-cracking haymaker.

In 2005, scientists were slowly, quietly learning about the effects of such blows among athletes. They were learning about a disease called chronic traumatic encephalopathy, eventually to become known simply as CTE. It was not caused by major blows to the head, necessarily, but by repeated blows, even small, forgettable blows, the subconcussive hits barely noted—the kind of hits that occurred across the sports landscape, from the youngest ages.

It was an affliction long recognized in boxers, dating back nearly 100 years, sometimes referred to as "dementia pugilistica." Aging boxers, often dismissively referred to as "punch drunk," were actually victims of a degenerative brain disease. By 2005, Derek's rookie year in the NHL, there was growing evidence that CTE was inflicting athletes beyond boxing. The focus had turned to football. Hall of Fame center Mike Webster died in 2002 after years of battling drug addiction, depression, and dementia. He was 50. And when his brain was examined after his death, he was found to have had CTE. A steady stream of other deceased football players, whose families donated their brains in a desperate search for clues to their late-life demise, were discovered to have had the disease, too.

Scientists found that repeated brain trauma could cause the buildup of tau, an abnormal protein that can lead to neurofibrillary tangles that interfere with brain functioning. The results of such degeneration could include memory loss and impaired judgment, aggression and impulse-control problems. Depression was a common symptom. In the long run, CTE—a scientific cousin to Alzheimer's disease—could lead to the early onset of dementia, scientists said.

But in 2005, evidence was spotty and sample sizes were small. The National Football League was denying the science and the impact that football had on the post-career lives of former players. And there was no link of CTE to the NHL. Not yet.

It was certainly not a concern for the likes of Derek. It was the hands, the back, the shoulder, the nose that he and those around him worried about, if they worried at all. Not the head.

THERE WAS NO way of knowing how many concussions Derek had had by the time he reached the NHL. The Wild knew of at least one, back in junior, and his family recalled several discombobulating blows that likely were concussions shrugged away. Surely there were more. What counts as a concussion, anyway?

Fighting, after all, was a relatively small part of hockey, and even the top enforcers in the NHL fought only once every few games, on average. They wore helmets. They were balanced precariously on skates, so the blows were delivered without much leverage. Fights were short. Doctors were nearby. It was more of a show than a danger.

That is what everyone thought.

Enforcers never complained about their role, and players rarely admitted to concussions. Enforcers, especially, did not concede to anything that could be construed as a weakness or a lost edge. Such an admission raised doubts about an athlete's commitment and toughness, the most important qualities for an enforcer. To admit to concussions was to commit career suicide.

There was too much to lose. The fall to obscurity was not a long one.

Trainers might have sympathy for a head injury, but most coaches and general managers did not. Either you could play or you could not. And while anyone could understand the seriousness of an injury when they saw a cast or learned about the rehabilitation time of a surgically repaired knee or shoulder, the debilitating effects of a concussion were not obvious to anyone but the injured.

There was no protocol for handling possible concussions then—no baseline test against which to measure the effects of an obvious blow to the head, no requirement to leave the game or move to the training room for examination. For the most part, players were on their own, left to decide for themselves whether they wanted to draw attention to the fogginess or strange symptoms in their minds.

There was a more immediate and practical matter. One thing that was understood about concussions was that one could easily lead to another, and then another. It seemed as if athletes who were knocked out once by a concussion often got knocked out again, and then again. Maybe that was a question of science. Or maybe it was because players known to be susceptible to concussions became targets for more blows to the head. Target an opponent's weak spot, whether an ankle, a shoulder, or a head—it was an understood part of the strategy.

In a sport where injuries were masked to laughable lengths—a broken toe in hockey might be described publicly only as a "lower body" injury—a known concussion was kept secret by teams, too. Such misdirection was common, meant to protect the player. But it had the effect of disguising a serious health issue afflicting all levels of hockey. No one kept track of the truth. Teams wanted to protect players from further injury. Players wanted to protect their jobs. It was a circular culture of concussion denial.

Yet, by 2005, there was a growing body of worrisome evidence across the NHL. The careers of bankable stars were ending because of concussions. Enforcers? No one paid much attention to why they faded away. But as an increasing number of well-known players had their careers shortened by concussions in the years leading up to Derek's arrival to the NHL, people began to notice.

The most noted case was that of Eric Lindros, the No. 1–overall draft choice in 1991 and the NHL's most valuable player in 1995. His potential was snuffed by a stream of concussions—eight of them, reportedly, beginning in 1998—that fanned the flames of criticism of his overall toughness. Some of the sharpest jabs came from his boss, Philadelphia Flyers general manager Bobby Clarke, a hard-nosed captain during the franchise's Broad Street Bullies heyday and a member of the Hockey Hall of Fame.

Brett Lindros, Eric's brother, was also a first-round draft choice, by the Islanders in 1996. He quit the game at age 20 after three concussions, each with deepening effects. Pat LaFontaine had a 15-season Hall of Fame career, but it ended bleakly in 1998, at age 33, after the last of at least six major concussions. New York Rangers goalie Mike Richter suffered a fractured skull and a concussion from a puck one season, then took a knee to the head the next. He retired 10 months later, in 2003, before the symptoms subsided enough to allow him to play another game.

Devils defenseman Scott Stevens, known largely for dishing out vicious checks, sustained a concussion from a puck in 2003 and retired in January 2004. That same season, the burgeoning career of Steve Moore of the Colorado Avalanche ended when Todd Bertuzzi of the Vancouver Canucks, looking for retribution, punched Moore from behind and drove him face-first to the ice.

Keith Primeau, one of the league's top power forwards, retired early in the 2005 season, unable to recover during the lockout from a string of concussions two seasons earlier. And Moore's Colorado teammate Adam Deadmarsh missed parts of two seasons because of concussions—the most debilitating one sustained in a fight—and retired in 2005.

"It's one of the most frustrating injuries I think you could possibly have from a sports aspect," Deadmarsh told the *Canadian Press*. "Unless you have concussions, it's kind of hard to explain to someone what it feels like. But you know it's something that's not supposed to be there."

Enforcers, too, were among those who left the game due to concussions. Dean Chynoweth, who bounced between the minor leagues and the NHL while fighting for the New York Islanders and Boston Bruins, retired in 1998 at age 29 after being diagnosed with 13 concussions. The better-known Stu Grimson, nicknamed "The Grim Reaper," was involved in about 200 NHL fights. He was concussed for the last time in 2001 during a bout with Georges Laraque and never played again.

That was the world of NHL hockey that Derek entered in 2005. Concussions were a growing concern, but not enough of one to alter the rules or greatly impact safety measures. They certainly were not enough of a concern to curtail fighting, the one part of the game where players intentionally tried to hurt one another with repeated blows to the head, while everyone else gave them room and watched.

No one knew whether concussions were occurring more than they ever had, or if players were simply more aware of them—if a name had been given to what had long been euphemistically called "having your bell rung" or "getting dinged." It was not a new problem, just an old one dressed in a more cautious, more scientific vernacular.

There was no rhyme or reason to those inflicted, it seemed— goalies or slick forwards, hulking defensemen or lumbering brawlers. Concussions could happen to anybody. You just hoped it was not you—that you were not a victim of bad luck or an unwitting owner of a soft head.

The least of the worries, if there were worries at all, was for the enforcers. They knew what they were getting into. They chose to fight, and they loved to fight. Why else would they do it?

· · ·

IN THE FIRST HALF of Derek's rookie season, the role of the enforcer was considered a dying one, on its way to slow extinction. It had nothing to do with the danger of the role, or concussions, or even fighting's sideshow characteristics that many purists felt detracted from the beauty of the game. The league did nothing to deter fighting from its long-held place in the sport. The NHL, returning from a canceled season, merely warned that rules for obstruction, hooking, and holding would be more strictly enforced. Teams interpreted that to mean that there would be a premium on speed, not brawn. There was no room for lumbering players in an increasingly fast game.

Teams that typically reserved a roster spot for a single enforcer were going without. They needed players who could chew up minutes, not opponents. Many of the enforcers who led the league in fights two years earlier were relegated to the minor leagues.

"When I think of a role of a guy that just can fight, it was gone for me years ago," Risebrough told the *StarTribune*.

Yet Risebrough had employed Matt Johnson, who had never tallied more than eight points in his four seasons, and replaced him with Derek, who had not scored more than one goal for a team in any season since he was 16.

But the league's fighting numbers were down. In 2003–04, before the lockout, there were 789 fights in the NHL, as measured by fighting penalties. In 2005–06, Derek's rookie year, there were 466. About 38 percent of NHL games had a fight, the lowest rate since the late 1960s and about one-third the rate of the late 1980s.

"I don't know if you'll ever take fighting out of the game or whether we really want to," Canucks coach Marc Crawford told reporters in Vancouver, offering an echoed refrain. "When emotions spill over, it's better to let it take care of itself right there than to have anything fester."

Derek fought 16 times during his rookie season, more than all but three other players. And, according to the online judges, Derek had the league's second-highest winning percentage (61 percent), trailing only Georges Laraque (64 percent).

On November 2, just as NHL followers started analyzing the diminished role of fighting in the game through the early weeks of the season, Derek pounded Vancouver's Wade Brookbank, a 28-year-old from Lanigan, Saskatchewan, not far from Melfort. With his left arm, Derek held Brookbank—who, along with his brother Sheldon, had been adversaries of Derek's in the minor leagues—and assailed him with a flurry of punches to the head. One of them broke Brookbank's helmet free. Another dropped his body to the ice.

Four nights later, in Anaheim, six-foot, three-inch, 230-pound Trevor Gillies made his NHL debut for the Ducks. Derek had already beaten Kip Brennan and dueled Todd Fedoruk in an earlier game with Anaheim. With Brennan nursing a shoulder injury, Gillies was promoted from the American Hockey League for the singular purpose of standing up to Derek.

Midway through the first period, the two began a fight near the boards. The crowd stood. Derek clutched Gillies's jersey on the shoulder and hit him several times with his right fist. Thirty seconds into the fight, the two twirled in front of the Anaheim bench. Derek pulled Gillies closer and clocked him in the face with a right-hand uppercut.

Derek knew immediately. Like a heavyweight moving to his corner knowing he had scored a knockout, he turned to skate toward the penalty box at about the time Gillies crumpled to the ice. The crowd responded with a mournful *ohhh*.

Gillies was helped to the dressing room. Sent back to the minor leagues when he recovered, he did not reach the NHL again for four more years.

"This kid is a monster, Boogaard," the television announcer said.

. . .

THE WILD BASKED in popularity, still in a honeymoon phase in the Twin Cities. Minnesota had been home to the North Stars from 1967 to 1993, when they moved to Dallas in hockey's southern migration. In 2000, the Wild began play as an expansion team, a franchise smothered warmly with newfound appreciation. The Wild made the playoffs in its third season, reaching the conference final. There was momentum in Minnesota. Derek both rode it and pushed it.

Fans latched on to something more complicated than Derek's ability to punish opponents. He was cheered for his fists, beloved for his humility. He was, in the kindest sense of the term, a beloved goon.

His on-ice manner was cool and humble. He carried none of the histrionics of some other top enforcers, who might blow on their knuckles after a knockout or make a pugnacious show of retreating to the penalty box. Derek seemed, somehow, more reluctant, more clinical. His face rarely showed anger. Even during ferocious fights, Derek looked like a man exerting himself, not one lost in a rage.

"But you get in his face, and the minute you do, it's on," his brother Aaron said years later. "And there's nothing you can do about it. He just took personal offense to people challenging him like that. I don't think he ever wanted to be bullied."

As in his fight with Gillies, Derek did not gloat over his knockouts. He was readily available to reporters in the dressing room and had a knack for self-effacing, humorous quotes. When the public-relations department needed players to attend off-ice events, from on-location radio spots to hospital visits, Derek volunteered. He was not covered in tattoos, he did not have facial hair, and did not cut or color his hair in some self-aware way, like many of his foes who felt a need to create or adhere to an image. He wore wire-rimmed glasses, like the kind he had worn since middle school, which gave him an unintentionally bookish, Clark Kent persona.

He was well liked by teammates, too. As he had as an outcast in high school, Derek gathered a misfit assortment of friends from all

Derek entertains young Wild fans during a summertime team event in Saint Paul.

corners of the roster. He quickly became close to Slovakian Marian Gaborik, the rising 23-year-old star, a fleet scorer whom Derek was expected to protect. On buses and during meals, Derek often sat with teammates from foreign countries, peppering them with questions about their homelands, playfully trying to learn words from their language. He had several friends from his playing days in Houston, such as goalie Josh Harding, from Regina, and defenseman Brent Burns.

But Derek knew that his roots in the NHL were not deep. Minutes were scarce and chances were few. A couple of losing fights might send him to the minors. An injury might lead to his replacement. A punch might change everything.

There may have been no fighter who gave Derek more problems than Georges Laraque. Bulging with muscles, six foot three and 240 pounds, Laraque was widely considered the league's toughest enforcer. Derek, brimming with confidence after his first few fights, wanted to measure himself against the best. His first chance came on November 23, 2005, in Edmonton. Laraque was 30, but he remembered his early years, when he tried to prove himself against the likes of Bob Probert, Tony Twist, and Tie Domi. He was receptive to accepting a challenge from a young, legitimate fighting talent.

Barely two minutes into the game, Derek and Laraque were side by side for a face-off. The puck and the gloves dropped. Fans stood. Flashes from cameras lit the arena like strobe lights. Laraque threw the first big punch, a right fist that came up short, but his fingers caught Derek's jersey by the collar. Derek lunged with a left hand that missed. Laraque swung a left that landed. Derek, still clutched by the collar, was off balance, his head down, trying to shake free from the man considered the strongest in the game. Laraque did not let go. He pulled Derek closer and hit him with another left. Derek slipped to the ice, Laraque fell on top of him, and fans cheered the reigning champion.

"It's not very often I feel like a midget," Laraque told the *Edmonton Sun* afterward. "He had to be 10 feet tall."

It did little to tarnish Derek's reputation. Veterans, as Derek came to know, tended to dismiss challenges from up-and-coming fighters, knowing that they had little to gain in a fight with an unknown player. That Laraque so willingly took Derek on only validated Derek's rising stature.

A couple of weeks later, Derek fought Donald Brashear, another of the vaunted heavyweights. Again, his opponent's raw strength kept Derek off balance. Brashear was eager to throw punches again and again before falling on top of Derek.

Those were hiccups, considered worthy bouts of experience, amid an otherwise impressive assortment of punch-out victories. Derek's standing grew in accordance with his string of fallen victims. There was Ottawa's six-foot, five-inch, Brian McGrattan, a fellow rookie and the league leader in fights. The two traded right-hand blows for 45 seconds before Derek landed one on McGrattan's jaw that felled him. There was a similar beating of Chicago's Jim Vandermeer, then a mauling of Columbus's Jody Shelley and a one-punch knockdown of Phoenix's Matthew Spiller. There were two more bouts with Laraque, more evenly fought than the first.

"TO TELL YOU the truth, I never really loved fighting," Chris Nilan, a noted fighter of the Boston Bruins and Montreal Canadiens, told *Sports Illustrated* in 1986. "You get sore hands. There have been nights when I've sat in the dressing room between periods with my hands in buckets of ice. Who in their right mind likes to do that? But to be honest with you, I don't think I'd ever have gotten the chance to play up here if I hadn't fought."

For generations, enforcers liked what the fighting brought them—respect and a career—but not the hidden costs. Their popularity grew exponentially when they battered another enforcer, but it was a small fraternity. There was no room for grudges. Unlike any other player in the sport, their success came at the expense of someone else's health, reputation, even livelihood. But the alternative was worse. Derek recognized that quickly.

"Derek was so big and powerful, he knew what he could do to people," Todd Fedoruk said. "And when it happened, in some cases he felt bad about it. But I always told him, 'You've got to understand, man, I would do the same thing. I would love it if I had your size.' But he had that strength and that power and that ability to really beat guys, and he didn't like it. He enjoyed it when he needed it, but some of it weighed on him."

All enforcers shouldered the weight of expectations, worry and unpredictability. The pressure was enormous.

"The thing about that job is that it's mental," Laraque said. "The fact that at any given time, you might fight somebody. Even if you're tired or something happens, even if the other tough guy doesn't play much, if the score of the game is out of proportion, you've got to go out and show up and fight, and show that you're there for your team. You always have to be ready at any time. And depending on who it is and what team you play, your level of nervousness might be higher from one game to another. You might not be able to sleep during your afternoon nap, or you might not be able to eat. You go to the movies, you might not be able to get into the movie because you know the next day you're playing this guy. You're worried. So many things that can happen, and it's mostly in the head. Because once you start fighting, it's different. It's okay. The adrenaline kicks in and you don't feel anything."

Outsiders, and some teammates and coaches, never understood. They underestimated the toll, both physically and mentally. They saw a player who played the fewest minutes on the team and who got into a fight only once every few games. They saw it as a job with few responsibilities, rewarded by lots of admiration. And they saw the enforcers as fearless.

If a scorer missed a good shot on goal, it rarely haunted him. There would be other shots and more goals, perhaps as soon as the next shift. But a fighter was keenly aware that every fight could be his last. The opportunity might not come again, particularly against a specific foe. A lost fight might mean a trip to the minor leagues. One big punch might end a career.

"Toward the end of my career, when I had a really good reputation, I started getting less and less nervous because I knew how the other tough guys felt," Laraque said. "I knew I had a mental advantage. Because if I was nervous, I knew the other guy was 10 times more nervous than me."

Most misinterpreted the enforcer. Despite their rugged reputations, many lived with an inferiority complex. They wanted to be more like everyone else, not less. They wanted to be all-around players trusted in every phase of the game. Nearly every young fighter who reached the NHL told the same story that Derek told all along: I know my role as an enforcer, but I know I need to improve my other skills, too, so that the team can trust me in all of those other game situations. Most of them, like Derek, remained fighters, first and foremost. Rare was the young fighter who grew into something more.

In early July 2006, the Wild announced that it had re-signed two of its young players to new contracts. Marian Gaborik had played 65 games that season, the same number as Derek. He scored 38 goals and recorded 28 assists, a point total that ranked him 58th in the league. Gaborik received a three-year contract worth $19 million. Derek scored two goals and fought 16 times, third most in the league. He signed a one-year contract for $525,000.

The lower pay, and the constant realization that fame could be fleeting, may be part of the everyman charm of the enforcer. But it ate at many who played the role.

Enforcers never knew for sure what a particular game might bring. The team might start slowly and need a fight as a momentum changer. A blowout might force the losing team to start a fight to restore its honor. An unexpected hit might light the match and quickly turn into an unpredicted brawl. Shift by shift, enforcers had to be ready to fight at a moment's notice.

Some games were almost guaranteed to have a fight. Those were the hard ones. Enforcers learned to look ahead at the schedule to see who and when they were likely to fight. Maybe there was a debt to be settled from last month or last year—retribution for a cheap shot that injured a teammate, payback owed for a beating during a fight. Maybe there was an up-and-coming enforcer who wanted to prove himself. Maybe there was a long history of acrimony between particular fighters.

The anticipation could be ignited by the media, showing high-lights from the last time and debating what would happen this time. But, mostly, enforcers internalized the pressure. They masked it behind their rugged, unworried faces.

Fans never saw enforcers curled up in a ball on the hotel room floor. They didn't see the food left on the plate during the pre-game meal. They didn't know that the enforcer tried to take his mind off of the fight with an afternoon movie or a long walk, and later had no idea what he had seen or where he had been.

Don't have the appetite to fight that night? Move aside. There are plenty of others who would love your job.

The role, and the pressures associated with it, could propel enforcers into a cycle of personal problems. Even as Derek arrived, the line of NHL enforcers was littered with broken lives. Alcohol and painkillers, especially, became the silent antidotes to the pain and pressure.

One of history's great enforcers, an idol to many players of Derek's generation, was Probert, who retired in 2002. He was a bru-tally effective fighter, a decent scorer, and a beloved teammate. He was also an alcoholic and a drug addict, he admitted in his autobiog-raphy, arrested at the United States-Canada border once for cocaine possession and suspended by the NHL for substance abuse multiple times. There were many other enforcers of the era who struggled through addiction, including Nilan and Brantt Myhres, whose career ended with a Laraque punch that broke his eye socket in the 2005 preseason, just as Derek arrived in the NHL.

Their problems, and those of many others that were not publi-cized, were dismissed as a side effect of their personalities, the kind of daredevil traits that led them to fight in the first place.

· · ·

TODD FEDORUK, "THE FRIDGE," wanted a piece of Derek. The puck had been sent to the other end of the ice, and as players chased it, Fedoruk tugged on the back of Derek's jersey.

It was early in the second period of a game between the Anaheim Ducks and the Wild, in Saint Paul on October 27, 2006. In the first period, Derek had kneed Anaheim's Chris Kunitz. Shane O'Brien came to Kunitz's rescue to challenge Derek. Derek pummeled him to the ice.

Now came Fedoruk, seeking hockey's convoluted brand of revenge. For several years, he had proved to be a willing and capable fighter in the NHL, with a bit of scoring punch. His grittiness had made him popular in Philadelphia, where he spent four seasons, and coveted by Anaheim, which traded a second-round draft choice to get him. Fedoruk was, in many ways, the type of all-around player Derek wanted to be—back when they were both in Regina, and here in the NHL.

Derek glanced over his shoulder and momentarily resisted the temptation. The whistle blew, and Fedoruk followed Derek into the corner. They grabbed one another, slipping their hands from their gloves as they glided toward the nearest face-off circle.

Derek popped Fedoruk in the face with a right hand. He had Fedoruk in his grip with his left hand, and Fedoruk ducked and squirmed to escape Derek's reach. He tried to keep his head turned away, out of range. Derek's next punch, cocked from his right hip, hit Fedoruk squarely on the right side of his face. Fedoruk dropped immediately. Derek skated away.

"Oh, ho, ho, ho, ho," one television announcer said.

"Oh, boy," the other replied over the din of the rollicking crowd.

Wild teammates banged the boards in front of their bench with their sticks, the ultimate ovation of appreciation for a fighter. Ducks players watched Fedoruk rise, one side of his face caved in, sickly demolished. Some turned away in horror.

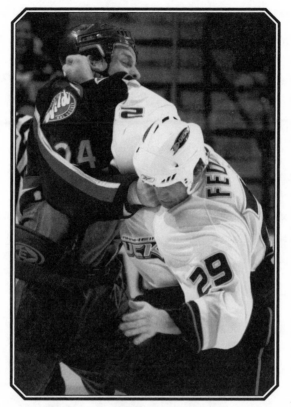

Derek breaks Todd Fedoruk's cheekbone.

As he stepped, expressionless, into the penalty box, Derek raised his left hand to acknowledge the crowd. It was a rare display for Derek. Len Boogaard called his son after the game. Do not ever do that again, he told him.

In the hallway outside the locker room, Derek spoke to friends with a pang of disbelief. His right hand was wrapped in ice inside a towel. It would throb for days.

"Oh, my God, I feel so bad for him," Derek said. "I crushed his face. My hand is killing me."

Derek bottled his astonishment and empathy in front of reporters.

"You never, ever wish that on somebody," Derek told them. "But you've got to look at it in a different way, too. What happens if he had you in that position? Do you think he would let up? You know he wouldn't."

The one punch altered the arc of both men's careers. For Derek, in his second season, it announced his coronation as the most feared fighter in the NHL. For Fedoruk, then 27, it irretrievably interrupted his career trajectory.

"I didn't see it coming at all," Fedoruk said of the punch, years later. "I was in a bad position and he hit me hard, hardest I've ever been hit. I instantly knew it was broken. I didn't lose consciousness, but I went straight on the ice. And I felt where it was, and my hand didn't rub my face normally. It was a little chunky and sharp in spots and there was a hole there about the size of a fist."

6

LEN AND DEREK BOOGAARD stepped out of the movie theater in San Jose, California, and went searching for something to eat.

It was less than two weeks after Derek's reputation had ballooned with his face-crushing knockout of Todd Fedoruk. The Minnesota Wild had invited the fathers of players to join the team on a West Coast road trip, and 16 of them came. They met at the Xcel Energy Center in Saint Paul, ate a full buffet meal on the team's charter jet and stayed at a high-end hotel in downtown San Jose. It impressed the fathers, but it was nothing different than the players typically enjoyed.

Len and Derek had spent all those years together, driving through the empty winter nights of Saskatchewan, warming themselves with rink burgers and the glow of the radio broadcasting faraway hockey. Len had visited Derek often in junior, where the buses drove a thousand miles at a time and only the oldest boys got a bunk. Derek and Janella and their bulldog, Trinity, had spent a couple of recent summers living with Len and his second wife, Jody, in Regina, where Len had added a room to the house.

Len thought he knew Derek's habits and creature comforts as

well as anyone. Derek was easy to please and unpretentious. His tastes
were simple. Len liked that about him.

"Pita Pit?" Len said, spotting a fast-food place across the street.

"No, I don't want that," Derek said. "We can just go back to the
hotel and order room service."

Len was not the room-service type, so the two parted. Len bought
a pita and a drink for six dollars and carried it back to the room.

Derek was there, waiting for his dinner. He joked about the fru-
gality of some of his teammates, especially the ones with wives and
children, who scrimped with the likes of Subway, Chipotle, and Pita
Pit so that they could squirrel away most of the $125 per diem that
players received.

Derek had ordered steak, some vegetables, and a bottle of Coca-
Cola. It came to the room. Derek signed the tab. It was $90.

Len protested. Ninety dollars? For dinner?

"Don't worry about it, Dad," Derek said, raising a dismissive
hand. "It's the lifestyle."

SEVERAL MONTHS BEFORE, the four-year relationship between
Derek and Janella had ended.

When Derek first made the Wild's season-opening roster in the
fall of 2005, Janella was still in Houston, living in the apartment they
had shared. She quit her job at a bank and pulled together the loose
ends of their lives. She arrived in Minneapolis in November for his
rookie year.

She already knew that Derek had cheated on her. She began to
snoop through pockets and phone records, their relationship spiral-
ing into distrust, and learned that he had done it again. Near Val-
entine's Day, while the Wild were on a road trip, she intercepted a
letter intended for Derek at their Minnesota apartment. Inside was

a note to him, from some girl writing about working things out. It mentioned Trinity and the truck.

Wow, Janella thought. This isn't just a fling. Somebody has seen our dog and been in our truck.

The card included a ticket stub from the night that Derek scored his first NHL goal, earlier that season. Janella had been stuck in Houston. The mystery woman had been at the arena.

Janella confronted Derek when he returned, and he begged her to stay and give him another chance. She did. But Janella knew that the NHL had changed Derek. He no longer went out in public without his false teeth. He bought designer glasses to replace the ones he had worn since middle school. He cared about where he got his hair cut. He upgraded his wardrobe to trendy brands.

He just wanted to fit in and look like he belonged. Janella understood that. She also understood how different Derek's world was from the time she met him, and she was willing to let that be an excuse for his behavior. He went from anonymous and poor to famous and rich. He went from having few close friends to having to fend off strangers desperate to get close to him.

Like many professional athletes, Derek did not have to grow up. He had never had a real job, anything besides being a hockey player. Teams told him what to do and where to be. His mother, or his billets, or Janella took care of things at home. Derek was just an oversized boy. And he behaved like one.

"We'd go to bars," Aaron Boogaard said, "and if you're there and the place is packed, and you can't get near the bar to get a drink, he'd shout, 'Submarine!' And he'd put his hands up over his head and duck down, going through the crowd. He'd be bumping into people, knocking drinks, pissing people off. Then he'd get to the bar and stand up and wave us over. We'd follow that path. He made me laugh, so, so hard."

There were times that Derek and Aaron, four years and about six inches apart, pretended to be twins. Derek loved it. "Who do you think is older?" he asked young women. And if they said Derek, he would feign disappointment and point to Aaron's retreating hairline.

At an outdoor concert one summer, Aaron found himself away from Derek, striking up a conversation with a couple of young women. Aaron pretended to be his brother, the cool enforcer of the Minnesota Wild. Later, as the same women approached, Aaron hid out of sight.

"Oh, you look so much taller with your glasses on," one of the women cooed to Derek.

He was confused. "Who are you?" Derek asked.

The boys must have told that story a hundred times.

Derek never denied anyone an autograph or a chance to take a picture with him. People bought him drinks, and Derek went along with it, accepting them and clinking glasses. Minneapolis, especially, was filled with young people who thought they were good friends with Derek Boogaard.

Part of him wanted to stay hidden behind the facade. Most of him could not resist the temptation. Aaron always thought Derek was like Shrek. Derek wanted people to know him as the big guy who could beat up anyone. That got him respect. But he really wanted to be liked, and he quickly established a reputation for being an approachable star. Even serious conversations in quiet corners of restaurants were routinely interrupted by someone asking for something from him.

Women, mature versions of the junior-league puck bunnies, wanted to know if the new Wild star was single. Men wanted to befriend Derek. Some wanted to drink with him, and some begged to be hit by him, to see if they could take one of his punches. Others, usually emboldened by alcohol, wanted to fight him, just to brag to friends. They usually settled for a fist bump and a cell-phone photograph of themselves with the Boogeyman, their fists raised in mock anger.

Weeks before training camp opened in 2006, Derek's second season with the Wild, he was at a Regina bar called the Pump Roadhouse. He was with his brothers, Ryan and Aaron, there to celebrate Aaron's birthday. In the late hours, long after anything good ever happens, Ryan turned away and lost track of the others. He walked outside to find Derek and Aaron in the middle of a scrum. Days later, Derek was charged with assault causing bodily harm, and the story soon echoed across the news wires. Derek declined to talk about the case publicly once he arrived at training camp, and not only to protect the upcoming legal proceedings. It was because he had been too drunk to remember what happened. Aaron, too.

The case, delayed until the following spring, was a soiled backdrop to Derek's everyman image for months. It was at Christmastime that Ryan ran into an old friend in Regina.

"I can't believe what happened at Pump Roadhouse, when Derek got punched by that guy," the friend said.

"Wait, you were there?" Ryan said. "You saw it?"

"Yeah, your brother got suckered," the friend said. He agreed to come forward as a witness. Charges were soon dropped.

Janella had grown used to the occasional shenanigans. When you have a thousand girls throwing themselves at you, she figured, eventually a man will break. When you have men wanting to cling to you, you might find yourself in unpleasant company. Derek was never good at saying no to people who wanted to get close to him. He was not adept at dissecting motivations.

Janella thought she could be the steadying influence for Derek, a sort of protector from the outside lures of money and fame. But weeks before the alleged assault in the summer of 2006, Derek cheated again, and she decided to teach him a lesson.

Derek had bought a loft-style condominium in Regina, just north of downtown, on a nondescript side street not far from a popular stretch of bars. He and Janella spent months designing it. It had exposed-brick walls and steel beams and high ceilings. There was a huge kitchen counter that opened to a big room. A large-screen television built into a wall could spin, flipping between the bedroom and the family room, with its monster-sized leather sofa. There was a den with a Murphy bed tucked into the wall and a large desk designed specifically for Ryan, to watch four NHL games at once so he could scout Derek's fighting rivals.

Derek wanted the loft to be for everyone, and he envisioned it filled with family and friends, maybe a precursor to the houses he dreamed of building in the mountains. He called the contractor continuously to check on the most minute of details. Finally, it was ready to move into.

Janella's mother had moved from the Portland suburbs to the Denver area, and Janella spent several weeks in Colorado early that off-season. She had plane tickets to return to Regina, but Derek called three days before her trip. He was upset. He had cheated again.

It broke Janella. That's it, she told Derek. She canceled her flight.

ON JUNE 26, after a few weeks apart and following a long and tearful phone call, Derek wrote the first in a string of rambling love letters to Janella, mostly on hotel stationery while spending time traveling Minnesota for off-season public appearances with the Wild.

"I am writing you this letter because I want you to know that I love you more than you think and that I do love you more than you love or loved me," one letter began.

The letters were written mostly in the late-night and early-morning hours. Derek misspelled some words and apologized for his grammar. Sometimes, he admitted to being drunk.

"I don't think I've ever cried that long in my life," he wrote in the first letter. "This year you have made me cry 4 times, that is the most that I have since I was 10 yrs old when I broke my brothers waterbed."

He talked about the condominium, how he had taken her design ideas to help make it something they could share, a place they could have friends and family.

"I feel like such a disappointment to everybody, you, my brothers and sister, my grandparents, the people in hockey, everybody."

He said he was writing in the dark with the lights off.

"I can't look myself in the mirror still," he wrote. "I feel like a failor [sic]. I wish I could have talked to you better and not just saying nothing is wrong when you asked me what was wrong. I know that you just cared about me and wanted to help. I want to give you the best life possible even if I stop hockey and you just want a normal life. If you really want that, I will do it and I will be happy with our decision."

He suggested that he could leave hockey behind and work the oil wells of Saskatchewan and Alberta. There was decent money in that, he reasoned, and he would be close to home.

He apologized to Janella for past arguments, including one where he criticized a "sexy white skirt" she wore.

"I get jealous but I don't show it until I just snap," he wrote. "Because everybody is looking at you! And they think why is she with that big idiot."

On June 29, in the afternoon, he wrote soberly about his excitement to see Janella the next day. He was coming to Colorado to visit.

"I am not going to let you go ever again if we get back together," he wrote.

Janella waited for him at the airport. It had been nearly four years since they met, awkwardly and nervously spotting one another at a tiny, rural airport in Minnesota. Back then, she had pretended not to notice him walking toward her. This time, through the crowd in Denver, she watched carefully. Janella was determined not to be a pushover. She told Derek that she had to think seriously about their future together. She needed more time. He went back to Regina. She stayed in Colorado.

Finally, near summer's end, she told Derek she was ready. We will make this work, she said.

Derek demurred. His friends and agents had been whispering to him that he needed to free himself of distractions. And Janella was a distraction, a girlfriend from long before he reached the NHL, someone Derek had outgrown and who threatened to hold him back. Focus on the future, Derek was told.

Derek told Janella that he needed to concentrate on the upcoming season. Camp was starting, and he wanted to keep his mind clear of personal issues.

The relationship was over.

Janella knew it was only temporary. She and Derek were meant for one another, and he would see that. He was just focused on the NHL, on an opportunity he had dreamed about and suddenly found himself living. He would be back. They would get married and build a life together, with a house and a family and a dog.

She took all of Derek's mementos—his notes, his pictures, even his medical records—and kept them locked in a safe place, holding them until they came together again.

She came to Minneapolis in the spring of 2007 to collect the last of her belongings. Derek's mother, Joanne, was there at Derek's condominium. Derek was not. Janella and Joanne talked, and talked, waiting for Derek to arrive. Janella was excited and nervous to see him. She did not know that Derek had no intention of seeing her. He waited for her to leave before he would return home. Finally, unable to wait for Derek any longer, Janella left.

Moments later, Derek and a guest arrived. Derek introduced his new girlfriend to his mother.

THE FIRST WILD game that Erin Russell attended was October 27, 2006—the game in which Derek shattered Todd Fedoruk's cheek. Thin and blonde, Erin was a 21-year-old who had grown up in Minnesota. She knew hockey well, had even played it as a girl. But she did not closely follow the Wild.

She met Derek at a nightclub in downtown Minneapolis called the Annex. Some of his friends knew some of her friends, and Derek spotted Erin right away.

"She's the one," he jokingly said to Tobin Wright, a former Wild employee who had become a sort of manager for Derek and one of his closest friends. "Yep, she's the one."

Erin asked why he was wearing a suit, and Derek told her that he was a bouncer. She believed him. She later found out that he was not a bar bouncer, but the Wild's young, popular enforcer. A meathead, Erin figured. But he seemed sweet—attentive and eager to please. And she was struck by how he was so interested in others, as if his priority was to make everyone else comfortable and deflect attention away from himself. Not the stereotype Erin had in mind.

Derek invited Erin to a game and gave her two tickets so she could bring a friend. Just as the women arrived and took their seats in the seventh row at the sold-out Xcel Energy Center, Derek was beating up Anaheim's Shane O'Brien. A period later, Erin saw Fedoruk tug on Derek's jersey, entice him into a fight, and collapse on the ice as the sellout crowd of 18,568 fans roared in wonder. This was the same humble, soft-spoken guy she had met at the club?

The Wild won, 3–2, in a shootout after neither team scored in overtime, improving the team's record to 9–0–1. Of the game's 65 minutes, Derek played 1 minute, 42 seconds. He had three penalties in four shifts and spent 12 minutes in the penalty box.

He had a throbbing right hand, a burgeoning reputation, and a new girlfriend.

STRATEGIES VARIED FOR fighting against Derek. Get close to him, to counter his reach advantage, and do not let him hold you straight out with his left hand. Hit him quickly and often, to keep him from setting up his one big punch. Switch hands and vary punches and dekes, to keep him off balance. You weren't going to knock Derek down. But you could make him slip to the ice.

And, after the fight with Fedoruk, the best strategy of all was to avoid him. Avoid his giant right fist, certainly. Better, avoid him altogether.

Derek fought 10 times in his second season, but only six after he knocked down Fedoruk. No one wanted to be his next victim.

But Derek was hurting, too. He played in only 48 of the season's 82 games. Most of the absences were due to injuries, but he was a healthy scratch from the lineup a few times, kept out because coach Jacques Lemaire wanted other players available for specific matchups. Maybe the other team had no true enforcer, or too much speed for Derek to handle. Maybe Lemaire wanted a boost on the power play or the penalty kill, and Derek rarely played on those special teams. Derek's average ice time dropped from 5 minutes, 23 seconds as a rookie to 4 minutes, 38 seconds in his second season.

But he was still prized by Lemaire. Years later, watching an NHL game after he retired from coaching, Lemaire wrote a Twitter message to his followers: "This is the kind of game I used to tell Boogey to find a face to smash with his fist. I'd say 'Go punch a face, then take a seat.'"

Derek's first fight after the Fedoruk takedown was against Laraque, then playing for the Phoenix Coyotes. Derek had missed a couple of games with a sore quadriceps, and a couple of others with a strained rotator cuff.

An ESPN player poll released later in the season called Derek the second "toughest player" in the NHL, behind Laraque.

"Here we go! Boogaard and Laraque! The heavyweights!" the television announcer said as the men stood in front of one net, fists raised. A graphic, entitled "Tale of the Tape," prepared in advance for the moment, quickly appeared at the bottom of the screen. It noted that Derek was six foot seven and weighed 270 pounds. Laraque was six foot three and 243.

Derek grabbed Laraque with his left hand and pelted him in the face with a couple of right hands. Laraque countered with a jab that dislodged Derek's helmet. Derek stumbled forward and nearly fell, sliding to one knee before standing again. The men clutched one another and tried to throw punches, but neither could get arms extended. It looked like they were boxing inside an invisible phone booth. Laraque jabbed Derek hard with a left hand to the side of the head. He wrestled Derek backward to the ice, folding his legs beneath him.

Derek was prescribed codeine that night by the Wild team doctor—one of the first times, records showed, that he was prescribed a painkiller. He missed the next 10 games with strained ankle ligaments.

He played through most of December, but did not fight again until January 9. In the days leading up to his next fight, according to pharmacy and medical records, a Wild team doctor prescribed Derek Ambien—20 pills on January 4, and 20 more on January 8.

On January 9, Derek was battered by Calgary's Eric Godard.

Godard and Derek had first fought in the Western Hockey League in 1999. Derek was 17 then, and it was his first fight for the Prince George Cougars. Godard was a 19-year-old from Vernon, British Columbia, who played for the Lethbridge (Alberta) Hurricanes.

Godard was never drafted into the NHL, but he signed with the Florida Panthers and was eventually part of a 2002 draft-day deal with the NHL's New York Islanders. In the summer of 2006, he signed with the Calgary Flames, a division rival of Minnesota's and a team in need of a capable enforcer to combat the likes of Derek. Calgary placed Godard with its minor-league affiliate in Omaha.

But he was promoted in time to make his debut with the Flames against Derek and the Wild. Starting near center ice at Calgary's Saddledome, two seconds after the Flames took a 1–0 lead, the two traded jabs and overhand punches with metronomic steadiness. Derek hit Godard with a couple of blows to the face and seemed to be in relative control before Godard hit Derek twice on top of the head with his right fist. Derek fell to one knee, stood back up, and was hammered twice more again. He dropped to a knee again, but Godard, clinging hard to Derek's jersey, did not let him stand a third time. He dragged him sideways to the ice and fell on top of him.

The Calgary fans cheered as the men stood and slid away. Derek, dazed, skated toward the wrong penalty box. Redirected, he slipped into the visiting penalty box, but quickly left for the dressing room.

Derek sat out a week. He missed three games. The team, required by league rules to publicly reveal injuries that might affect a player's chances to play, reported that Derek had a "head" injury.

The Wild and Flames played again on January 26, this time in Saint Paul. During a television timeout in the second period, Derek and Godard lined up next to one another, awaiting a face-off. They spoke calmly, like two men discussing the weather.

The puck dropped. Gloves flew. The two took turns swinging right fists, rhythmically, like lumberjacks working a two-man saw. A few punches connected. Godard jabbed Derek with a left fist full of Derek's jersey, knocking Derek's helmet to the ice. The chorus of the crowd lowered an octave, from a collective *ahhh* to an *ohhh*. A hard right hand to Godard's face loosened his helmet, and the response of the crowd rose in anticipation again.

Derek hit Godard with another hard right, then pulled the back of Godard's jersey up over his head. Another punch sent Godard to the ice. As officials converged, Derek dropped to his knees to get an angle to throw a couple of low uppercuts—emphatic, spiteful punctuation to the end of the brawl.

"That's un-Boogaard-like, but he does get a couple of extra ones in there," the Wild's television broadcaster said.

Derek skated away with blood on his lip and a scrape on his cheek, road rash from the rough cut of his own jersey being rubbed into his face.

"It wasn't from his fists," Derek explained to reporters later.

The season continued in fits and fights. Derek sat out four games in March because of lower-back pain. But he was on the ice again on March 22 against St. Louis, ready to fight D. J. King.

The two had much in common. King was 26, a native of tiny Meadow Lake, Saskatchewan, part of a First Nations tribe. He and Derek had crossed paths years earlier, in the Western Hockey League, but never fought. King was not a big fighter then, but he showed an affinity for it, and certainly had the size for it, at six foot four and 230 pounds. Coaches steered him toward a role as a brutish enforcer, and King was willing to do it, seeing it as his only chance to reach the NHL. He was drafted by St. Louis in the sixth round of the 2002 draft. Like Derek, he graduated from the WHL and built his skills and reputation in the East Coast Hockey League and the American Hockey League.

He had been promoted to the Blues, and already had beaten up a string of respected enforcers: Shawn Thornton, Scott Parker, and Darcy Hordichuk. Now, midway through the third period of an easy Wild victory, it was time to face the Boogeyman.

It was no contest. Starting in front of the St. Louis bench, Derek pounded King with a battery of right hands. The two got tangled tightly, which was King's strategy, before Derek escaped enough to unfurl two overhand fists to the back of King's head. With King's face ducked, Derek crushed him in the jaw with an uppercut, then swung wide with his right hand for a series of blows to King's ribs, below the armpit.

It was as if Derek wanted to display his full arsenal. For 60 seconds, Derek battered King, but could not knock him out. He threw about 30 punches and landed half of them, some squarely.

"It's time to go down, son," a television announcer said.

Finally, like boxing referees stepping in to save a fighter and declare a technical knockout, the officials barged in during a lull.

King had proved his fearlessness. He would get more chances at Derek.

Derek had proved that he was, in just his second season, an enforcer to be measured against.

THE PINNACLE CAME on the night of Tuesday, April 17, 2007. It was Game 4 of a first-round playoff series with the Anaheim Ducks, and Derek's last name—*Boo-guard*, not *Bow-guard*—echoed through the Xcel Energy Center.

He was on the bench. Minnesota was on its way to a victory, the game paused as officials sorted through a series of rough hits and cheap shots. Derek stood against the wall, jabbering through a straight face at the Ducks players. Fans grew louder and louder. Lemaire gave Derek the signal to get on the ice.

Derek stepped over the boards and glided effortlessly in a graceful arc, as if propelled by the deafening cheers that engulfed him. He kept his kind, sad eyes on the Ducks bench. He smirked. He shrugged. There was no fight. But the message had been sent.

The Ducks had 71 fighting majors that season, 20 more than any other team. When one brawler went down—as Fedoruk had, to Derek's right fist, in October—the Ducks merely reloaded. At the time they traded away a broken Fedoruk, they received six-foot, five-inch George Parros, as if to specifically counter Derek.

Before the series began, the Ducks bragged of having six players willing to drop the gloves. They were a modern vision of the Broad Street Bullies, finding success in planting intimidators across the roster.

The Wild really had just one fighter. The team accrued only 14 fighting majors during the season, of which Derek was responsible for 10. And one of the storylines before the series was which side had the better philosophy toward intimidation.

In Game 1, in Anaheim, Derek took the ice for the first time and barreled over Anaheim's Corey Perry within seconds. He was penalized for charging. The Wild lost by a goal. In Game 2, Derek compiled 14 penalty minutes, none of them for fighting. The Wild lost by a goal again.

Game 3 was in Saint Paul. Derek had the flu, and team doctors fed him intravenously with two liters of prescription fluids and electrolytes. Lemaire scratched Derek from the lineup and tried to replace him with scoring punch to spark the Wild's meager power-play unit. The Wild lost by a goal for the third game in a row.

There was nothing to lose in Game 4. Derek was back in the lineup. It was his assist, on a pass to Pierre-Marc Bouchard, that helped tie the game in the second period.

That turned the game. The Wild scored three times in about eight minutes of the third period to secure its first playoff victory in four years. The contest then devolved into one of bombastic surliness, the Ducks bent on avenging the loss by leaving the Wild bruised and battered. Derek was saddled on the bench for most of it, including a fight between Minnesota's Brent Burns and Anaheim's Perry. Another fight steered most of the players into duels. That was when Anaheim's Brad May approached Minnesota's Kim Johnsson. He gave Johnsson a shove and hit him in the face. Johnsson dropped to the ice with a concussion.

Derek, an attack dog on a leash, was unable to rush to the defense of his falling teammates. Many of them adored Derek. About half a dozen of them had played alongside Derek back in Houston, when they had five-figure salaries and drank Bud Lights in sports bars and $700-a-month apartments. They respected how hard he had worked to reach the NHL and were thankful for his willingness to defend them through fighting, a job they could not imagine for themselves. They appreciated Derek's humility, his eagerness to help young players, his penchant for handling media and public-appearance requests. There was nothing Derek would not do for them. Yet here he was, caged in the bench, unable to get out.

The chant began.

Boo-gaard, Boo-gaard, Boo-gaard, Boo-gaard . . .

It grew louder, like something heard over the horizon that slowly moves closer, a wave that rises in the distance and builds as it approaches the shore.

Derek looked back. Lemaire nodded. Derek, needing no further assurance, slid effortlessly over the half-boards and onto the ice. Never had Derek soaked in such adulation. People loved him not for what he did, but for who he was.

In the off-season, he signed a three-year contract worth $2.63 million. His $750,000 salary the next season ranked Derek among the highest-paid enforcers in the NHL, trailing only the likes of established bruisers like Laraque ($1.3 million) and Donald Brashear ($1.1 million).

But it did not place him among the top 500 highest-paid NHL players. Nineteen of Derek's own teammates made more.

THE IDEA FOR the "Boogaard Fighting Camp" for children wasn't really Derek's, but he was the one to answer for it.

Todd Ripplinger, the Regina Pats scout who had discovered Derek in the old Main Arena in Melfort a decade earlier and helped rekindle his love for the game after he quit during junior, was a partner in an indoor rink and training center in Regina. The place hosted a constant stream of camps, filled with children learning the skills of hockey—skating, shooting, goaltending. Two of Derek's Minnesota teammates, goalie Josh Harding and defenseman Nick Schultz, ran youth summer camps at the center.

Someone wondered aloud if there should be a similar camp for another hockey skill: fighting. Ripplinger called Derek, who was spending parts of his summers in Regina. Derek and his brother Aaron, the former draft pick of the Wild who had recently signed with the Pittsburgh Penguins, were glad to do it.

About 30 boys, aged 12 to 18, came to the first of several camps that summer. They paid $50 each. They watched a 25-minute video of Derek's best fights, including his knockout of Fedoruk, compiled by Ryan Boogaard. They learned examples of following "the code"— fighting's unwritten rules. Know when to start a fight. Know what is allowed and fair. Know how to win with grace and lose with dignity.

The boys were taught some keys to fighting. Get a strong stance. Grab the jersey. Tuck the chin. Each boy partnered with another boy, roughly the same size and age, and practiced the lessons—with their gloves on.

They were given a T-shirt that read "Boogaard Fighting Camp"; what looked like red drops of blood dribbled from the letters. Their parents wielded cameras and autograph pens.

"The kids love it," Derek told the *StarTribune*. "It's fun to see how excited they are and how pumped up the parents get."

He explained that nearly every young hockey player would find himself in a fight eventually, maybe just a spur-of-the-moment scrap with one of the sport's countless agitators—"rats," as Derek called them. It was prudent to learn how to protect yourself. The camp was not about beating up opponents, but preventing them from beating up you, Derek said.

"The people who say this is a bad thing—because it's going to happen—just tell them to cool it, relax, sit back and watch," Derek told the Regina *Leader-Post*. "It's not a bad example. A bad example is letting a kid go out there and fight and get himself hurt. This is to protect the kids, bottom line."

But some called it "goon school," and the camp made national news. It was debated and widely panned across the Internet, on talk shows, even in newspaper editorials. Derek appeared on news channels to defend himself. He did his best to dismiss the critics, but the backlash took its toll.

Enthusiasm for the camps waned. Derek declined to do them again. He did not like to be the bad guy, at least beyond the rink. His job was to protect, not to hurt. He had wanted to show people that he was not a thug—that there was an art to his craft, a method and meaning to the madness.

AMONG THOSE WHO lent the fight camps credibility was a boxing instructor named Frank Fiacco. Derek spent several summers working at Fiacco's gym in Regina, learning and rehearsing the nuances of the sport. It was Fiacco who worked with Derek to develop the body blows that he used on D. J. King. It was Fiacco who helped develop Derek's uppercut, not unlike the one he used to knock out Fedoruk.

Fiacco was a small, tightly wound man—"a short Italian," he

called himself—whose day job was as a building coordinator for the city of Regina. His brother was Regina's mayor.

But Fiacco was also an international boxing referee and judge. His Lonsdale Boxing Club was in a cavernous building on a grim industrial street beyond the north edge of downtown, not far from Derek's condominium. The ceiling hummed with fluorescent lights, and the walls were covered in mirrors. The large room had mats on the floor and heavy bags suspended from above. A regulation-sized boxing ring was in one corner.

On any given evening or weekend, the ring would host a revolving cast of boxers—men and women, adults and children—learning how to use their padded fists. Many of the participants were hockey players. Teenagers from the local teams, like the Pats and the Pat Canadians, sometimes brought in groups for team-mandated training sessions.

Derek arrived wearing jeans, a T-shirt, and glasses. People did not always recognize him.

"You look like a schoolteacher instead of a hockey player," Fiacco said to him.

When younger hockey players approached, Derek knelt down to talk to them eye to eye. He was soft-spoken and quick to smile. Fiacco could tell his good-naturedness was genuine, and he appreciated how Derek spoke so kindly and gently to his young daughters.

But he felt for Derek, whose fame grew in Regina in step with his fame in Minnesota. He struck Fiacco as a shy young man who now always had to be "on." He had to be in a good mood and he had to be social. He had to make being hockey's most-feared man look easy. It had to appear that there were no drawbacks. Who would ever feel sorry for a rich, famous professional hockey player, especially in the gritty outposts of Saskatchewan?

Once the workouts began, Fiacco donned thick mittens called "focus" pads. He held his hands up, as if under arrest, providing targets for Derek and Aaron to punch. The Boogaards would throw 10-pound medicine balls from their chests to strengthen the motion of a punch. They would shadowbox in front of the mirrors to practice technique and pound on the heavy bags to improve stamina.

"He had fast hands," Fiacco said of Derek. "Really, really, really, really fast hands. And power. Without really having to unload."

Then the boys would climb into the ring together, wearing boxing gloves. It was a formalized extension of their not-so-brotherly battles in the basement and the yard at the house in Melfort.

"Don't hit my nose," Derek said. "Don't hit me in the—"

Bam! Aaron hit Derek in the nose.

"I swear to God, Nick, if you hit me if the nose again, I'm going to kill you."

Bam! Another shot. Aaron always knew how to make Derek mad.

Nearly every NHL enforcer had had his nose broken too many times to count. Most had surgery at least once to rebuild the breathing passages.

Derek hated getting hit in the nose. He rarely complained of injuries and pain, but the nose was an exception. He'd had it broken at least six times, probably double that. After getting his nose broken once during a game in Minnesota, a friend of Derek's found him lying on his back in the training room. A trainer was straddled on top of Derek, pulling and twisting his nose back into position with all his might.

Bam!

The fights descended from workouts to brawls. Derek chased his brother around the ring. People in the gym stopped what they were doing to watch. Boogaard family members, sometimes accompanying the boys to the gym, had seen it all before. Joanne winced through the punches, but was happy that they at least had gloves on.

Fiacco tried to break Derek of his early habit of swinging wildly for the knockout. Don't just grab with the left. Hit with it, too. And don't waste movement. Don't go wide with the right. Shorter distances. Keep yourself protected. And learn new moves.

"If you plateau, everyone else is catching up," Fiacco told Derek.

If Fiacco were ever to instruct an opponent on how to fight Derek, he would advise them to go after Derek's body—something most fighters did not think to do, wanting to hit him quickly with a big blow to knock him off balance. But Fiacco thought the body blows would force Derek to drop his left hand down, exposing his head. That was what Aaron did.

Opponents, especially smaller ones, usually tried to get in tight with Derek, to prevent him from holding his opponent at arm's length and pounding him with his near-lethal right fist. But Derek was strong enough to wrestle many of them away. Once he grabbed the collar of the other man's jersey, he could thrash them side to side or sway them rhythmically until he timed his fist with their face.

But larger enforcers, men like Laraque, could not be throttled. Laraque would muscle in close to Derek, wait for Derek to try to shove him away, and punch as Derek's hands were out of position. Aaron, smaller than Derek but more technical, did that, too.

Laraque, like most others, hated to fight Derek. Just the thought of an upcoming duel caused restless nights and bouts of anxiety. He knew that he was one punch away from the end of his career. And if anyone would land that punch, it would be Derek.

"There's not that many guys that did that to me, but because of his punching power, and his height, his size, and the fact that he liked fighting," Laraque said. "You know, he broke Fedoruk's face, and he's fucking tough. And the scariest thing for me was the pressure. People expected us to fight. I knew sooner or later he would get the better of me, and I just—I like my face, and I just didn't want to have it broken."

· · ·

TODD FEDORUK CAME back too soon. After being crushed by Derek, Fedoruk's face was surgically rebuilt with small metal plates and a swatch of mesh.

"The angle that I was hit at and stuff like that, the cheekbone came all the way over to my nose and crumpled up," Fedoruk said. "The orbital—that's the shell behind your eye—was completely blown out. The doc said, 'I've fixed a lot of faces from car accidents that weren't as bad as this.' And he was trying to tell my wife to prepare her for it, and he said, 'I really don't know if he's going to be able to play again.' I was like, 'No, no, I'll be fine. I can still see.'"

About two weeks later, Fedoruk was traded back to the Philadelphia Flyers, where his NHL career had begun, for a future fourth-round draft choice. Five weeks after the punch, he was in the Philadelphia lineup.

He felt internal pressure to get back on the ice. He was 27, supposedly in his prime, but embarrassed to have been on the losing end of a brutal highlight and afraid of being forgotten entirely. In late February, he fought Chris Simon of the Islanders.

"Simon recracked some stuff in here," Fedoruk said, touching his cheek. "And I didn't tell anybody, because I'm still young, I've got my best years in front of me, and I just had a good year in Anaheim. I shouldn't have been fighting. But I wanted to get back on the horse."

In March, he fought Colton Orr of the New York Rangers. An Orr punch drilled Fedoruk in the face. He sank to the ice, unconscious. A stretcher carried him off the Madison Square Garden rink.

Fedoruk was damaged goods. He signed with the Dallas Stars that summer, but barely played early in the season. He tried to make an impression, getting into a fight in the season opener and then battling George Parros in an October game against Anaheim. He was soon demoted to the minor leagues, a willing fighter but a broken enforcer.

That was when the Wild called. Minnesota, looking for a wider range of toughness through its roster, wanted to sign him. Fedoruk called his wife, Theresa.

"Don't they have Boogaard?" she said. "Now you won't have to fight him anymore."

"I wasn't going to fight him again, anyway," Fedoruk said.

Fedoruk welcomed the Wild offer, but envisioned the awkward reintroduction: "Hey, buddy, remember me, the guy whose career you almost ended last year? See this dent in my face? Want to be roomies?"

Derek hoped that the video board at the Xcel Energy Center would finally stop playing replays of the punch.

"They show it before the game, during the game, after the game," Derek said.

The Wild did not want any discomfort to simmer. The team assigned Fedoruk a dressing-room stall next to the corner one that Derek used. The tension was palpable when Fedoruk arrived.

After a few moments, Fedoruk broke the silence with a joke.

"Do you want to switch sides?" he said to Derek, loud enough for others to hear. "Because this is the side you hit, and I don't feel comfortable with you on that side of me."

Derek laughed his familiar laugh, a deep, guttural *heh-heh-heh* chortle. Teammates laughed in relief.

Derek apologized for the damage he had caused. Fedoruk told him not to. That is part of the enforcer's code, never having to say you're sorry.

"I would have done the same thing to you if I could have," Fedoruk said.

DEREK'S SEASON, his third in the NHL, began strongly. He had six fights in the first 20 games, and his place in the ranks of enforcers—on the top tier—was secure.

But that sixth fight, against Jody Shelley of the Columbus Blue Jackets, the night that Fedoruk first played for the Wild, was the last Derek would fight for nearly four months.

Derek's back problems flared up again. He missed all but two of Minnesota's next 24 games. Even before that, medical reports later showed, Wild doctors diagnosed him with facial lacerations, a bruised foot, and cuts to his hand.

Derek already had received more prescription drugs from team doctors than he had in his first two seasons combined, according to medical and pharmacy records later obtained by Len Boogaard. Ambien, 30 of them at a time, came with regularity. There were muscle relaxants and anti-inflammatories. There were regular dosages of Tylenol with codeine, then Endocet, a mix of acetaminophen and oxycodone.

By the middle of winter, in January of 2008, Derek was receiving prescriptions from Wild medical director Sheldon Burns for hydrocodone, sold under the brand name of Vicodin, a powerfully addictive narcotic pain reliever mixed with acetaminophen, the active ingredient in pain relievers such as Tylenol. Generally consumed on an as-needed basis, Derek received 20 one week by prescription, then 20 the next, according to pharmacy records.

And for the first time, records showed, a Wild doctor prescribed oxycodone, usually marketed under the brand name OxyContin, another highly addictive opioid (narcotic) used as a round-the-clock treatment for moderate to severe pain.

The Wild was desperate to get Derek back onto the ice. When it became clear that he might miss much of the season, the Wild went looking for reinforcements. In February, at the NHL trading deadline, the Wild added a surprising bit of punch: the notorious veteran enforcer Chris Simon.

In the previous 12 months, Simon had received a 25-game suspension for slashing the New York Rangers' Ryan Hollweg and a

30-game suspension for stepping on Pittsburgh's Jarkko Ruutu, two of the longest suspensions ever doled out by the NHL. The Islanders had given Simon a personal leave of absence earlier in the season, and Simon—with a known bout with alcohol addiction as a junior player in Canada—entered the league's Substance Abuse and Behavioral Health Program. After a league vice president said that Simon was receiving drug-and-alcohol treatment, the league backpedaled. A spokesman pointed out that the program also addressed other behavioral issues and cited the league's privacy policy.

The Islanders no longer wanted the 36-year-old and were glad to get a sixth-round draft choice out of the deal with the Wild. Simon would play 10 regular-season games and two playoff games for the Wild and end his NHL career before playing a few more seasons as a bruiser in Russia.

But at the time, the Wild's additions of Fedoruk and Simon boosted the team's air of toughness and provided security in case Derek's injuries, particularly his balky back, kept him out of the lineup.

"There's no doubt we're bigger and stronger, and that was a factor last season in maybe not being No. 1 in our division or advancing in the playoffs," Doug Risebrough, the general manager, told reporters after the trade was announced. "We needed to make sure we could compete physically, and these changes we've made, I think they're a positive."

They did one other thing that the Wild never fully considered: they provided Derek with personal examples to follow. Both Simon and Fedoruk were intimately familiar with the strange life of an NHL enforcer, and the private demons that could undermine a career.

Derek's usual roommate on the road was defenseman Brent Burns. After Fedoruk's arrival, though, players shuffled themselves, and Fedoruk and Derek, traveling sporadically because of his injuries, shared hotel rooms.

"I don't know if he was my friend more because he felt sorry for what he did to me, or he just liked my jokes," Fedoruk said later. "But I think there's a level of respect that he had for me for not trying to hold anything over him for doing what he did."

They quickly became close friends and confidants. Fedoruk saw how strangers reacted to Derek—usually by commenting on his size, which made Derek uncomfortable. Young men often raised their fists and dared Derek to punch them. When Derek asked why, they said, "So I can say I took a punch from the Boogeyman."

Fedoruk experienced firsthand the disconnect between Derek's persona and personality.

"He got along with my kids better than he did with some adults," Fedoruk said. "Luke was four in Minnesota, and Derek really enjoyed Luke, because Luke always sat between me and him when he was at the rink. Luke was always scared and shyer when he was at the rink, and I think Boogey liked that shyness about him. He liked that he felt real safe beside the Boogeyman."

When Fedoruk's son was scared of the dark, Fedoruk told him not to fear the Boogeyman. "You know the Boogeyman," he'd say.

"And Boogs liked that. I think you can really judge a person's character by how they are around kids who've got that innocence and unsafe feeling."

Derek played just two games in December and three games in January, nursing his injuries. He was desperate to return to the lineup, not wanting to disappoint the Wild or give the team a reason to replace him. He tried to conceal the pain from teammates and coaches, but was receiving medication from team doctors.

"He couldn't sit on the bench," Fedoruk said. "He was in a lot of pain—a lot of pain. He couldn't walk around being the guy he was. He couldn't show that pain."

With each man eager to hide their problems from others, Derek and Fedoruk grew closer. Their bond reached all the way back to their similar boyhoods in western Canada and their brief overlap as members of the Regina Pats, to the misunderstood role that they played in hockey and the one punch that had altered the arcs of their careers.

In the time-killing tedium of hotel rooms in unfamiliar cities, Derek leaned on Fedoruk for advice. Derek knew that Fedoruk understood him more than most teammates ever could. He felt he could trust him. Derek was naturally curious, and now, on this day, he was curious about prescription pills.

"He was kind of in and out of the lineup that year," Fedoruk said. "That's when he needed these things, the pills, the painkillers and stuff. I knew he needed them because I was roommates with him."

Derek asked Fedoruk about some of the drugs he was taking, too, including oxycodone.

"They really work," Derek said. "Are you taking them because you need them, or because you like them?"

Fedoruk saw trouble brewing. It was so familiar. He had seen it with other hockey players, and known about it with other enforcers. Fedoruk had lived it. He, too, had been in the throes of addiction, first with alcohol, then with pills, keeping it all secret and exploring his own counseling off and on for years. The worst bout was ahead of him.

Now his teammate, his friend, was asking for advice.

"It was kind of a sick, unhealthy relationship," Fedoruk said later. "I was up front with him about my issues. I was in rehab and all this stuff and he knew it. I was trying to balance how I could hold on to the addiction part of it, live that style of life, be a dad at home and be a hockey player. I was trying to balance it all when, really, the booze and drugs had priority over everything at that time."

The hotel room they shared was a virtual pharmacy, both men holding prescription bottles filled with pills to allow them to play, and to fight, and to feel good during all the slow, dull, difficult hours in between. Some were on the bathroom counter, others hidden from view in their bags. Part of an enforcer's code was to keep your problems to yourself.

"I know you've got pain," Fedoruk told Derek, "but be careful."

Derek, a young apprentice, was an earnest listener. To him, the pills were something to help him do his job, a tool handed him with the tacit approval of his employers, under the direction of team doctors who had his best interests in mind. Hockey players often had pills. Enforcers, Derek was learning, probably needed that kind of help most of all. It was normal.

Derek loved Fedoruk's company. He thought Fedoruk was hilarious, and Fedoruk liked to hear Derek's low-octave *heh-heh-heh* chortle. Over plates of room service, the television on, each splayed on a bed, they traded stories about home and hockey.

There were times that season when it was simply too hard for Derek to move his giant frame without feeling stabbing pain in his back or hips or shoulder. In the privacy of the hotel room, far from the arena lights and the outside world's expectations of fearlessness, Derek needed help.

"Todd," Derek asked, "can you put a couple of pillows under my feet?"

7

THE FIGHT DID NOT seem different than all the others, except that Derek lost, which was unusual, and he lost a tooth, which no one really saw. Only in hindsight did any of it seem significant.

It was October 16, 2008, an early-season road game against the Florida Panthers. The Wild won, 6–2, and Derek recorded an assist. It was his first point of any kind—goal or assist—since the playoff game against the Anaheim Ducks two seasons earlier.

The fight Derek lost was against Wade Belak, an affable defenseman with a shock of red hair. Belak was born in Saskatoon, just like Derek, and grew up mostly in Battleford, Saskatchewan, not far from Melfort. As a teen, Belak played in the Western Hockey League for the Saskatoon Blades, whose general manager was Daryl Lubiniecki, later the Prince George executive who traded for 17-year-old Derek. Belak was a first-round NHL draft choice in 1994. Like Derek, he had a younger brother, Graham, drafted into the NHL, in the optimistic hope that the family name and a willingness to fight would carry him into the league and to similar stardom.

By the time that Derek and Belak fought in South Florida in Minnesota's third game of the season, the six-foot, five-inch, 225-pound Belak was 32, an improbable age for someone making a living as an enforcer. But teams viewed him as a solid defenseman with a willingness to throw punches with the heavyweights of the league. He could play decent minutes, fight when necessary, and keep the team loose. Belak seemed to enjoy his role. Others in the fighting fraternity liked Belak and respected him, Derek included.

Belak clutched Derek's jersey near the bottom, while Derek grabbed Belak's near the collar. The players yanked themselves into a slow-motion spin, throwing spot-on punches with their free hands while trying to keep their balance. Like a campfire that smolders before suddenly crackling with flames again, the fight slowed several times before another punch reignited it.

Each man took fists to the face, many times. Along the way, one of the punches knocked a false tooth out of Derek's mouth. He never winced, not even as the officials slid between the exhausted fighters and nudged them toward the penalty boxes.

A team doctor for the Florida Panthers examined Derek and noted that the post of the false tooth hung in his mouth by a piece of skin. He removed the hardware and recommended a visit to the Wild's team dentist when the team returned to Minnesota.

Derek in the penalty box after a fight for the Wild.

The injury did not prevent Derek from playing the rest of the game. His assist came in the second period.

The Wild played two nights later in Tampa, and Derek again played his usual number of shifts and minutes. On October 20, back in Minnesota, Derek was given a prescription for 15 hydrocodone pills from Wild team dentist Kyle Edlund, pharmacy records showed. It was just a start. Over 33 days, Derek received at least 195 hydrocodone pills from six NHL team doctors, according to medical reports and prescription records later collected by Len Boogaard. The records, and others collected, did not say how often Derek was to take the pills, or how many to consume each time. But it was a far greater quantity of prescription painkillers than Derek had been prescribed in his first three seasons combined.

Five of the doctors were affiliated with the Wild. The sixth was a team doctor for the San Jose Sharks, Arthur Ting, who prescribed 40 hydrocodone pills for Derek when the Wild arrived two days before playing a game in California. While it was not unusual for team doctors to treat opposing players, since not all teams traveled with team doctors of their own, Ting, a former doctor for baseball player Barry Bonds, was under probation from the Medical Board of California, which said that he "prescribed dangerous drugs and controlled substances to friends and acquaintances, particularly athletes, for whom he kept no medical records or for whom the medical records were fictitious, inadequate, or inaccurate," according to the Associated Press.

A second spurt of prescription pills came in December. Sheldon Burns, the Wild's medical director, and Dan Peterson, a Wild team doctor who shared a practice with Burns, prescribed 110 more hydrocodone pills to Derek over 27 days, the last on New Year's Day, usually with no notation in Derek's medical file to explain the reason, according to records. Amid those prescriptions for painkillers, Peterson also prescribed 30 pills of Ambien, the sleeping drug.

That flurry of prescription pills began with one punch from Belak, who was on his way to becoming undone by demons of his own. On this night, though, it was just another hockey fight, barely noted.

WHEN DEREK STEPPED into Sneaky Pete's, familiar faces looked up to him and smiled. The bar's owners and bartenders gave him high fives and shoulder pats. Everyone knew Derek. Like the character of Norm in *Cheers*, the owner said.

When things got too crowded, or Derek just wanted to escape, he slid behind the bar, where a Derek Boogaard bobblehead doll was prominently displayed on a shelf. A stuffed bison head that Derek bought hung from a wall.

Sneaky Pete's opened in 2007 on North Fifth Street, on the northwestern edge of downtown Minneapolis, part of the Warehouse District that was quickly becoming a gentrified center of bars and nightclubs. A light-rail station was outside Sneaky Pete's darkened-glass front wall. The new baseball stadium for the Minnesota Twins, Target Field, was just a block away, out the door to the right. The popular pedestrian-only Nicollet Mall was a couple of blocks the other direction.

Sneaky Pete's was operated by a couple of brothers of the Hafiz family, which also owned several other bars in the area, including a couple of adult clubs featuring topless dancers. Derek became friends with Stewart Hafiz, who managed the place. He also became friends with Dillon Hafiz, Stewart's son, several years younger than Derek, who sometimes supervised and worked the bar.

During the day, Sneaky Pete's was a typical sports bar and restaurant, with tall tables in the front and booths in the back. A long, snaking bar curled along the left side in the back half of the room, and televisions flickered from all corners. The men's room had two-way mirrors looking toward the bar, so that people at the urinals could voyeuristically scan the crowd.

At night, especially on weekends, Sneaky Pete's took on the feel of a nightclub. Bouncers stood outside, keeping people waiting behind velvet ropes. A throbbing beat escaped through the walls and open door. Tables were stashed away to create a large dance floor. Brass poles were bolted to the ceiling and floor for women to climb and contort themselves. Dancing atop the bar was encouraged. Attractive women were stationed behind large troughs, offering ice-cold beers. Others female workers roamed the crowd, enticing patrons with sweet-flavored shots.

Downstairs was darker and mellower. With a straight bar hugging the entire right side, it had the feel of a speakeasy.

In 2010, the *StarTribune* called Sneaky Pete's "downtown's most popular party bar." *Maxim* magazine made a habit of declaring it one of America's top sports bars.

There were stretches when Derek was at Sneaky Pete's several nights a week, especially in the off-season. He was easily recognized. Sports fans knew who he was because of his stature in the Twin Cities. Everyone else assumed he was an athlete because of his size. They called him "Boogey," or the "Boogeyman," and sometimes an impromptu chant of his nickname broke through the din.

Derek smiled sheepishly and agreed to every autograph request. He stood for photographs, often with young men, everyone raising their fists like prizefighters at a weigh-in. Derek was embarrassed by the attention, but he soaked it in, too. He managed to be both approachable and awe-inspiring. Friends constantly tugged him away from conversations because Derek was not good at walking away.

He often sat at a table in the back, his back to the wall, where he could see people approaching and where friends could provide a buffer when he wanted one. He sipped on Bud Light.

Derek tried to drag teammates to Sneaky Pete's, but most had more private lives, or they lived closer to the team's headquarters in Saint Paul, or they were married with children and did not frequent the bars. Derek insisted one spring that the Wild hold an end-of-season party at Sneaky Pete's, and so the team did, renting out the lower level.

But most of the time, Derek went to Sneaky Pete's by himself or with some his non-hockey friends. As in high school, Derek found himself a magnet to people who were not hockey players. One of his best friends was Tobin Wright. Eight years older than Derek, he worked in hockey operations for the Wild at the time that Derek was drafted. Wright left the club during the lockout and became a certified player agent, aligning himself with Ron Salcer, a veteran Los Angeles–based agent whose Minnesota clients included Derek, star forward Marian Gaborik, and defenseman Brent Burns.

Wright was a sort of business manager for Derek and the others, organizing their public appearances and handling whatever daily headaches they encountered. Wright's relationship with Derek spanned many years and places. He knew Janella from Derek's days in the minor leagues. He was with Derek the night he met Erin.

In the summer of 2007, Wright introduced Derek to Jeremy Clark, who soon became Derek's closest friend in Minnesota. Clark, a taut and tightly wound former mixed-martial-arts fighter, raised in a small town in northern Ontario, owned a gym called Top Team. It began in a cramped end of an industrial building hidden off a small road in suburban Eagan, but Clark slowly took over the space next door, and the space next to that, creating a maze of rooms filled with mats and heavy bags and gym equipment. One room had a full-size boxing ring.

Clark slowly found a niche training hockey players. Eventually, entire teams were sent to be trained by Clark, and Clark was being summoned across the country to train teams, including some in the NHL. Derek was his most famous client.

"I get to train this monster," Clark thought to himself when they met. Derek could lift enormous kettle bells that Clark could barely budge, and stretch rubber strength bands twice as far as anyone else. The first time he stepped into the boxing ring with Derek, Clark was scared. He moved like a moth, trying to avoid Derek's fists. Derek had a switch, and Clark saw it flip a few times while boxing, usually when Derek's brother Aaron hit him in the nose. Clark came to recognize it when he watched Derek fight in the NHL. Saying that Derek snapped implied that he lost all control. It was a switch, and Derek knew when to throw it.

Derek liked the art of the fight, and he liked studying and practicing technique, but Clark could see how the teeter-totter of emotions could get to a man. Not knowing when the fight would come, but knowing that it always did, and that it might be the last, and that it had to be done within the boundaries of written rules and an unwritten code, and that the long stretches of time between the fights were a blend of private worry and tedious training, hidden behind a veneer of invincibility and the persistence of public graciousness— well, there might be nothing like that in sports.

"You think of getting in an argument with a driver on the road, or you have a confrontation with somebody, and you're all riled up and you think about the confrontation for the next two days," Clark said three years after he met Derek. "It eats at you. 'I shoulda, I coulda, if he would have just stepped forward I woulda . . . ,' and you boil it over in your head. And you've got to think these guys got to do that. And they've got to get themselves to the point where it's man on man, full out, and then they've got to shut that off and come and talk to the press and be part of the team and take pictures with kids and handshake and go home to a girlfriend, wife, kids, whatever the case is. And then, the next night, bring that emotion back up and be the toughest guy in the league and the one that wants to eat somebody alive. And then repeat 80 games a season."

There's a toll, Clark thought. There has to be. He never could quite pull it out of Derek. But he knew it was there.

Aaron had come to spend the summers in Minneapolis with Derek, sharing an apartment between his seasons as a minor-league hockey player, trying to reach the NHL. Clark took to calling Aaron "Nick," like his family members did. They fell into the lazy rhythm of summer. Summer, not hockey season, was Derek's favorite time of year.

For a Brooks and Dunn country music concert at Xcel Energy Center, the three men spent a day shopping for matching shirts, hats, Wrangler jeans, and belt buckles. They arrived looking a bit like backup singers at a Western chuck-wagon show, with a hint of Steve Martin, Chevy Chase, and Martin Short in *Three Amigos*.

Derek and Aaron became fixtures at Clark's house, and good friends with Clark's wife, Jennie. Derek sat on the back deck, chatting away as Clark worked in the yard. He was, in many ways, like the neighbor kid who just hung around, looking for company. When Clark had training assignments for a team in Russia for a couple of weeks in the summer, Derek went with him. He was always up for an adventure.

More than anyplace, though, Clark's gym became Derek's second home. Derek's pictures soon adorned the walls. Clark eventually converted a loft space into a small apartment for Derek, with a refrigerator and a shower, a couch, and a bed, a place where Derek could nap during the day or sleep overnight.

In the warehouse-like room with the boxing ring, giant dock doors rolled up to allow daylight and fresh air to enter. Between training sessions, the men sat on folding chairs, chewing sunflower seeds and talking, sometimes through the afternoon and into the dusk.

They climbed to the roof, using a ladder on a chair to pull themselves onto the fire escape. The view stretched over the trees and marshes of the Minnesota Valley National Wildlife Refuge, south of the Minneapolis-Saint Paul International Airport. The downtown skylines of the Twin Cities gleamed in the distance. Clark and Derek turned on music, usually country music, and talked until deep into the night, often about growing up.

"If Boogey could have come off the ice and hit a switch, and become 5-10 and 185 pounds and a normal guy, he would have," Clark said. "In a heartbeat. In a heartbeat."

DEREK'S THIGHS. Pat O'Brien had never seen anything like them. When Derek sat down in a chair, his thighs arced upward, as if he were smuggling a ham in each pant leg.

O'Brien, a Minneapolis chiropractor, had worked on hundreds of athletes, many of them NHL players. In some ways, Derek had a prototypical build, with thick legs and a broad backside. But he also had abnormally huge hands. His arms were not rounded with bulging muscles, like those of a compact bodybuilder. They were long, like massive pistons. If he ever punched me, he'd kill me, O'Brien thought.

Derek, persistently bothered by a back that might need surgery, first came to O'Brien at the recommendation of Gaborik. For a couple of years, O'Brien saw Derek at his office several times a week, using his hands-on, non-surgical remedies to keep his body in working order—massage, acupuncture, whatever made Derek feel better. He worked on his jaw, his neck, his shoulders, back, and wrists. He saw the hands, scarred by cuts and teeth marks.

The two became friends. Derek called from the grocery store, reading a label and wondering if it was something he could eat. He worried about what he put into his body.

Derek became an avid cyclist during the summers, strengthening those thighs with long rides along the bluffs of the Mississippi River with O'Brien, Aaron, and several others. Derek's size made him look a bit like a clown atop a tiny bike. He would fall behind the group as it climbed hills, then fearlessly whiz past on the way back down, pulled by gravity and his own weight. O'Brien and others marveled at how his thin-wheeled bike held him up. One morning, after a long ride, they found that it barely did. The rims on the wheels of Derek's new bike were bent out of round.

Another excursion had just begun, up an incline, with Derek at the rear. The peloton came to a stop when the riders heard a crash behind them. Derek stood about 50 feet back, holding the frame of his bike in one hand and the crank in the other. His strong legs had snapped the pedal assembly off. The bike-shop owner had never seen it happen before.

"I don't know about this biking thing," Derek said through his crooked grin.

Something about Derek told you not to worry for him. He'd take care of you, not the other way around. He was the guy you went to when you needed help. To O'Brien, Derek had that persona, the kind that deflected attention: I'm fine; let's talk about *you*.

O'Brien's third son was born with Down syndrome, a shock discovered in the delivery room. Derek arrived at his next appointment and asked how everything went. O'Brien could barely speak.

"It's going to be okay," Derek said, his smile a burst of reinforcement. "It's going to be fine." O'Brien never forgot.

What amazed O'Brien most about Derek was not his body, but his personality. He brought a powerful calm to situations—an ability to soothe people and assure them that everything would be okay in the end.

O'Brien knew some of the owners of the Twins, and they invited him to bring Derek to a game on a Monday night. Just as O'Brien arrived at Derek's apartment, his wife called in a state of panic. Their three-year-old had fallen in the driveway and knocked his two front teeth out.

O'Brien explained to Derek what happened. He had to rush back home.

"Bring him over here," Derek said calmly.

He pushed a few buttons on his cell phone and spoke to a team dentist for the Wild.

"He'll see you," Derek told O'Brien.

O'Brien's wife arrived with the boy in the back seat, his face covered in blood, his teeth gone. Derek stuck his head in to talk to him.

"Hey, buddy, how you doing?" he said to the boy. "I heard you knocked your teeth out."

The boy nodded and stopped crying.

"I've lost so many teeth in hockey from getting punched," Derek said. "I just lost a tooth today eating a sandwich, and went to the dentist and he put it back in. You're going to be fine. I'm going to send you to this dentist who works on me, who puts my teeth back in."

BUT SOMETHING WAS changing with Derek, and the Wild coaches noticed. To those on the outside, Derek was still a good quote, a jovial presence at his corner stall in the dressing room, a team leader by virtue of his tenure and standing among those at his position. Increasingly, he supported the fledgling charity work of Defending the Blue Line, a Minnesota-based organization aimed at getting the children of military members involved in hockey. "Boogaard's Boogaardians" raised money to send children to hockey camps.

Defending the Blue Line's founder, Shane Hudella, a first sergeant with the Minnesota Army National Guard, found Derek to be unlike most stars he met—a guy who just as easily could have been a best friend working at the factory. Derek, beyond autograph sessions and meet-and-greets with the military, sometimes spent days with the National Guard, donning fatigues and shooting weapons. He told Hudella that someday, after he retired and took care of his family financially, he might join the military.

Derek's reputation as the everyman, underdog overachiever was intact. But things were different at the rink. Teammates and coaches saw a darker Derek emerge. Sometimes it took someone who had not seen Derek regularly to notice it.

Matt Shaw had been the assistant coach in Houston when Derek played two years there in the minor leagues. He watched Derek run the hills outside the rink, spend an extra 30 minutes on the ice after practice, and always come back asking for more. Shaw watched Derek's first two seasons with the Wild from a distance, proud that he and Aeros head coach Todd McLellan had helped mold Derek into something they initially did not think he could become: an NHL player.

Shaw was promoted in 2007 to become an assistant for the Wild. He was surprised to learn that Derek had grown into a source of frustration for other Wild coaches.

Derek was frustrated, too. Fewer of the league's other enforcers wanted to engage Derek, so his number of fights declined. He thought he could be trusted to play an expanding role. But his average time on the ice fell from 5:23 in his rookie season to 3:56 in in his third year. He thought he had shown enough to deserve more respect.

Shaw saw that Derek was sulking.

"What's up?" Shaw asked Derek one day. "What's up with you? Where's the Derek that I know?"

Derek would not look Shaw in the eye. Guilt? Shame? Shaw could not tell. He just knew that the player he once trusted to work harder than anyone else on the team was not there anymore. Derek was no longer the first one on the ice and the last to leave. He was still relaxed away from the rink, still threw playful barbs from his corner of the dressing room. But something was gone. It was hard to pinpoint it. Derek was just . . . distant. He would sleep for 12 hours in hotels on the road. He fell asleep in the middle of card games on the airplane. Teammates looked at one another, smiled, and shook their heads.

The dressing room was an insular place, a clubhouse for players. Coaches tended to pass without stopping and team executives rarely entered. Their primary link to players—their moods, their attitudes, their concerns—resided in a web of people like team trainers and equipment managers, unsung grunts in the background of every organization that kept the day-to-day operations moving.

That is how coaches or executives would learn that one player arrived in the mornings smelling of alcohol, or another was having trouble at home, or another was not working hard to rehabilitate an injury, or another was poisoning the positive attitude inside the dressing room.

Wild management had not heard bad things about Derek. But something had started percolating in the back of Tom Lynn's mind. The assistant general manager, a former Yale hockey player, and part of the Wild's original staff, Lynn began to note an unspoken trend around the league. While evidence was anecdotal, enforcers were more likely to have personal problems, he thought. Lynn saw it mostly from afar, through roster moves and whispers, but the tallies of names could not be ignored. Something about that role, it seemed, made players more susceptible to problems like addiction to alcohol and drugs.

Maybe it was the role itself—the pressure of the job, the eternal spot at the bottom of the roster, the pain hidden behind a facade of fearlessness. Or maybe the role attracted a certain devil-may-care personality, young men from rough backgrounds who were more susceptible to personal problems whether they fought or not.

Lynn had not connected it to Derek, who seemed to be different than other enforcers in so many ways—quiet, a kid with an admirable work ethic and from a good family. But then Lynn started hearing things from the dressing room. Derek was taking Ambien, and not just the usual amounts. Most players used it as a short-term solution to sleeping problems caused by rugged travel schedules or discomforting injuries, but Derek was constantly asking for it.

THE WILD WAS desperate to keep Derek on the ice, but injuries made it increasingly difficult. In December 2008, before a game in Calgary, doctors administered an injection of Toradol into Derek's sore right shoulder.

Toradol, the brand name for ketorolac, was a non-steroidal anti-inflammatory used to treat acute pain over no more than a few days. It is what athletes of all kinds sometimes received as a last resort to mask severe pain in places and joints like the knee, ankle, elbow, and shoulder.

Such an injection came with heroic undertones. For decades, athletes gamely took last-minute, painful shots to get them on the field, the court, or the ice, and myths had been built around such acts of brave desperation. Basketball player Willis Reed of the New York Knicks cemented his legacy by making a surprise start in Game 7 of the 1970 National Basketball Association Finals, a selfless return credited to his ability to withstand a huge needle filled with painkillers.

But Toradol, a blood thinner, could increase the risk of life-threatening heart conditions or circulation problems, and it could cause serious stomach and intestinal bleeding. One warning was to never use Toradol if the patient suffered from any sort of closed-head injury or bleeding on the brain—something such as a concussion. In 2011, a group of former National Football League players sued the league for its widespread use of Toradol, saying that its dangers had never been fully explained to players and arguing that the masking of pain—including symptoms of a concussion—was dangerous. By 2013, most teams in Major League Baseball had stopped using it. Several European countries had banned its use entirely.

For Derek, the shot on December 29, 2008, was the first of at least 13 such game-day Toradol injections over two seasons, records showed, several from doctors of other teams while the Wild was on the road. Many of the injections to his shoulder came on nights when Derek expected to fight.

He took the first shot before the game in Calgary, after missing Minnesota's previous game, because he had had a fight with the Flames the last time. The second Toradol injection came two nights later, when the Wild hosted the San Jose Sharks on New Year's Eve. Derek and Jody Shelley had fought four times before, and it was early in the second period that they ran into each other again. After a big check by Shelley—a man from Manitoba who was six years older than Derek and measured a beefy six feet, three inches and 230 pounds—he chased Derek from behind, soon getting Derek's attention. The gloves were off. The fans were up. Derek pounded Shelley quickly. His right fist shattered Shelley's helmet, and a piece of it flew through the air clearly enough for television cameras to capture and replay.

Four days later, at practice, Derek was "blind-sided by a teammate along the boards and hit the right side of his head against the glass," a team medical report read. "Derek felt momentarily dazed," had "some fogginess to the right field of vision." The symptoms persisted. Derek missed five games with an apparent concussion. Publicly, the team reported that Derek was out with an "upper body" injury.

Derek's season ended early, 10 games short of the scheduled 82-game conclusion. Derek finished with three assists in 51 games. He had nine fights, only two more than teammate Craig Weller. Rookie

Cal Clutterbuck stepped in for several fights, too, and the Wild signed six-foot, eight-inch defenseman John Scott during the season to help fill the void created by Derek's injuries. Derek's importance to the team was slipping.

The Wild finished two points out of the eighth and final playoff spot in the Western Conference. After the last game, coach Jacques Lemaire resigned. Within days, Doug Risebrough was fired as general manager. The two men most responsible for building Derek's NHL success were gone.

DEREK AND ERIN were engaged, but it felt more like the end than a beginning.

When they first met, it did not take Erin long to see past the brutality and folklore of Derek's public persona. She met him at a club, and soon watched him crush the face of Todd Fedoruk. Boogey was a folk hero, the opposite of Derek. Derek was shy and patient, rarely angry. He was a go-with-the-flow type, aiming to please. He worried about everyone else's comfort and happiness. He wanted to be liked.

And he was deeply in love with Erin.

He bought her expensive gifts. He gave her a car and helped pay for her courses at a Minneapolis art institute. He was protective of Erin, proud to call her his girlfriend, still surprised that someone so beautiful would want to be with him. He liked that other men left her alone, knowing that she was the girlfriend of the Boogeyman. He liked to have someone who depended on him.

She loved that it made him so happy to see others so happy.

"He was like a puppy dog," Erin said. "You didn't have to say anything. You just had to be there. You had to be next to him. Sometimes he preferred that you didn't say anything. He was a very quiet person. He just wanted somebody to be with him."

She worried about him getting hurt, but Derek seemed to injure others more than he got hurt himself. Erin did not follow the NHL closely, and Derek would not tell her when the Wild played a team with an enforcer that he expected to fight. He did not want her to worry.

Their relationship took a course much like Derek's four-year relationship with Janella. Derek and Erin spent quiet hours wandering shopping malls and eating at restaurants. They dreamed about places to live and went to open houses. They, too, shopped for a dog—and bought one, only to find that their high-end apartment building would not allow it.

And as with Janella, Derek's relationship with Erin unraveled over bouts about money, fears of distrust, and the fact that Derek, especially, seemed to become something different than what he was.

Erin recognized the toll on Derek's body, especially his lower back. Derek declined suggestions for surgery, partly because his father had had back surgery, and it had only seemed to make things worse. Len was eventually relegated to desk work, unable to continue as a beat cop in Regina, and ultimately transferred to the RCMP's headquarters in Ottawa.

But Erin, over a couple of years, began worrying less about Derek's physical injuries and more about his mind. Derek began to repeat himself. He would tell a story, and soon tell it over again. His sentences occasionally came out muddled. His memory slipped. Erin noticed. Concussions, she thought, collecting those episodes in the back of her mind.

Derek dismissed it all with a laugh.

"Yeah, I got hit in the head too many times," he joked.

Their worlds never seemed to completely blend. Erin did not know the Boogaard family well, and the family was persistently and, in Derek's view, unfairly skeptical about Erin. The Boogaards had never been sure about Janella, either, wondering if she was good for

Derek's hockey career. But they had respected that Janella's relationship with Derek began when he was a poor, unknown teenager. Erin arrived just as his career bloomed with fame and wealth.

Despite the completion of Derek's customized condominium in Regina, intended for use in the summers, Derek spent less time there every off-season. Erin was not a fan of Regina and had little interest in being there. That did not endear her to Derek's family.

But Derek was there enough to create some memorable times, like when Aaron shot a rubber-tipped dart that struck Derek in the neck, leading Derek to shove Aaron through the drywall. There was a time that one of Derek's high school friends from Regina came to a party and pulled out cocaine, and Derek kicked him out because he did not want drugs in his home.

Summers were a time when Derek reconnected with family. He would box and train during the days, and occasionally play recreational hockey at a Regina rink. He would call his father and ask him to watch—watch the toughest guy in hockey, a well-known player in the NHL, play a couple of hours of rec-league pickup games without any fighting. Len did.

But the pull toward Minneapolis was an ever-stronger one. Derek, now in his mid-20s, had less contact with his mother and father and his siblings. Ryan was a young RCMP member, assigned to far-flung posts in Saskatchewan the way his father had been a generation before. Aaron was a professional hockey player, playing in Pennsylvania in the American Hockey League. Krysten, at six feet, five inches, was a starting center for the University of Kansas women's basketball team.

Derek had grown closer to Curtis, the half-brother he did not know he had until he was 18. Curtis was 10 years older, worked as an operations manager for an oil-and-gas company, and lived in Lloydminster, Alberta, on the border with Saskatchewan. He came to Derek's games when the Wild played in Edmonton and Calgary. Curtis and his wife were raising three children, and when the youngest was born, Derek rushed there and held the boy in his arms.

But family was far away, and age had a way of widening the distance. The rest of the Boogaards increasingly worried about the strangers who, like meteors, drifted in and out of Derek's orbit in Minnesota. Derek would call and mention another name that his parents had not heard before, and they worried about that person's motivations and influence.

They knew Derek was in love with Erin. But they noted how she talked about Derek—she focused on what he bought, what they did together, where they planned to travel. Sensitive to how others treated Derek and what they expected from him, they worried that Erin did not love Derek for who he was, but for what he did for her.

The family's concerns about Erin only drew Derek closer to her. After Derek and Erin had been dating for about two years, Derek made a call to Mike Tobin, his former billet father in Prince George, asking about wedding rings. Tobin, owner of a jewelry store, was surprised at the size and extravagance Derek considered—custom designs, two-karat diamonds. He remembered Derek as the jeans-and-T-shirt teenager who never had more than few dollars in his pocket.

Derek and Erin went to a Minnesota jewelry store and designed a ring. It cost about $55,000, according to the Boogaard family. Derek and Erin were informally engaged for months, until the ring was ready in the spring. When it arrived, Erin took pictures of it on her finger from several different angles and e-mailed them to friends and family. "We're engaged!" she wrote.

By then, Erin admitted later, she had reservations about getting married at all.

. . .

BETWEEN THE END-OF-SEASON departures of Lemaire and Rise-brough, Derek had nose surgery to repair the airways that had been crushed from blows to the face. He was prescribed 40 pills of oxyco-done by the oral surgeon.

A week later, on April 21, Derek had surgery to repair the labrum of his right shoulder. It was the day of a farewell press conference for Risebrough, held at a sports bar called Tom Reid's Hockey City Pub, two blocks from Xcel Energy Center in Saint Paul.

"In a touching scene," the *StarTribune* reported, "Derek Boogaard, in pain after being discharged from shoulder surgery Tuesday, was driven to Tom Reid's by his fiancée, Erin Russell, because he wanted to thank Risebrough."

Derek arrived just as the press conference ended. With his right arm hanging from the passenger window, he asked someone to tell Risebrough that he was outside. Risebrough came out. Derek thanked him.

"You have no idea how much I owe him and Jacques for playing in the NHL," Derek told reporters.

That same day, records showed, Derek picked up a prescription at Walgreens for 40 oxycodone pills, prescribed by the Wild's team orthopedist. Three days later, team doctor Dan Peterson prescribed 30 more. Three days after that, the orthopedist prescribed another 40. Over 16 days, Derek was prescribed 150 oxycodone pills and 40 hydrocodone pills—both considered Schedule II controlled substances under the Controlled Substances Act, "with high potential for abuse." Generally, the recommended doses for the types of pills that Derek received were one pill every four to six hours, as needed for pain. But because the records obtained later by Len Boogaard do not detail the recommended number of pills to take at a time, or how often they were to be taken, it is unclear if Derek did anything other than follow the doctors' advice.

In total that season, Derek's fourth in the NHL, he received at least 25 prescriptions for oxycodone and hydrocodone, a total of 622 pills, from 10 doctors—eight team doctors of the Wild, an oral surgeon in Minneapolis, and a doctor for an opposing team. It is unknown how many other pills he might have received directly from the doctors, or in transactions unnoted in pharmacy records and medical records later obtained by the family. But Derek quickly discovered that team doctors did not communicate with one another when it came to prescriptions. There was no tracking system in place to tell one doctor what another had previously prescribed. He could get pills from a doctor one day, and more from another the next. He also learned that team doctors might dole out drugs without an office visit. Derek had their cell-phone numbers and could call or text them and ask for a refill. He could then pick up the prescription at his nearest pharmacy.

By the time Derek had the nose and shoulder surgeries a week apart in April 2009, he realized that he preferred oxycodone to hydrocodone—OxyContin and Percocet (a combination of oxycodone and acetaminophen) to Vicodin (hydrocodone and acetaminophen). He told doctors that Vicodin made him feel strange. They began to prescribe him the others instead.

His building tolerance for the pills fed his appetite. Aaron had a similar surgery on his shoulder at the same time as Derek that spring. Doctors said it took twice as much anesthesia to knock out Derek than it did Aaron. Like Derek, Aaron was prescribed oxycodone to combat the pain. But while Aaron took three or four pills at a time, Derek gobbled eight or 10.

Team doctors continued to prescribe Ambien for Derek all through the summer of 2009—210 pills between late April and early September, records showed. But prescriptions for painkillers appeared to stop during the off-season.

By then, Derek had found other sources.

· · ·

AARON BOOGAARD RETURNED from his season with the Wilkes-Barre/Scranton Penguins of the American Hockey League. His ambitions of being an all-around player had faded. After scoring two goals and fighting 16 times, his goal of reaching the NHL rested largely in his fists.

Aaron ended the season with shoulder surgery, just like Derek. He moved into the apartment that Derek and Erin shared in Lilydale, across the river from downtown Saint Paul.

Between hockey seasons in which they rarely saw one another, the two brothers were virtually inseparable. They went to Jeremy Clark's gym. They rode bikes. They played video games for hours. They went to bars at night. Almost every errand, from filling the car with gas to buying groceries, was done together, because Derek hated to be alone.

On occasion, Derek stopped the car at a check-cashing store. Aaron never quite understood what was happening. He just knew that Derek sent money to someone in New York.

Aaron, four years younger, revered Derek. He wanted to follow him to the NHL. But four years was a strange distance in age. In the summer of 2009, Derek turned 27 and Aaron turned 23. Aaron was old enough to recognize what was best for Derek, but too young and obedient to tell the mightily successful Derek what to do.

Aaron was a hockey enforcer, too, and he understood the pain and quiet desperation. But he never quite understood why Derek always had so many pills. Maybe it was just different in the NHL.

Aaron once saw a package arrive for Derek that looked like a book, only its pages were carved out and filled with pills. Aaron came to learn that Derek also got pills from at least a couple of sources in the Twin Cities, including a young woman near Saint Paul and people he met at Sneaky Pete's. When Aaron asked, Derek offered the same reply.

"Don't worry about it," he would say.

It was Erin, more than Aaron, who found Derek uncharacteristically mysterious and undependable that summer. On sunny days, he would keep the blinds closed and black out the room and play video games or sleep. He spent less time at the gym than ever. Surgery was a good excuse for his lethargy, but Derek seemed sapped of his drive. A zombie, she thought sometimes.

The two drifted apart, and their lives, even within the apartment, crossed with fading regularity. Erin left for a family wedding, and heard stories about Derek's nights at Minneapolis bars while she was gone. She canvassed social media and found photos of Derek out at night, often smiling amid pretty women.

During a time together, Erin, Derek, and Aaron visited the jewelry store where Derek had purchased the engagement ring. Erin wanted something looked at, so Derek and Aaron made amicable small talk with the owner in the back room while Erin's ring was fixed. After 30 minutes or so, they came back out to the showroom. Erin had found a ring she liked better. She wanted to trade in the one Derek had helped choose for her and bought her. Aaron was furious.

"I don't think she's in it for the right reasons," Aaron told Derek later. "I don't think she's right for you. I think she's more into the money than she is into you."

"Yeah, I know," Aaron recalled Derek responding. "I've noticed that, too. It's just hard to admit."

Erin was having second feelings about the whole relationship. Derek was changing, and she did not like who he was becoming. He slept during the day and went to bars at night. He showed a grumpy side she had not seen. His moods swung wildly. His memory seemed frayed.

She began to question him about the pills, the Ambien that was being constantly prescribed in the off-season by Wild doctors, the pain pills that Derek always had by the handful, and he waved her off, the way he waved off Aaron when he dared to pry.

"He joked about it a lot," Erin recalled in an interview two years later. "But I worried even when he joked about it, especially when he started to take more and more of them. And he would say he was in pain—'It's OK.' The biggest thing that made me worry was that he was in denial about it. He wasn't saying, 'I know I shouldn't be doing this, I know it's a problem, but I'm in pain.' He wasn't even being honest with himself about it. I was angry more than anything. There was nothing you could do. You can't do anything with somebody who can't even admit it's a problem. More than anything, it was just really frustrating. I felt like there was no outlet for my frustration because of who he was. There were so many favors. They give him so much more slack than the average Joe."

He was the toughest man in the NHL. Who was she to question that? The relationship deteriorated, though Derek was slow to recognize it. Erin wondered about the long-range future: What will it be like when he is not playing hockey? What's going to happen when he finally admits to a problem and no longer has the resources available to him? Marriage? Children? Where will this all end up? She had met Derek when everything was going perfectly—a future bursting with possibility. She shuddered at the thought of where it was all headed.

DEREK'S LIFE UNSPOOLED quickly in small episodes. In August, during a phone conversation with Ryan, Derek slurred words and spoke incoherently. Was it alcohol? Drugs? Concussions? Ryan called his parents. His mother and father had had similar experiences, too.

Near the end of August, Derek, still volunteering for public appearances to help the Wild, unveiled the team's new third jersey at the Minnesota State Fair. He was unshaven and wore sunglasses.

Even in pictures and videos from the event, Derek's friends and family could tell he was not right. Was he drunk?

September came. Aaron left for the start of his hockey season, back to Pennsylvania with the Wilkes-Barre/Scranton Penguins. Derek called his agent, Ron Salcer.

"Ronnie, my shoulder's still not right," Derek said. "Think I should go see Chuck and tell him I need another month?"

Chuck was Chuck Fletcher, the Wild's new general manager, who had taken the place of Doug Risebrough. Salcer was aghast.

"You kidding me, Derek?" Salcer replied. "What have you been doing? You've got to be doing whatever it takes to get yourself ready for training camp in two weeks. Call them and tell them that you need another month? That doesn't sound like someone with an NHL mindset."

Derek showed up to training camp overweight and out of shape. On September 20, the day of a home preseason game against the Chicago Blackhawks, he was found asleep in the driver's seat of his Denali along the side of a road. A police officer stopped behind the car and recognized Derek. He brought him home to Erin. The Wild reported Derek as a healthy scratch for that night's game.

Derek had no recollection of any of it. Erin could not figure out what was wrong with him. There were times when she found pills loose in his jacket pockets. Derek told her they were anti-inflammatories, but when she looked them up online, she found they were prescription painkillers. It was late one night when she watched him bump into walls and stumble over things, like a drunken sleepwalker. Derek spoke, but his words made no sense. Through the haze he said something about taking four Ambien—Wild team doctors prescribed him 90 of them between September 1 and September 16—but Erin knew it was something more than that. She was scared. She called Joanne Boogaard in Regina.

Tobin Wright, Derek's friend and manager, hurried to the apartment. He had been suspicious of Derek's drug use for months, but Derek adamantly denied that anything was wrong, and Wright said that he could never catch Derek buying drugs or taking them. But there were times when they were together, like in a restaurant or in a car, when Derek's phone rang, and he would speak in some strange, suspicious code to someone on the other end. All the small episodes were beginning to make sense.

Wright cried as he sat in front of Derek. He was scared to confront him.

"I'm putting you in the substance abuse program," Wright said, recalling the conversation with Derek. "Enough is enough. If you don't do it, you're going to be suspended, probably without pay, and it's going to be public knowledge. Everybody's going to know about it."

Calls bounced between Erin and Joanne and Len and Salcer. Dots were connected, and the message was clear: Derek was addicted to something. There was talk of OxyContin and Percocet and Ambien, drugs that sounded familiar but that no one knew much about.

Ryan Boogaard was with his mother in Regina while he attended a training session at the RCMP Depot. A few miles away, at the Agridome, now renamed the Brandt Centre, an NHL preseason game between the Tampa Bay Lightning and Ottawa Senators was underway.

Wait a minute, Ryan thought. He had read a newspaper story about the return of Todd Fedoruk, the former Regina Pat, now with the Tampa Bay Lightning. Ryan rushed to the arena and arrived just as the game ended. He managed to work his way to the tunnel where players walked between the ice and the dressing rooms, and he shouted at Fedoruk, whom he had never met.

"Todd!" Ryan shouted. "I need to talk to you! I'm Derek Boogaard's brother! I need to talk to you!"

Fedoruk said he would change clothes and come back out. He did. Ryan explained the situation, and Fedoruk was not surprised. He had seen the arc of Derek's troubles bending more than a year earlier. But he had his own problems. By the end of the season, Fedoruk would be drunk at a game that proved to be his last in the NHL.

"He has to admit he has a problem," Fedoruk told Ryan. "He has to want to get help."

Ryan booked a flight for the next day to Minneapolis. He had no passport with him, so his girlfriend drove several hours to meet him with it at the airport in Saskatoon. While he waited for his flight, Ryan received a call from someone in the NHL's substance abuse program. Derek was scheduled to go to a clinic in California, Ryan was told. And you can go with him.

THE NHL'S SUBSTANCE ABUSE and Behavioral Health Program began in 1996, co-founded by Dr. David Lewis, a psychiatrist based in Los Angeles, and Dr. Brian Shaw, a clinical psychologist in Toronto. The men created and oversaw a similar program for Major League Soccer. Salcer had sent players their way before.

"I need to get Derek out here," Salcer told them.

In Minnesota, Ryan sat on the end of Derek's bed. Derek was curled under the sheets. It takes a big man to admit he has a problem, Ryan told his brother. The family will support you. Get the best possible treatment, get better, and put this behind you.

Derek was embarrassed. He was afraid that people would find out. He was afraid that the Wild would replace him. He was adamant that he had no problem, but if the league insisted that he do something, Derek wanted to stay home and go through detoxification in Minneapolis, and keep Ryan around for support. He would be fine, he said. He just needed a little bit of time.

But plans were set. A day later, Ryan and Derek were on a plane to Los Angeles. Derek called Risebrough, the deposed general manager, to apologize for letting him down.

Salcer met Derek and Ryan at the airport. They stopped for lunch, where Salcer told Derek that other clients of his had had the same issues, but they had gotten help and made it through.

"You've got a pot of gold here," Salcer told Derek. "Don't piss in it. You are one of the most unique guys in the world. How many guys are six foot eight, 270 pounds, and can skate like you and play hockey? People are supporting you. You know how expensive this place is? It's, like, $50,000 a month. But they're paying it for you. They're paying for you to get better. Don't piss in your pot of gold here."

"Yeah, yeah," Derek said.

Salcer, like an exasperated father, hoped the message sunk in. He could never quite tell with Derek.

They drove less than an hour to the Canyon rehabilitation center, set in the serene hills above Malibu. Lewis was on the staff there, listed as a consulting psychiatrist. Derek and Ryan were given a tour of the facilities, its grounds pristine as a country club, its atmosphere as relaxed as a spa. Ryan sat in on an introductory meeting.

Derek was admitted. Ryan left the next day.

In notes from the Canyon later obtained by Len Boogaard, Derek provided his "substance abuse history" upon admission. He said he had been taking eight or nine tablets of OxyContin and three tablets of Ambien daily. He admitted to recent use of Vicodin and Percocet, up to 10 pills per day. He said he regularly used Vicodin and Ambien throughout the previous season, to combat a sore back and sleeping problems, and sometimes chewed them.

The Minnesota Wild announced that Boogaard was out with a concussion. It was the only time that he was publicly diagnosed with one. It just happened not to be the reason for his absence.

"We don't know the extent of it," first-year Wild coach Todd Richards told reporters, when asked how much time Derek would miss. "It could be a week, two weeks. It could be a month, two months. We don't know."

He said he did not know how the concussion occurred.

Players figured out the truth. The Wild never told Derek's teammates, and Derek never told them, either. But they knew. One day, Derek was there. The next, he was gone. It was not hard to understand why.

8

DEREK HAD NO TIME for this. The regular season was starting. He had teammates to protect. He had a job to do. And when he heard that John Scott, the young six-foot, eight-inch defenseman, had been elevated to the primary enforcing position in his absence, Derek got especially anxious.

Scott crushed Chicago's Danny Bois in a preseason fight, then Columbus's Jared Boll in another. In the second game of the regular season, against the hated Anaheim Ducks, Scott battered George Parros.

Derek looked suddenly expendable. He worried about what people were saying about him. And he felt stranded and forgotten in Malibu, sentenced to the five-star accommodations of the Canyon and its celebrity clientele. He told people, both friends and counselors, that he had no reason to be there. He had nothing in common with the other patients, people with real drug problems to sort out and, apparently, with plenty of time to burn. The sessions were a joke, he thought. Admit to an addiction? Come on. There are more important things to do, especially right now.

Derek felt like a child on a time-out, quarantined while the world moved on without him. Time slipped away. But it was not just the unease over his role on the team that bothered him. He worried about his broken relationship with Erin.

Ron Salcer came to visit. Tobin Wright came from Minnesota. They, along with others, told Derek he needed to focus on getting himself together and not worry about Erin. They told him that she had canceled plans to come see him in California.

"Everybody in his life was telling him, 'This girl isn't good for you,'" Wright later recalled.

Derek had real-life problems to fix and jobs to do. He couldn't do anything as long as he was stuck in Malibu. Every day he asked when he could leave.

It wasn't long. Derek spent three restless weeks in rehabilitation. He was dismissed, conveniently, just after Scott's winning fight in Anaheim with the Wild during a five-game road trip to the West Coast. Derek attended the next game, against the Kings in Los Angeles, before he began to skate with the Wild, eager to reassert himself as the top enforcer—not just in the league, but on his own team.

He played his first game of the season about a week later, at Edmonton on October 16, 2009. News reports said, without further explanation, that Derek had returned from a preseason concussion.

There were no fights in Derek's first two games. He would have to wait until the Wild, loser of six of its first seven games of the season, played at home on October 21. Early in the second period, away from the puck, Colorado's David Koci needled Derek with his stick. Derek agreed to a fight. He casually flipped aside his gloves and positioned himself at center ice. He stood upright and steady, his fists raised stoically. Koci, a six-foot, six-inch Czech, crouched and circled around him. Fans stood.

Derek jabbed Koci in the chest, then grabbed his jersey near the collar. Koci jabbed at Derek's chin, but Derek seized the opening with a hard overhand right fist to the left side of Koci's face. He hit him again in the same spot, dropping Koci to his knees momentarily.

Derek, still clinging to the jersey, helped lift Koci back up. Koci scrambled to get away, turning his face as far from Derek as possible. They held each other by an arm and swung, trading simultaneous left-hand punches before Derek hit Koci again with his closed right hand. Koci fell to his knees, got up with Derek's help, and stepped into another right fist. He tried to flee Derek's grasp. Derek, without a hint of malice or any trace of an expression, stopped and let the officials step between the two.

"Derek Boogaard needs to do this, and he needed to do it soon," the television announcer said over the replay of the fight. "Just to continue to keep that belt, if you will."

It was his first fight since January. There was no mention of rehabilitation, and no word of the impending breakup with his fiancée. Derek simply beat up another man. Fans cheered. Teammates banged their sticks against the half boards. The fight was replayed in slow motion. Derek was in the penalty box.

By all appearances, everything was in perfect order.

WHEN HE WAS discharged from the Canyon in early October, Derek signed an "aftercare plan" with the NHL/NHLPA Substance Abuse and Behavioral Health Program. The form had the logos of the NHL and NHL Players' Association at the top. It listed 10 requirements.

1. I will remain abstinent from all medications, drugs and alcohol unless specifically approved by Program Doctors or prescribed by Minnesota Wild Team Physicians.

2. I will not attend adult entertainment centers, strip clubs, men's clubs, or massage parlors.

3. I will not gamble, attend or enter gambling establishments.

4. I will attend a minimum of three 12 Step meetings per week. The Program Doctors will approve the meeting schedule. I will document my attendance at all 12 Step meetings.

5. I will submit to random urine testing. Schedule of testing will be determined by the Program Doctors. If I miss a test, I understand it will be deemed a positive test.

6. I will choose a Home Group from my 12 Step meeting schedule. I will be active in this Home Group.

7. I will keep in regular contact with the Program Doctors and Dan Cronin and will return all phone calls on a timely basis.

8. Any and ALL changes in this schedule must be approved IN ADVANCE by the Program Doctors.

9. This contract shall be in effect until altered by Program Doctors.

10. I understand and agree that failure to meet the conditions of this Aftercare Plan may result in a permanent suspension at the sole discretion of the Program Doctors.

The two-page contract was signed and dated by Derek, program counselor Dan Cronin, and the program's founders and co-directors, Dr. Dave Lewis and Dr. Brian Shaw.

Derek was considered in "Stage 1" of the program's four defined stages of substance abuse. Under Stage 1, players continued to receive their full salaries, provided they met the obligations of the program. A player was moved to Stage 2 if he violated the aftercare program. A Stage 2 player would be suspended, without pay, during active treatment of substance abuse and not be reinstated until approved by Lewis and Shaw. A player who violated the plan while in Stage 2 would be moved to Stage 3, with a mandatory six-month suspension.

The program, jointly overseen by the league and the players' association, had been cloaked in secrecy since its inception in 1996. Confidentiality, the doctors argued, was critical to counseling, because players would not come forward if they thought there was a chance that their struggles could become public—or, even, known around the league to executives, coaches and other players.

There was an oversight committee, also responsible for management of the league's performance-enhancing-drug program. The committee was made up of one executive from the NHL, one from the NHLPA, and one expert chosen by each of those entities. One chosen expert was Lewis. The other was Shaw.

Privacy was such an overriding concern that Bill Daly, the NHL's deputy commissioner and the league's lone representative on the oversight committee, said in 2011 that even he was not told which players were in the drug-rehabilitation program. That would change, presumably, if there were cause for suspension. Such a step was rare; through the years, only a handful of substance abuse cases became known to the general public, and usually only after the fact, when word leaked or the player felt the need to explain his long absence.

Shaw and Lewis directed team medical staffs on how to treat players in the program. During the 2009–10 season, following Derek's return from rehabilitation, Wild team doctors prescribed Derek no oxycodone or hydrocodone. There was just one prescription for Ambien, on December 10, the day before Derek fought Calgary's Brian McGrattan.

There were dozens of prescriptions for other drugs, however—anti-inflammatories (many to treat a torn labrum in January), more moderate painkillers like tramadol, and a lot of trazodone, meant to fight depression and anxiety. Derek never went more than two weeks—and rarely more than a few days—between prescriptions from Wild team doctors.

He sometimes missed drug tests, and scheduled most of them directly with the sample collector, phone records show, usually through text messages. He had at least one positive result, and bank records reveal that he frequented bars and strip clubs. Any one of those could have been considered a violation of his aftercare plan and resulted in his suspension, but none did.

Lewis and Shaw, in notes later obtained by Len Boogaard, each expressed concern over Derek's attitude and his missed drug tests. By April, they were asking Derek's agent and program counselor Dan Cronin to "intervene."

While the public never caught on to Derek's problems, teammates suspected all along. They could tell something about Derek was different, because he showed up late to the practice rink and left early, and because he sometimes said things that did not make sense, and because he occasionally slumbered in a heap near his locker.

Teammates traded knowing glances and smirks. That's Derek. Big, goofy, invincible Derek. You don't worry about Derek. He worries about *you*.

But they also knew that his problems were related to drugs. That was because, when Wild players were prescribed painkillers for their own ailments, as most of them were, the drugs came with a new warning: Do not give your pills to Derek.

THE STRING OF conquests was an impressive one. Derek delivered three beatings in 10 days of December, all against heavyweights of hefty reputations, each victory more impressive than the last. If the past couple of injury-riddled seasons and the missed time from a "concussion" at the start of the season eroded any of Derek's standing as a bruiser, it was rebuilt in late 2009.

The first victim was Wade Belak, the fellow Saskatchewan native who had knocked out Derek's tooth a year before in Florida. Belak had since moved on to the Nashville Predators. The men spent 30 seconds staring down one another theatrically with raised fists, then

60 methodical seconds throwing occasional punches. There was no antipathy or urgency. Derek finally steered Belak against the boards and, after a couple of halfhearted punches, let him go, allowing the patient officials to casually step between them.

Two nights later came George Parros, the Anaheim enforcer with a Princeton education, whom Scott had hammered while Derek sat in rehabilitation. Derek slammed another Duck into the corner, and Parros responded with a shove. Derek looked unimpressed and uninterested as Parros shook his gloves away. Finally provoked by some words, Derek jabbed Parros with a gloved hand, igniting a ruckus. The men danced tightly, squirming through clutches. They eventually unfolded mirror-image rights. Derek landed a couple of shots to the side of Parros's ducked head, and the players fell together in a clump.

A week later, Derek's hard check crushed a Calgary Flames player named Brandon Prust, who would become a teammate and friend a year later, and drew the ire of McGrattan, a big, bombastic bruiser. The preamble lasted longer than the fight. Derek jabbed McGrattan with a left, then hit him with two hard rights. McGrattan fell to his knees, and Derek pounded down on him twice more, as if driving in a stake. The fight was over in 10 seconds.

It was more than enough to re-establish Derek's league-wide reputation. Derek was in the final year of his contract, on his way to playing 57 games, the most he had played since his rookie season four years earlier. A 2010 poll of NHL players showed that 44 percent considered Derek the "toughest fighter."

Those who knew Derek best, including his family and closest friends, believed that he had emerged from his addictive throes of summer. Maybe it was a one-time issue, now resolved. His care was overseen by a Wild franchise that always seemed to have Derek's best interest in mind, counseled by the NHL/NHLPA Substance Abuse and Behavioral Health Program. There was reason to think that the worst was behind him.

Then again, there was no one close to keep tabs. Len and Jody lived in Ottawa, both working at Royal Canadian Mounted Police headquarters. Joanne was still in Regina. The Boogaard children were scattered over Saskatchewan, Pennsylvania, and Kansas. Curtis, Derek's half-brother, lived in Alberta. Ron Salcer, Derek's agent, lived in Los Angeles. In Minnesota, Erin, the ex-fiancée, was out of the picture, and the Wild was run by an entirely new group of executives and coaches. Doug Risebrough, the general manager who drafted Derek and envisioned his rise, was gone. So was Tom Lynn, the assistant general manager, who wondered about Derek's changing personality. Jacques Lemaire was coaching the New Jersey Devils. Most of his assistant coaches had scattered to other corners of the NHL.

Even one of Derek's closest friends on the team, Marian Gaborik, was gone. He signed a five-year, $37.5 million contract with the Rangers after becoming a free agent in July. Derek moved into Gaborik's empty, expansive apartment in downtown Minneapolis, having left his own apartment to Erin when he returned from rehabilitation.

In the weeks and months after privately submitting to the league's substance abuse program, Derek was re-established as the league's toughest man. And he was as alone as ever.

DEREK AND JOHN SCOTT seemed to have little in common, other than size and a willingness to fight. Scott was from St. Catharines, Ontario, on the southern shore of Lake Ontario near the American border at Niagara Falls. He played a season of junior in the relatively low-level North American Hockey League, and spent four college seasons at Michigan Tech. While fighting was rare in college hockey—rules against it were far stricter than in junior—Scott managed to rack up 347 penalty minutes and just 19 points.

At the same time that Derek was working his way through top-level junior teams in Regina, Prince George, and Medicine Hat, then moving on to minor-league hockey in Louisiana, Scott earned a degree in mechanical engineering. He became one of several well-educated enforcers in the NHL, a fraternity that included George Parros and Kevin Westgarth, both of whom went to Princeton and helped blur the stereotype of the mindless hockey goon.

After Derek reached the Wild in 2005, Scott signed with the Houston Aeros, Derek's old American Hockey League team. A six-foot, eight-inch defenseman, he had Boogaard-like size, but little experience as a fighter.

He got to know Derek because they were part of the same organization, through training camps and a common role. But he mostly got to know him through videos of his fights. Scott played them again and again, awed by Derek's calm demeanor and relentless attack. Outside the Boogaard family, Scott studied Derek's fights more closely than anyone. He imitated Derek's upright stance, which made the men appear even taller and more daunting. He, too, learned to be the aggressor in fights, to try to end them quickly, but he struggled to emulate Derek's ability to patiently absorb punches to the face while waiting for an opening to put a brutal end to a fight.

So engulfed in that violent dimension of Derek on videotape, Scott presumed him to be a bully off the ice, too. He was surprised to find that Derek had barely a rough edge. There was no need to steer clear of him; if anything, Derek drew you in. He was funny and curious. He befriended arena workers and low-level team employees. Scott loved that about him.

After Scott was promoted to the Wild during the 2008–09 season, to add beefiness to a roster that had lost Todd Fedoruk and Chris Simon from the season before, the two became workout partners and road roommates. They occasionally went to restaurants with teammates, but mostly ordered room service, often platters of chicken wings. They watched movies and relaxed. They talked about fighting and joked about the next rival enforcer on the schedule. You take him this time, Derek would say. And so Scott would.

Scott noticed that Derek had pills. Most hockey players had pills, though, and to pry about their origins or their purpose would be like visiting someone's house and rifling through the medicine cabinet. Scott did not know what they were or where Derek got them, and it never felt like his business.

Scott had a close look at Derek's tangled decline. There were the surgeries and the pills and the rehabilitation during training camp. There was the teetering relationship with Erin, and Derek's frustration that his family did not accept her or trust her. There were the personnel changes among the Wild, and Derek's growing concern over the size of his role and his long-term future. His reputation was intact, but nothing else was the same.

Over time, Scott saw a hollowed shell of a man, like a spirit risen from the departed.

"It just left him," Scott remembered. "He didn't have a personality anymore. He just was kind of a blank face."

Whatever Derek's teammates thought of him, none of their worries had the benefit of hindsight.

"It was not like he's going to die," Scott said. "He's still going to play hockey, he's still going to be the toughest guy in the league. There's nothing that's going to happen to him. It's just like he was kind of our big brother—like, okay, nothing's going to happen to him."

. . .

IT WAS MARCH 14, 2010, and Derek and Scott were on the ice together in the early minutes of a home game against the St. Louis Blues. There was a whistle, but Scott, as if he did not hear it, smashed a Blues defenseman against the boards behind the net.

St. Louis forward D. J. King, 230 pounds of gristle, skated toward Scott. Derek stood in his way. He shoved King—an old adversary, another fighter from Saskatchewan, with the shaft of his hockey stick. The two had fought, but they had never truly met.

Let me get to him, King said casually to Derek, unless you want to go instead. Derek, his shoulder numbed and pain-free from a pregame injection of Toradol, was happy to oblige. He would handle this one.

King slid backward, a showman understanding that such a bout belonged at center ice. Derek stopped and froze, too proud to be a follower. The men stood and posed comically far apart. King drifted closer, as if pulled by the bigger man's gravity. Each player dropped his stick from his right hand and instinctively shook away his gloves. They pushed up their sleeves.

Teammates and officials backed away.

"The referee just looked at them and said, 'Okay, boys, let's get it going here,'" one television announcer said.

"This is a super-heavyweight bout," his broadcast partner said, his voice rising with excitement.

Derek stood in place, turning slowly. King orbited, clockwise, like a moon around a planet. King used the time to consider his strategy: Get in close, to avoid the full heft of Derek's right hand. Punch with the left, to keep him off-balance. Goad him into lefts of his own. Spot the opening and come back with the right. He batted at air, like a cat at a toy, gauging the distance to Derek while staying safely out of reach. Finally, King stabbed with his left and, head down, charged the bigger man with a wild right fist. Derek blocked it. King managed to get close to Derek, as he wanted, and delivered a pair of left-hand punches to Derek's face.

Derek, six inches taller, seven feet high on his skates, immediately thundered down a couple of right fists on top of King's head, blows that King only felt after the adrenaline of the fight faded later. The television announcer's voice raised to a shout.

"And then Boogaard fighting back!" he said.

King, his head still down, threw a couple of wild right hands that pierced the air. But one of them blindly bashed Derek in the nose and broke it.

"Oh! And King stuns Boogaard," the announcer shouted. And just as he said it, Derek threw a right hand that struck King in the forehead. King's white helmet flew from his head. It spun, like a saucer, completing a dozen revolutions before it landed and skittered across the ice.

In a fight for the Wild, Derek knocks off
D. J. King's helmet.

They had been swinging at each other for only eight seconds.

The men traded right hands, Derek hitting King on top of his bare head, King tagging Boogaard in the face again. They slid into one corner of the rink, against the boards, and grabbed each other's shoulders. The television broadcast displayed a "Tale of the Tape" graphic, showing the combatants' heights and weights.

Derek and King, as if roped together, drifted around the ice for 30 more seconds. King tried to steer the bigger man into the boards, where the fight might stall and be interrupted. Derek, his face throbbing in pain, tried to hit King a few more times, but King was content to hang on in a hug. Finally, as the men came to rest behind the goal, officials slipped between them. Derek's nose was bleeding, and blood was smeared across his forehead.

"That was a dandy!" the announcer said, and his broadcast partner laughed.

Fans cheered. Teammates on both benches watched the replay on the overhead scoreboard and banged their sticks against the outside of the half-boards fronting their benches. Rink workers arrived to repair the gouges in the ice and use shavings to cover the blood. At HockeyFights.com, fans were soon evenly split in declaring a winner.

King went to the penalty box. A tiny remote camera in front of him, used for the television broadcast, showed him gingerly wrapping a towel around his bloodied knuckles. Scar tissue had torn off in chunks.

Derek walked with his head down to the locker room, the roar within the Xcel Energy Center echoing behind him.

It was his last fight for the Minnesota Wild.

THE WILD MADE a meager attempt to re-sign Derek when his contract expired at the end of the season. Even before that, quietly in March, the team nearly completed a trade for Derek, sending him to Tampa Bay for league-fighting leader Zenon Konopka. It fell through at the last minute.

Among fans and media, there was wide-ranging discussion about Derek's value. His importance to the team was intangible and difficult to measure. On one hand, he was enormously popular, a good representative in the community, a respected voice in the dressing room. The stands at the Xcel Energy Center were filled with fans, young and old, wearing his No. 24 jersey. No player could make fans cheer the way the Boogeyman could. While he rarely scored, his presence probably made it easier for others to negotiate the ice. Derek would command a million-dollar-per-year contract, a lot for an enforcer, but his salary would pale compared to those of most teammates. Besides, he would be just 28 the next season. He probably had several years left in him.

The counterargument was just as strong. Derek had averaged only 51 regular-season games, out of 82, in his five years in Minnesota. Injuries, from his sore back to his surgically repaired shoulder to the mounting number of concussions, were taking a slow toll. Even when healthy enough to play, Derek averaged little more than five minutes of ice time. In his Wild career, over 255 regular-season games, he had two goals and 12 assists. He had not scored a goal since his rookie year.

He had 544 penalty minutes, about half stemming from five-minute fighting majors. But those were not the types of numbers associated with the nastiest players. Derek, playing more minutes than he ever had in the NHL, fought just nine times during the 2009–10 season—far fewer than Konopka's 33 fights for Tampa Bay.

Derek's reputation as one of the fiercest fighters, so quickly established in his first two seasons, prevented him from attracting many fights. And more teams padded their rosters with pugnacious, mid-sized players, the type who could play on second and third lines but were willing to fight when needed. Rather than a single enforcer, teams were finding value in an army of scrappers. In June, before free agency began on July 1, the Wild signed one such player, forward Brad Staubitz. Derek, increasingly, was a heavyweight fighter in an era of middleweights.

Of course, those were just the key points of the public discourse. Internally, the Wild knew all about Derek—the drug addiction, the attitude shift, the injuries that were never publicly noted. The team had no desire to re-sign him; not at the prices he would command. To guard against a public-relations hit, the team merely asked for a chance to match what other teams offered, knowing that other suitors would likely overpay for a damaged enforcer.

They did. The New York Rangers offered a four-year contract worth $6.5 million. The Edmonton Oilers, a division rival of the Wild, offered four years and $7 million. The Washington Capitals and Calgary Flames, another Wild rival, were interested, too, and willing to come close to those sums.

For Derek, the decision was between Edmonton and New York. There could not be two more different teams and two more different markets in the NHL.

His family urged him to choose Edmonton. It was western Canada, and it was familiar. It was close to home—a day's drive from Regina, close enough that his mother and relatives and friends could attend games semi-regularly. His half-brother, Curtis, lived in Alberta. Any of them could be there to help Derek through whatever personal problems he faced.

Edmonton was one of the NHL's smallest markets, they argued, but the Oilers were the No. 1 sports franchise, with a voracious fan base, a loud arena, and a history of Stanley Cups. It was Wayne Gretzky's old team, one of the most successful in the league. Derek might enjoy being a proverbial big fish in the small pond of central Alberta. The Oilers and Wild were division rivals. Derek was familiar with the roster and the facilities. He would be able to return frequently to Minneapolis and Saint Paul, play in front of his fans and friends, and show the Wild what they gave up when they set him free.

Ryan Boogaard, still Derek's unofficial scout, saw it from the on-ice perspective. He thought the Oilers were a far better fit than the Rangers. He liked Edmonton's core of young players. He told Derek that Oilers coach Tom Renney, recently arrived after several seasons with the Rangers, had shown a willingness to rely mostly on a single enforcer. And Renney was from British Columbia and coached junior in the Western Hockey League. Derek, with his lifelong clashes with authority figures, might like Renney's relatively mild-mannered coaching approach.

New York coach John Tortorella, Ryan told his brother, rarely relied on one enforcer. His previous teams in Tampa Bay—especially the later ones, after the Lightning won the 2004 Stanley Cup—featured a few pugnacious toughs, but not one well-known fighter. And the temperamental Tortorella was from Boston and had never played or coached in Canadian junior. He was a notoriously prickly personality.

Besides, the Rangers were nowhere close to the leading sports franchise in New York. Baseball, football, and basketball were all more popular than hockey. In the hierarchy of New York franchises, the Rangers, despite their long history and deep fan base, fell somewhere in line near the Jets, Nets, and Mets, below the Yankees, Giants, and Knicks. Derek would be a small fish in an extremely big pond.

But Derek was intrigued from the outset. Doug Risebrough, the former Wild general manager who had drafted Derek and shepherded his rise to the NHL, had been hired the previous fall as a consultant to Rangers general manager Glen Sather. The Rangers were interested in an enforcer to beef up their roster. Risebrough knew just the man. As Derek was about to become a free agent, Derek and

Risebrough met for lunch. He wanted to make sure he could recommend Derek in good conscience.

Sign him, Risebrough told the Rangers. Derek is the toughest enforcer in the league, comes from a good family, and is beloved by teammates. Marian Gaborik, the Rangers' scoring star who had spent years with Risebrough and the Wild, could attest. He had joined the Rangers the year before, and he told Derek how much he liked the city and the team. Derek would be reunited with his good friend and serve, again, as his primary protector.

The Rangers had sent Derek a DVD, placed inside a wooden box engraved with the team logo and delivered to him by courier in Minneapolis. It was a promotional video that the team used to seduce prospective players. It showed stirring scenes of Manhattan, the skyline, Times Square, Broadway, and Madison Square Garden. And it featured a roster of New York celebrities—Regis Philbin among them—encouraging the viewer to come to the Big Apple.

The decision was a cinch. Derek chose New York.

What could be bigger? he thought. It would be the pinnacle of his career, a chance to represent an Original Six franchise at Madison Square Garden—"The World's Most Famous Arena," as it's called, home of the Rangers and Knicks in the middle of midtown Manhattan.

For anyone who still wondered whether Derek Boogaard had arrived—anyone from Melfort or Prince George or anywhere else that Derek imagined those people might exist—playing for the famed Blueshirts would be the final word.

Derek, despite the pleas from his family—all but Aaron thought Edmonton was a better idea—never seriously considered the Oilers. He never liked the city, and he never liked the team. Derek also held out hope that his relationship with Erin was salvageable. He knew she wouldn't want to live in Edmonton, either. It wasn't that much different than Regina. But she would love New York.

"Derek is obviously the biggest and the toughest, and I think we needed that presence here," Sather told reporters during a conference call on July 1, 2010.

"It's one of those things," Derek said that day, "where New York knows what type of player I am and what I bring to the table. I love doing what I do, and I wouldn't trade it for the world, you know?"

PART III

NEW YORK

9

DEREK WAS NERVOUS ABOUT playing and living in New York, but he tried not to let on. In the two months before he left Minnesota, after he signed with the Rangers, he told people how excited he was to play in Madison Square Garden. He told friends about his 33rd-floor apartment at the Sheffield on 57th Street, between Eighth and Ninth Avenues, with views of Central Park through the skyscrapers of Columbus Circle. The apartment was rented for $6,900 a month from Aaron Voros, a former Wild teammate who had spent the previous two seasons as a forward with the Rangers.

No. 24 was taken by another player, so Derek deftly chose jersey No. 94, representing 1994, the last year that the Rangers won the Stanley Cup. That team broke a 54-year championship drought behind the likes of captain Mark Messier, winger Adam Graves, goalie Mike Richter, and defensemen Brian Leetch and Sergei Zubov. It was a tough team, backed by enforcers Joey Kocur and Jeff Beukeboom. Derek knew the history.

In New York, there would be sponsorship opportunities he had never fathomed. He would bring the burgeoning Defending the Blue Line charity to New York to establish roots. He would find endorsement opportunities and business offers he never would have received in places like Edmonton. Derek saw the potential. But it still scared him.

In the summer of 2010, Derek lived in one side of Gaborik's cavernous apartment near the Walker Art Center on the edge of downtown Minneapolis, while Aaron lived in the other. They had to shout to hear one another. Tobin Wright, the business manager for both Derek and Gaborik, also had a real-estate license and made preparations to sell the unit for Gaborik. He stepped into Derek's bathroom and saw a crystal wine stopper, with a Wild logo, on the counter. Why would Derek have a wine stopper in here? Wright wondered to himself. He picked it up. It had a bulbous handle on one end and a smooth, flat surface on the other.

When Wright touched the flat end, white powder rubbed off onto his fingers. Wright looked around. Nearby on the counter was a dollar bill, rolled up. Derek, he surmised, was crushing pills and snorting them.

When summer began, Derek and Aaron, both single, celebrated with several weeks of parties and barhopping. They spent several weeks in Manhattan Beach, California, visiting Derek's agent, Ron Salcer, and getting into a routine of workouts and parties. On the beach, Derek lifted, pulled, and coiled shipping ropes, giant spaghetti noodles as thick as logs, in a one-man tug-of-war to build strength. He tried to get a tan. The brothers shot videos that showed Derek, a bit heavier than usual, making jokes, playing in the waves, learning to use a stand-up paddleboard, and driving a convertible Maserati he had rented.

Wright called Salcer and told him what he had found in Derek's apartment. When Salcer confronted him, Derek denied anything unusual. He took Ambien on occasion, he said, but he would never crush it. Somebody must have left that in there during a party or something.

But then Derek showed up to the apartment one day, around the first of August, with 100 OxyContin pills.

"Where did you get those?" Aaron asked.

"Don't worry about it," Derek replied.

"What are you doing?" Aaron said. "We've worked our asses off."

Their relationship had grown increasingly tangled. It was weeks earlier, at a bar in Minneapolis, that Aaron had met a young woman he began dating. Derek liked her at first. But as he saw Aaron's one-night fling evolve into a relationship, he was not happy. The more Aaron saw his girlfriend, the less Derek saw of Aaron.

Derek had not gotten over his love for Erin, and, as if filling a void of his own, he began to contact her with increasing regularity as his final weeks in Minneapolis loomed and anxiety rose in advance of his move to New York. Erin could not fully resist the overtures. "Magnets," she called them.

Aaron began to worry. He had grown increasingly protective of Derek. Now, less than a year after Derek was in rehabilitation, as he nervously awaited his move to New York, he was coming home with bags of prescription pain pills. He was contacting Erin. He was hanging around people that Aaron didn't like. Every summer, it seemed, the number of people who elbowed their way into Derek's life grew, and Aaron was skeptical of their motives. He saw how Derek surrounded himself with people at restaurants and bars, people he considered friends, and when it came time for the bill, they all looked away.

He told Derek that those friends—"leeches," he called them—were taking full advantage of Derek's wealth and fame.

"I know," Derek would say. "I just can't say no."

One summer night, when Aaron and his girlfriend were at Sneaky Pete's, Aaron saw Erin. She asked to talk, to let her explain everything that had happened between her and Derek. Aaron did not want to hear any of it. He walked away.

Within an hour, Aaron's cell phone rang. It was Derek, furious, demanding that Aaron apologize for his rudeness toward Erin.

On Aaron's 24th birthday in mid-August, in the presence of their friend Jeremy Clark, Aaron and Derek bickered about Erin again. Aaron screamed that he was not the only one who felt that way about Erin; Jeremy thought so, too.

Derek stopped. His head turned slowly toward Clark. You do? Suddenly, the three of them—Derek, Aaron, and Clark, like boyhood brothers back in the Melfort basement—were in a fist-swinging scrum on the lawn of the apartment building.

By then, the first batch of 100 OxyContins was gone. Derek replaced it with another 100. He told Aaron that he bought them for $6,000—$60 a pill.

Aaron did not trust his brother with the pills, and he worried about the speed with which Derek went through them. Derek let Aaron take the pills and divide them, stashing them in drawers or closets. Only when Derek came to Aaron and asked for some, insisting that his back ached and that he needed the pills to combat the pain, would Aaron hand any over.

"What am I going to do?" Aaron explained later. "Deny this guy the pills that he just spent six grand on? Is his back really that hurt?"

Derek tried to hide his anxiety about the move to New York. He wanted summer to last forever. Friends promised to visit, and Derek talked about making a big, immediate impact with the Rangers. Privately, he worried that he would be unable to live up to the expectations.

Derek wanted Aaron to quit hockey and come live with him in New York. But Aaron had his own aspirations to pursue, even if the long-term prospects looked shaky. After being drafted by the Wild, Aaron had joined the Pittsburgh Penguins organization. He played three seasons divided between the American Hockey League and the

East Coast Hockey League. Now he had a contract in the lower-tier Central Hockey League, for a franchise in Laredo, Texas, on the Mexican border. Like Derek, he did not know what else he would do if he could not make a career out of hockey. He did not want to give up now.

In early September, Derek left to catch his flight to New York to join the Rangers. When he arrived at the Minneapolis–Saint Paul airport, though, he panicked. He could not remember whether he had packed his latest batch of OxyContin pills. He wanted to rummage through his suitcase, but worried about doing it in the terminal, in front of people who might recognize him. He walked back out of the airport. He arrived back at the apartment, missing his flight, and dumped his suitcase. The pills had been packed, after all.

Derek rebooked his flight to New York for the next day. But he was suddenly worried about getting caught with the pills.

"Send these to me in a week or so," Derek told Aaron, handing them to him.

For a few weeks, through Rangers training camp and before Aaron left for his own hockey season, Derek texted and called his little brother from New York to ask the whereabouts of the pills. But Aaron knew it was a crime to ship prescription pills, and he worried about his status as a Canadian resident living and working in the States. For several weeks, Aaron waffled—torn between getting caught and disappointing his older brother.

Finally, Derek erupted. Forget it, he said. Just take them back to where I got them, and give them to a friend who is coming to visit me soon in New York. Aaron carried the bag of prescription painkillers to Sneaky Pete's, he said later, and handed them over.

He was relieved to be rid of them. Aaron left for Texas for the hockey season. He and Derek barely spoke for many months.

· · ·

LEN BOOGAARD SENT the e-mail on the evening of October 13, 2010.

"I am the father of Derek BOOGAARD and need to make contact with Doug RISEBROUGH ASAP," he wrote to an administrative address for the New York Rangers. "I can be contacted via the noted e-mail as well as my work e-mail."

He provided two e-mail addresses and two phone numbers. "Regards, Len Boogaard," the note ended.

Aaron had told Len about Derek's late-summer slide and the pills he wanted shipped to New York. Len had presumed that Derek's addiction had been resolved a year earlier, in rehabilitation, and had trusted that his son was being closely monitored by the substance abuse program. He sent a note to Salcer, Derek's agent, but when he did not receive an immediate response, he went straight to the Rangers.

Len knew that Risebrough had a close relationship with Derek, dating all the way back to when Risebrough drafted the 19-year-old for the Minnesota Wild. Risebrough knew about Derek's troubled past.

Len's e-mail message was forwarded from the website manager at Madison Square Garden to an assistant in the Rangers' front office. In a reply on the afternoon of October 14, two games into the season and the day before the Rangers' home opener at the Garden, she assured Len that the message had been sent on to Risebrough.

About then, Risebrough called. The men were acquaintances, having met several times, and they exchanged pleasantries, Len recalled later, before Len told Risebrough that Derek was abusing prescription drugs again. Len relayed what he had heard from Aaron—that Derek was taking painkillers, and he had sources on the street, maybe even in New York.

Risebrough said he needed to think about how to proceed, Len later recalled.

Len awaited a response. It came two days later, when Derek called. He told his father that Glen Sather, the general manager of the Rangers, had called him into his office and berated him.

"He said, 'Tell me what's going on,'" Len recalled Derek saying. "'And if you're lying, I'll trade you so fast.'"

Derek also called Aaron and told him the same thing. He wondered if Aaron had told anyone about the incident at the airport, because Salcer asked about it, he said. Aaron denied telling anyone.

Derek never realized that it was his father who had prompted the Rangers to question him. Len listened to Derek as if he had no clue. Lying about what? Len asked. Derek turned typically evasive. He never admitted he had an addiction problem, and he was not about to now, over the phone to his father. It did not matter. Len was happy and relieved. He had told the Rangers, and the Rangers were taking action. Derek would get help.

What Len didn't know was that Derek had been asking a Rangers trainer for Ambien and painkillers—requests that made their way to Lewis and Shaw of the substance-abuse program. According to their notes on Derek later obtained by Len, each warned Derek about his use of the drugs.

Len also did not know that, within two weeks, a Rangers team dentist would give Derek the first of five prescriptions for hydrocodone.

DEREK IMMEDIATELY MISSED the life he had left in Minnesota. He had parted with Aaron, headed to another minor-league assignment, on unsettled terms, divided over girlfriends and pills. Derek had left behind Erin, the ex-fiancée he still hoped to marry. He had left behind friends he had made over five years, including Jeremy Clark and the suburban gym that had become a second home. He had left behind his creature habits, from restaurants to gas stations to grocery stores to Sneaky Pete's. He had left behind the familiar relationship he had with the media. He had left behind the goodwill of the charity work he had done and the legions of fans who spontaneously chanted his name, whether by the thousands at the Xcel Energy Center or by the handful at bars or on city sidewalks.

But Derek never fully disconnected from Minnesota. He begged friends to visit and stay with him in New York. Early in the season, several of them did. Erin came and stayed with Derek several times, for up to a week at a time, spending many of the days shopping in Manhattan with a friend she knew in the city.

On October 11, just as Len Boogaard learned about his son's relapse into addiction, Derek welcomed some acquaintances from Minnesota—among them, Dillon Hafiz, his father, Stewart, and his uncle Peter. They attended the Rangers' road game against the Islanders on Long Island that afternoon—Derek played one shift, and the Rangers lost—and then the Monday night football game in New Jersey between the Minnesota Vikings and New York Jets. They traveled in a limousine, and Derek paid the bill for $1,508. He supplied the tickets and bought No. 94 Rangers jerseys with BOOGAARD on the back. The men posed for pictures in front of the new football stadium at the Meadowlands.

Rob Nelson, Derek's financial advisor from Minnesota, brought on to help him manage his money and control his increasingly erratic spending habits, brought his girlfriend to visit Derek at the beginning of the season. Nelson had become another sort of big brother for Derek, someone to support him but also steer him straight. He did not know that Derek was abusing pills again, but found him nervous about the start of the season in New York and still unsettled about living there.

It was awfully big, Derek told him. When they went out, walking the streets of Manhattan or having dinner in restaurants, no one recognized Derek—or at least did not say anything to him if they did. He was not a star, not the way he was in the Twin Cities. He was one person among eight million.

Clark, too, came to visit, bringing his wife, Jennie. Derek and Clark were two small-town Canadian boys who appreciated the simple pleasures of life—a few friends, a couple of beers, a setting sun. Clark quickly decided that he did not like New York. He could not imagine Derek liking it, either, no matter how much of an optimistic spin Derek put on it.

Derek was welcomed at Madison Square Garden, but he was relatively anonymous everywhere else in New York, a city that shrugs at celebrity. Derek put more faith in his old friends from Minnesota than he did in his ability to make new friends in New York.

Among the connections he kept were those with some of the Wild's team doctors. Medical director Sheldon Burns gave Derek a final physical on July 13, after Derek signed with the Rangers, and completed both a medical form and one for an insurance company that covers professional athletes. Under the pre-printed category of head injuries ("including concussions"), Burns noted two: one in January 2007 ("headaches" and "missed 4–5 days," he wrote) and another in September 2009 ("headaches," "dizziness," and "missed 2½ weeks"). There was no mention that the second absence was for substance abuse rehabilitation. Burns noted several past injuries, such as broken fingers, a "fractured nose this year," a high ankle sprain several years earlier, and the bulging disk in Derek's back, but gave Derek a clean bill of health. "I do not see anything that would be a long-term concern or threatening his career at this point," he wrote.

On August 11, Burns's medical partner and fellow Wild team doctor Dan Peterson prescribed 30 Ambien pills to Derek, pharmacy records showed. Another prescription was dated September 5, the day Derek went to the airport to fly to New York.

· · ·

DEREK DID NOT make a good first impression with the Rangers. Once in New York, a week before training camp began, Derek went to dinner with Gaborik and Salcer, the players' agent. After dinner, Gaborik and Derek agreed to meet at a corner coffee place at eight the next morning. They would go together to the practice rink where most of the veteran Rangers worked out together in preparation for the rigors of training camp. Attendance was not mandatory, but it was a sign of solidarity and commitment.

Derek did not show up the next morning. Gaborik fumed.

"Don't worry about it, don't worry about it," Derek told Salcer later. "Training camp starts next week. I'll be okay."

He was not. He was overweight, pushing 300 pounds, and the Rangers were not pleased with his condition. When the preseason games began, Derek received little playing time—enough to try to coax him into shape, but not enough for Derek to prove his worth on the ice.

Preseason games in the NHL tended to have about twice as many fights as those in the regular season, as young players tried to fight their way onto rosters by demonstrating their scrappiness. With the Rangers, Derek did not fight.

On September 29, the *Wall Street Journal* featured Derek in a story, noting that he had not scored a goal since January 7, 2006, a streak of 222 regular-season games, the longest among active players. The story raised the age-old question of whether there was a benefit to enforcers. It asked Derek's new teammates. One of the unspoken axioms of the NHL was that no player degraded the position of enforcer, and no one argued for its demise.

"It's not just that he makes our guys comfortable," Rangers captain Chris Drury told the paper. "It's that he makes the other guys uncomfortable, and now maybe they make the wrong play, they turn it over and we score—that's the sort of thing just his presence can mean."

Rangers coach John Tortorella offered a succinct answer to whether enforcers—the *Wall Street Journal* interchanged the term with "goon"—had a place in the NHL.

"It's still part of our game," Tortorella said.

Publicly, despite training camp reports about Derek's poor conditioning, the season began with great promise for Derek.

"I think Boogaard is going to be an absolute superstar in New York," Darryl Wolski, who created the made-for-TV *Battle of the Hockey Enforcers* tournament in Prince George, told the New York *Daily News*. "I don't think the Rangers have seen a guy like him in a long time, maybe back to the Tie Domi era."

Derek told the reporter that fans should not expect Domi's notorious post-fight celebrations.

"You have to have respect for the guy that you just fought," he said. "I think it's absolutely ridiculous when guys do the showboating and all that. What if the other guy gets hurt? Everyone wants to watch the fight, but it's just a respect factor. I don't like it. I don't like to do it."

Tortorella told reporters that the Rangers expected Derek to be more than a fighter, someone who could play extended minutes as a power forward. It was a tease that Derek had heard most of his life.

In his first regular-season game as a Ranger, a 6–3 victory at Buffalo, Derek played a tentative seven shifts, for 6:03 of ice time— more than his career average, but less than anyone else in the game. Two nights later, in a 6–4 loss at the Islanders, Derek played three shifts in the first period, one in the second (for 22 seconds), and none in the third. His ice time was 1:34.

On October 15, the day after Len Boogaard spoke to Doug Risebrough about Derek's latest pill problems, the Rangers played their first regular-season game at Madison Square Garden. The Toronto

Maple Leafs, an Original Six rival and a team off to a hot start, were in town. Most expected a duel between Derek and enforcer Colton Orr, the former Ranger, now in Toronto thanks to a four-year, $4 million contract.

The Rangers lost in overtime, 4–3, and Derek recorded a third-period assist, the 13th of his NHL career. But that was overshadowed by how the Rangers lost. The Maple Leafs knocked Gaborik out of the game with a separated shoulder; he would miss four weeks. They charged and knocked down goalie Henrik Lundqvist.

Derek played eight short shifts. His lone contribution was the assist—not the kind of physical contribution he was paid to make. It was undersized sparkplug Brandon Prust who fought for the Rangers, and agitator Sean Avery who tried to ignite the team with combative hits and penalties for roughing and slashing.

Derek faced criticism like he had not had before.

"This isn't really about Derek Boogaard even though it is," long-time *New York Post* hockey writer Larry Brooks wrote, "but if Friday's calamitous night at the Garden doesn't expose the fatal flaw in the concept of hiring the biggest, toughest, most feared puncher pound for pound in the NHL to act as a deterrent, then nothing does and nothing will."

Brooks used the game as an example of how the notion of an enforcer had changed over the years, until it had become something cheapened, with little value.

"The idea a fourth-line player—who gets a mere handful of fourth-line shifts a night and who is essentially in the lineup to punch it out with the opposition's fourth-line heavyweight—can be a deterrent is flawed," he wrote. "The idea this presence will create more skating room for his team's stars is misguided.

"The heavyweight as a deterrent is an anachronism, proven so for the latest time before our very eyes Friday night," Brooks concluded. "Unfortunately, the Rangers have invested $1.625M in cap space to be lost in time."

IT WAS THE day after the Toronto game that Derek phoned his father, complaining about Sather. Derek saw it as a slight, proof that the Rangers did not believe in him. Derek's playing time plunged the following game.

Derek looked for a scapegoat, and found one in Tortorella, the coach. The positive reinforcement from coaches—from Floyd Halcro in Melfort to Jacques Lemaire in Minnesota—that Derek thrived upon over the years never materialized in New York. Tortorella was not unlike the coaches that Derek detested as a teenager, the ones Derek believed treated him without faith and respect. Derek came to joke with friends about the rare days that Tortorella exchanged a greeting when they passed. Quietly, among friends, he called Tortorella "Little Hitler."

He complained to Salcer and others about Tortorella's treatment. They don't like me here, Derek said. They aren't playing me, and they don't even want me. The retort was simple and obvious: The Rangers wouldn't have signed you to a four-year contract worth $6.5 million, Derek, if they did not believe in you.

Salcer, though, called Sather for an assessment. He found the general manager's words as haunting as they were surprising. Derek is in the worst condition of anyone on the team, Sather said, according to Salcer. He's in no condition to be playing in games. He's lucky to be playing at all. We're just trying to get him into shape.

Quite frankly, Salcer remembered Sather telling him, I'm really worried about Derek. There are a lot of big guys in this league, a lot of guys in really great shape. And I'm afraid someone's going to hit Derek and end his career.

Derek's first fight for the Rangers came in the rematch with the Toronto Maple Leafs on October 21. That morning, the *Globe and Mail*, the nationally distributed Canadian newspaper based in Toronto, contained a column by hockey writer Roy MacGregor. He had grown weary of the latest debates over the role of fighting in hockey.

"Surely the time has come to make fighting a penalty," Mac-Gregor wrote. "It is not a penalty, no matter what the rulebook pretends. Two players fight—usually as staged as the intermission T-shirt giveaway—and the game comes to a grinding halt.

"And here I must apologize, as I suggested higher up that fighting had no effect on the momentum of a game. It does. It kills momentum.

"Whistles blow, gloves are picked up, the long WWE grand march to the penalty box is held and, presto, the game begins again as if nothing has happened.

"Not only is neither team penalized in any imaginable capacity, but the two fighters count their majors as the skilled players count goals and assists. The fighters use their number of majors to argue in favour of a salary increase the next time their contract comes up.

"Fighting, therefore, has been deemed a reward by the league that would have you believe it is actually a penalty.

"So let us all strike a deal here. We agree to accept that fighting is part of the game. So long as the NHL accepts the same. And makes fighting a real penalty with real consequence."

Colton Orr was a former Ranger who, in 2007, knocked Todd Fedoruk unconscious at Madison Square Garden. He also was a foe of Derek's from the Western Hockey League and a good friend in Saskatchewan of Mat Sommerfeld, Derek's boyhood rival. Derek and Orr had fought twice in a month nearly a decade earlier, when Derek played for Prince George and Orr for Kamloops.

The game between New York and Toronto at the Air Canada Centre was scoreless and only two minutes old. As the puck and the rest of the players headed down the ice, Orr pestered Derek, asking for a fight in front of the team benches. He did not wait for an answer, throwing a punch before Derek removed his gloves. Derek demurred before engaging. He soon popped Orr in the face with his right fist, loosening Orr's helmet, then hit him again in the side of the head. Holding Orr around the collar with his left hand, Derek finally shook his right glove free. Orr got in a firm shot of his own, raising the volume of the crowd, then managed to fling Derek onto his back and to the ice. The noise rose to a crescendo. Players on both teams banged their sticks.

Len was in the arena that night. Like friends and family of Derek who watched on television, he could see that something was not right. Derek should have been eager to make amends for the disappointment of his first matchup with Toronto. Instead, he fought with uncustomary nonchalance and an expression that exuded more than its usual poker-faced tautness. There was a reluctance to engage, and then a fight without fury.

They came to know something that most witnesses did not: one of Orr's punches dislodged a three-tooth bridge in Derek's mouth.

Two nights later, Derek fought Boston's Shawn Thornton, a fearless pit bull. The game was still in the first period, the visiting Rangers leading 2–0, when Thornton wrapped up Derek in front of the Boston net just as the Rangers were firing shots on goal. Whistles blew. Players stepped back. Fans stood.

The predictable "Tale of the Tape" graphic appeared on television screens before the first punch was thrown. It showed that Derek had an advantage of five inches and 48 pounds—a conservative estimate, really, thanks to Derek being listed, graciously, at 265 pounds.

The two stayed knotted as Thornton steered the encounter into one corner. Thornton grabbed Derek's outstretched right arm and jabbed him in the face with a couple of punches. Derek finally freed his right hand and delivered several shots to Thornton's ribs. Officials pulled the men apart unusually early.

After the game, Derek was diagnosed by a team doctor with a cut on his right index finger. The wound became infected, and the injury was serious enough to be cited in at least eight subsequent internal injury reports.

On October 26, three days after cutting his hand on Thornton and five days after having his bridge damaged by Orr, Derek was prescribed 20 hydrocodone pills by Rangers team dentist Joseph Esposito. The dentist's notes that day described Derek's mouth injury, including a "nerve exposed," as an "EMERG."

That same day, at 3:08 P.M., Derek received a text message from Dan Cronin, the director of counseling for the NHL/NHLPA substance abuse program. It was, according to Derek's cell-phone records, their first phone interaction since June 24. The two exchanged five more text messages that afternoon, the last at 5:35 P.M.

Derek also exchanged six text messages with Dr. Esposito, between 4:38 and 4:57 P.M. And between 6:26 and 6:33, Derek called Cronin six times. If Cronin answered at all, the conversation never lasted more than a minute, cell-phone records showed.

Derek received a second prescription of hydrocodone from Esposito on November 13, plus three more through early December—a total of 64 pills, records show.

Whatever pain Derek was in did not prevent him from fighting. On his first shift of a November 4 game in Philadelphia, Derek got into a fight with veteran heavyweight enforcer Jody Shelley. The men had a twisted history, through years of bouts when Derek was with the Wild and Shelley was with the Columbus Blue Jackets and San Jose Sharks. Shelley had spent the previous season with the Rangers, but was cast off in favor of Derek. He now played for the Flyers, one of New York's biggest rivals.

The two circled one another near center ice. The public-address system heralded the raised fists with a bell, as if it were the start of a bout between Rocky Balboa and Apollo Creed. Derek opened with two overhand rights, then jabbed with a left fist filled with Shelley's jersey. Shelley never got comfortable and balanced enough to pose a knockout threat. Derek hit him in the back of the head a couple of times before Shelley slipped to a knee and officials intervened.

Despite the momentum that a victorious fight is supposed to bring, the Rangers lost, 4–1.

But Derek's minutes on the ice began to climb. His career with the Rangers peaked on November 9, against Washington at Madison Square Garden. He was on the ice early in the second period of a 2–2 game. Washington defenseman Tyler Sloan missed the puck along the boards in the New York zone, and Derek chased it down in front of the team benches. There was no one in front of him besides the goalie.

He heard teammate Brian Boyle shout a simple instruction: "Shoot!"

Derek cocked his stick and released a slap shot from just above the face-off circle. Washington goalie Michal Neuvirth lunged with his stick and missed.

The red lamp lit behind the net. The crowd lifted as one. Derek raised his arms and smiled—an emotional exhalation he never displayed when he beat someone up. He cruised behind the net and stopped against the boards in an embrace with teammate Erik Christensen. Others quickly swarmed him. Derek, his stick raised—the rare time he was cheered with a stick in his hand—returned to the bench as the arena still buzzed.

It was Derek's first NHL goal since his rookie season, five years earlier, a streak of 234 games. It fell 21 games short of the NHL record. Derek told reporters in the dressing room—a losing one, as the Rangers fell, 5–3—that it was his first goal on a slap shot since he was 20, playing in the East Coast Hockey League.

Derek spent most of the night talking to friends on the phone and returning congratulatory text messages. They all had seen the highlight, across the sports channels of Canada and the United States, of big, bad Derek Boogaard lumbering down the far side of the ice, barely slowing to unleash a ferocious shot, raising his arms in triumph and surprise, then soaking in the affection of a suddenly adoring crowd.

Unexpectedly, the biggest cheer he ever received in New York came on a goal.

IN THE THIRD period of a Sunday afternoon game on November 14, Derek fought twice against Edmonton's Steve MacIntyre.

MacIntyre was from a small town in Saskatchewan, too. He was two years older than Derek, but they crossed paths as teenagers in the Western Hockey League. Mat Sommerfeld was Derek's first-ever fight in the WHL; Steve MacIntyre was his second.

Unlike Derek, MacIntyre was not drafted by an NHL team. After the WHL, his odyssey took him through eight franchises in seven minor leagues over seven seasons before he finally reached the NHL with the Edmonton Oilers. One of the six fights he had his rookie year was considered a draw against Derek.

This one was Derek's first fight at home for the Rangers. But the crowd at Madison Square Garden knew the protocol. Fans chanted "Boo-gey, Boo-gey" as Derek pummeled MacIntyre with nearly 20 right hands to the head, each eliciting an *ooh* from the crowd. It took most of the punches to knock MacIntyre's helmet free, and the fight ended with MacIntyre looking as if he could absorb more.

MacIntyre, fresh from the penalty box, wanted a rematch. It goes against the unspoken code for enforcers, and Derek had no reason to oblige. The Rangers were on their way to an 8–2 victory. Still, after MacIntyre sidled up to Derek during a face-off, he provoked him with a cross-check. Derek flipped the switch.

They wasted no time shedding their gloves, instead just clutching and punching and trying to shake free their fists. They drifted against the Rangers bench, exhausting themselves with uppercuts and jabs from close range.

Without a haymaker blow, few realized that one of the shots broke Derek's nose and probably gave him a concussion. The Rangers' medical notes made no mention of the injury. But a few hours after the game, at 6:21 P.M., Derek sent a text message to the cell phone of Sheldon Burns, the Wild's medical director back in Minnesota. He exchanged seven texts with Dan Peterson, Burns's partner and Wild team doctor, over nearly three hours. In one six-minute span in the middle of that, Derek traded six texts with Esposito, the Rangers' dentist.

By Tuesday, Derek had a prescription from Esposito for 12 more hydrocodone pills. He also had a prescription from another Rangers team doctor, an orthopedic surgeon, for 40 pills of tramadol, a narcotic-like pain reliever. The two prescriptions were picked up from two different Manhattan pharmacies—both on 57th Street, close to Derek's apartment.

He missed the next night's game in Pittsburgh, but took time to photograph his right hand and send it to a few friends. It showed the knuckles and fingers grotesquely swollen and scabbed from the repeated bashing against MacIntyre's helmet.

The injuries continued. On November 24, in Tampa, Derek fell hard on his left shoulder, an injury that surfaced in internal medical reports for a couple of weeks. Derek missed three games. When he returned to the lineup, Derek was injected with Toradol.

On December 2, he deconstructed Trevor Gillies of the Islanders in a long-lasting fight instigated during pregame warmups. The next night, also against the Islanders, Derek was inadvertently struck in the face with a stick. During the intermission after the second period, a team doctor used three nylon sutures to close the cut. No anesthetic was used, the doctor noted.

Derek, as he had been the season before in Minnesota, after his trip to rehabilitation, was randomly drug tested. The latest one showed positive results for two types of decongestants, plus Xanax—despite no known prescriptions of Xanax from team doctors. Later in the day of that drug test, Derek was prescribed hydrocodone by Esposito, the dentist, for the fifth and final time.

Another drug test came on December 8—results would be reported as "negative" six days later. The test was taken on the same day that Dr. Ronald Weissman, a team doctor, gave Derek two prescriptions that Derek had filled at a pharmacy not far from the Rangers' suburban practice facility. One was for six pills of azithromycin, an antibiotic. The other was for 30 pills of trazodone, an antidepressant.

The timing was peculiar. Erin had been in New York. She had come several times through the fall, staying for most of a week here and there. She shopped, spent time with an old girlfriend, and stayed with Derek. Most of Derek's family and close friends did not know. Derek rarely talked to them, and he knew what they would have said, anyway.

Erin could tell all fall that he was lonely, by the calls and text messages he sent to her and others, asking for visits. And he seemed happy when she was around. But she came to realize, just as she had more than a year earlier, that there was no future with Derek. She could not picture the two of them raising a family and growing old together. Part of it was that they were so different; something Derek's family recognized but Derek either did not or never minded. And part of it was that Derek was different than he used to be. Erin struggled to explain it. He was more distant, more forgetful, more . . . something. It was hard for most people to notice in short bursts of time with Derek, because he was adept at disguising his shifting moods. But those who came to stay with him, especially, began to see that something was not right.

Erin accused Derek of taking drugs—more than he was supposed to, at least—but he always pointed out that he was being prescribed them by team doctors and passing his drug tests. He complained constantly about the tests, about having someone come to his apartment periodically to collect a urine sample, and Erin never understood why it was such a big deal—it was merely the cost of having a past addiction problem, she thought.

There was more than that for Erin. Derek was increasingly hurt, and he seemed to be lazier than he used to be, and his mind seemed to be slipping, and his family did not like her, and none of this felt like the makings of a lifetime together. Finally, in New York in part to celebrate her friend's birthday in early December, Erin did it again: she told Derek it was over. This time, she said, it was for good. This time, she left New York and did not come back.

She never could have known that Derek's next hockey game would be his last.

THE FIGHT BEGAN with little of the customary pageantry. Derek and Matt Carkner were still skating down the ice in Ottawa, Derek gliding backward, when they threw the first punches.

There were about two minutes left in the first period. The score was 1–1. Derek had plowed into Ottawa's Jesse Winchester, a low-line center, and knocked him down with a late, hard check. Carkner, looking for retribution, chased Derek down.

"Uh-oh," one of the television announcers said, interrupting his partner. "Boogaard and Carkner. Two big men have dropped the gloves."

Carkner was a six-foot, four-inch, 237-pound tower of muscle from Winchester, Ontario. Two years older than Derek, he played junior in the Ontario Hockey League and, built like a model power forward of the era—a bit like Eric Lindros or Keith Tkachuk—was drafted by Montreal in the second round of the 1999 NHL draft. He and Derek first met in 2004, in an unmemorable fight in the American Hockey League, when Derek played for the Houston Aeros and Carkner for the Cleveland Barons. Unlike Derek, though, Carkner did not break into the NHL in a meaningful way for 10 years after he was drafted, a rookie enforcer for the Senators at age 28. He had something to prove.

The entire episode lasted 20 seconds. Carkner had given Derek a shove at mid-ice. By the time their momentum carried them to the top of the face-off circle, they were swinging wildly. Derek landed a strong right hand, but Carkner immediately responded with a punch to Derek's face just as Derek was swinging again.

Derek's nose was broken again. He turned his face away, his spirit shattered. Carkner hit Derek with a series of short left-hand jabs. The men clenched near the boards, grappling for dominance, pawing at one another's face. The crowd in Ottawa cheered.

Carkner had one arm around Derek's neck, the other under his left arm. He tried to lift Derek up, but it was like trying to uproot a sequoia. He took a quick breath and tried again. Two officials swirled within a few feet, helpless and unwilling to interrupt due to the unwritten codes of tradition. Carkner pulled Derek to one side, until all of Derek's body was off the ice. He rotated him over his hip. Derek landed hard on his right shoulder. The fans cheered his fall.

Carkner landed on top of Derek and was slow to get off of him. The two officials tried to pry them apart. Carkner knew Derek was

Derek and Matt Carkner exchange blows in the last fight of Derek's career.

hurt. On his way off the ice, he gestured to the Rangers' bench—
some Rangers said he flicked blood at them—and was penalized with
an extra 10-minute misconduct penalty.

Derek clambered uneasily to his feet, hunched over in pain. The
fight had occurred near the gate at the end of the Rangers' bench,
and Derek quickly stepped through it, past backup goalie Martin
Biron, and shuffled toward the dressing room.

"He landed a quick punch and I got lucky to land one real good
one, as well," Carkner said the next morning. "I didn't really know
I hit him flush like that. I noticed he kind of stopped fighting and I
took him down and landed on top. Obviously, if you land a punch
on a guy like that, it feels good. It feels good to take down a big man
like that. But he's definitely one of the toughest guys in the league,
and I'm fortunate to get the upper hand in that one."

The game took place at Ottawa's Scotiabank Place, about 20
minutes from where Len and Jody Boogaard lived. But they were
not at the game. Len had driven down to Ann Arbor, Michigan, to

watch Krysten play basketball for the University of Kansas. He spoke to Derek after the game on the phone. Derek told him his nose was still broken from the MacIntyre fight a few weeks before, and doctors had just set it again a few days earlier. The punch damaged it again.

And Derek had landed on his perpetually aching right shoulder, the one that had been surgically repaired about 18 months earlier. He also landed on the back of his head, though camera angles made it hard to see.

Derek was out indefinitely, the Rangers reported publicly, due to a shoulder injury.

"His shoulder's pretty sore," Tortorella told reporters several days after the game. "He won't even be in the building. It's not a day-to-day thing, it's recurring."

The issue was not Derek's shoulder. The Rangers had privately sent Derek to see a neurologist the day after the game.

"Mr. Boogaard suffered moderate blunt facial/head trauma without loss of consciousness," New York neurologist Dr. Claude Macaluso wrote after an examination of Derek that included a magnetic-resonance exam. "The constellation of symptoms following the injury, even in the absence of loss of alteration of consciousness, qualify as a cerebral concussion."

The report noted that Derek "suffered nasal fractures on several occasions, the last time as recently as three weeks ago," a reference to the broken nose at the hands of MacIntyre.

Derek soon told a story to friends about a doctor asking him his history of concussions. Derek had no idea how many he has suffered. A few, probably. The doctor framed the question differently. How many times, would you say, have you been struck in the head, and everything went dark, if only for a moment? Five? Ten?

No one had ever defined a concussion that way to Derek. He laughed.

"Try hundreds," he said.

. . .

THE SYMPTOMS IN his head not only persisted, they worsened. Within days, Derek displayed all the signs of post-concussion syndrome. He complained about bright lights and loud noises. He kept the blinds in his apartment closed, obscuring the million-dollar views. He wore sunglasses when he left the apartment, even at night. He could not ride in cars or taxis, because the motion made him queasy. At times, he struggled to form coherent thoughts and speak in sensible sentences.

Still, the Rangers listed Derek out "indefinitely" with a shoulder injury. It was nearly two weeks before the Rangers publicly acknowledged that Derek had sustained a concussion and was feeling its aftereffects. Tortorella said Derek's problems "started off" with his shoulder injury, and Derek now had "some problems" "with headaches and stuff like that." The news of a concussion became a short notebook item in news reports.

"With Derek Boogaard continuing to experience headaches that started during his rehab from a shoulder injury suffered in a fight with Ottawa's Matt Carkner on Dec. 9, the Rangers are sending the enforcer to see a neurologist," the New York *Daily News* reported on December 23—13 days after he had been fully diagnosed by a neurologist.

But even the Rangers did not know what else had happened on December 10, the day Derek returned to New York from Ottawa for further examination. Derek received a phone call from a man on Long Island. The two exchanged dozens of text messages. The man told Derek that he could get him prescription painkillers. And on December 12, Derek did something he rarely ever did: he withdrew $700 from an ATM. It was telling, if only anyone had known. Derek rarely carried cash, and was known among his friends for his flippant use of his credit card. He would buy a bag of chips at a convenience store and put the $2 sum on his American Express gold card.

Then Derek went to another ATM and withdrew $700 more. Then he did it again. Over the next several months, it became a pattern—ATM withdrawals on his Wells Fargo bank account timed with charges for tolls for bridges, tunnels, and roads between Manhattan and Long Island. Sometimes he stopped to grab something to eat or fill his car with gas. The withdrawals and charges created a secret financial footprint that indicated when Derek bought drugs.

The Rangers and the substance abuse program remained focused on Derek's acquisition of pills from prescriptions written by team doctors. Weissman contacted Derek on December 14, five days after his injury, to check on him. Derek complained of "chronic insomnia," the doctor wrote in his notes.

"At a previous conversation with Dr. Lewis from the NHL substance abuse program we suggested use of trazadone 25 mh h.s. the patient had a prior history of abuse Ambien CR," Weissman noted. The Rangers had not given Derek Ambien all season, and program doctors were careful not to recommend it now.

Derek instead would be given Restoril, a different sedative. "Limited quantities will be given to the player and it will be dispensed directly from the team trainer," Weissman wrote.

He also noted another request from Derek: Xanax. Derek asked to have some for when he traveled on airplanes. Weissman wrote in his notes that he discussed the request with the team trainer and with Dr. David Lewis of the league's substance abuse program. Derek had tested positive for Xanax twice already in December, despite there being no record of it being prescribed by team doctors. If Lewis or Weissman had seen Derek's positive drug tests for Xanax, it did not stop them from prescribing it to Derek now. Weissman wrote a prescription for 20 pills.

Derek was out of the lineup indefinitely. He was told by the

Rangers to hibernate, essentially, the recommended method for recovery from post-concussive symptoms. But the symptoms came and went more than Derek let on. At 6 in the morning on December 24, he flew to Minnesota for Christmas, arriving shortly after 8. At 9:46 A.M., his cell phone records showed, he sent the first of four text messages to Dan Peterson, a doctor for Derek's former team, the Wild.

Later that day, Derek picked up a prescription at a Minneapolis Walgreens for 30 zolpidem—Ambien. Peterson was listed as the prescribing doctor.

IT WAS CHRISTMAS EVE, and Derek had a 5 o'clock appointment scheduled with Pat O'Brien, the Minneapolis chiropractor who had done work on him when he played for the Wild. Nobody made Derek feel better than Dr. Pat, as he was known. But Derek did not show up.

O'Brien wondered if he had missed his flight, because Derek had never missed an appointment and had made a special request to be seen on Christmas Eve. O'Brien called Derek and sent a text message. Derek did not respond. O'Brien was hurt and disappointed. Derek, of all people, he thought.

Derek was with a woman named Laurie whom he had met a couple of years earlier when he sat courtside at a Minnesota Timberwolves basketball game. He had asked a server to deliver his name and telephone number to her. Someone had to explain to Laurie who Derek Boogaard was. They went to Sneaky Pete's after the game, where Laurie was smitten by Derek's boyish kindness—a gentle man and a gentleman. But Derek was still involved with Erin, and Laurie moved out of state for work.

But after Derek moved to New York, he heard that Laurie was back in Minneapolis, and he called her before he came for Christmas. He landed at the airport, and the two met at the Mall of America. Laurie found Derek standing there, wearing a big grin and a Russian-style fur hat he had bought. Outside, it was below freezing, and the forecast for Christmas the next day called for a high temperature below 20 degrees Fahrenheit.

Derek checked in at the Hotel Ivy, a luxury hotel in downtown Minneapolis, and ate dinner at Seven, an upscale steakhouse and sushi bar, on Hennepin Avenue at Seventh Street. It was where he had eaten his last big meal before leaving for New York in September, nearly four months earlier, and had run up a $243.59 bill.

Derek spent Christmas Day at Sneaky Pete's. He paid a tab—his own and that of many other people, apparently—of $840.

He returned to New York early on December 26. Before he left, though, Derek withdrew $500 from an ATM. Upon landing, he made more withdrawals.

The Rangers trainer made a note in the log that day—"Complained of headache today"—and wrote that Derek "continued rest/follow-up with Dr. Macaluso," the New York neurologist who had been analyzing Derek since his concussion on December 9. On December 28, Macaluso's thorough examination of Derek noted "post-concussive syndrome, mild but with persistent symptoms." He also wrote that Derek had "persistently blurred vision from left eye" and a "nasal fracture." He advised Derek to use Breathe Right nasal strips, Nasonex spray, and Simply Saline to aid the difficulty of breathing through his nose, and referred him to an ophthalmologist to assess Derek's complaint about "blurred vision from the left eye."

An ophthalmologist later noted "there is no evidence of any ocular trauma."

On January 4, Derek made nine ATM withdrawals, for thousands of dollars. Five of them were in Manhattan. The other four were in and around Huntington, New York, the Long Island town where Derek often drove to exchange cash for prescription painkillers, returning to Manhattan with them in a Ziploc bag.

On January 6, Derek filled a prescription for five pills of Ambien from Weissman, the Rangers' team doctor who, weeks earlier, had declined Derek's request for Ambien after consulting with the league's substance abuse program. Weissman prescribed Ambien to Derek at least seven more times, a total of 179 pills through early April, according to pharmacy records.

On January 7, the urine collector arrived at Derek's apartment. Nearly a week later, the result from the screening laboratory of Quest Diagnostics in Santa Ana, California, was returned. Derek tested positive for oxymorphone, an opioid known under the brand name Opana. The result could not have been a surprise to Lewis and Shaw, the substance-abuse administrators. They were in regular contact with Derek, and Lewis wrote in his notes on January 10 that Derek had made an admission. "DB reports buying oxycodone from person in MN," Lewis wrote. "Refused intervention or therapy. Refuse to fly to CA for treatment. Doesn't want to leave apartment."

Derek's behavior was increasingly erratic, and his good-natured pleas for visitors became incessant. He called some friends 10 or more times a day. During the month of January, he exchanged about 10,000 text messages, and his cell-phone bill consumed 167 pages. And, to his closest friends—including the men, from Jeremy Clark in Minnesota to his half-brother, Curtis, in Alberta—Derek began signing off in a way he never had before: *I love you.*

He sometimes told friends that his head hurt. Over several weeks, when Laurie and Derek spoke on the phone, Derek sometimes groaned and cried, saying his head hurt so badly. From a thousand miles away, she screamed at him, worried that he was having an aneurysm or something.

His behavior was considered symptomatic of the recent concussions. But there probably was some lingering effect of his breakup with Erin and the loneliness of New York, and the frustration that he was too hurt to play hockey. That's what everyone thought—Derek is lonely and bored—but they had their own lives to attend to. They had come at the beginning of the season, to watch Derek play and see New York. He wasn't playing now, and most couldn't drop everything and come just to keep Derek company.

Derek will be all right, they thought. It's Derek.

Rob Nelson, Derek's financial advisor, and Tobin Wright, Derek's manager in Minneapolis, each visited for a few days in January. They found Derek in his apartment, looking as if he had not showered in days, his hair matted and his face unshaven. Fast-food packages littered the apartment. Blinds were closed.

But Derek, typically, did not want to burden others with his problems. He never disclosed his ongoing reliance on pills, and few connected his issues to drugs. Derek merely wanted someone around. Nelson assumed Derek's fragile emotional state stemmed from the latest concussions, plus his general unhappiness in New York. And when he left to return to Minnesota, Nelson felt that he had helped improve Derek's mood and outlook. Wright, who had confronted Derek in Minneapolis on the eve of his trip to rehabilitation, was more skeptical. He placed calls to Salcer and to Derek's parents. Something is not right, he said.

Len Boogaard had been on the receiving end of some of Derek's calls. When Len was not home, Derek talked to Jody, his stepmother. Years before, Derek had been the first of the Boogaard children to accept their stepmother into their lives, and their relationship remained close. Derek told Jody he wished Len could come and visit. Just ask him, Jody told Derek. You know he would.

Derek got Len on the phone. Dad, he said, I want you to come stay with me. Can you?

· · ·

LEN ARRIVED IN New York on January 11. His son looked horrible. The apartment was a mess. It was a surprise to Len, who had never seen the worst of Derek's problems. When Derek had gone to rehabilitation 18 months earlier, it was during the Wild's training camp; Len was far away. When Aaron called the previous fall to tell his father about Derek's descent back into the drugs, it was weeks after the episode at the airport.

Now Derek was in the throes of something real, calling out for help but still trying to conceal the problems. He wanted his father there, but he never explained why. It wasn't his style. And Len did not always push Derek to open up. Derek hated to be prodded with questions. It made him feel doubted or untrusted, and it often spun him into a mood of irritability and sulkiness. Len, like others close to Derek, knew what kinds of things upset him, and those things were best avoided.

But Len did not like what he saw. Derek was irritable and complacent. He talked badly about the Rangers and complained about bright lights. The mood was dark. Derek slept for long stretches of daylight hours. He never opened the blinds. He complained of headaches. A dried, dying Christmas tree still stood in the corner. Len offered to take it out of the apartment, but Derek insisted. It left a trail of brown needles. When Derek cleaned them up, he sweated profusely and stopped to throw up.

The concussion, Len thought.

But Derek also complained about the drug testing. It was a Tuesday, and Derek told his father that the urine collector was coming on Friday morning. Len realized that the drug tests were not "random."

Len saw a prescription bottle on the bathroom counter. Weissman had prescribed 14 Ambien pills the day before, the label showed. There were 10 left.

Salcer, Derek's agent, was in New York, too, where he had been raised and where his mother still lived, on Manhattan's Upper East

Side. Marian Gaborik had called Salcer in California and told him that he was worried about Derek, that he seemed "out of it." Salcer flew across the country. He and Len accompanied Derek to Madison Square Garden that night to watch the Rangers play Montreal.

When Derek stepped out of earshot, Len told Salcer about the Ambien on the bathroom counter. What's that about? Derek's not supposed to have Ambien; it had helped send Derek to rehabilitation in the first place. Salcer said he would report it to the substance abuse program.

But Salcer had information to relay to Len, too. He told Len about Derek not showing up for the pre–training camp workout with Gaborik back in September. He told him about the Rangers' November game against the Wild in Saint Paul, when Derek received a warm ovation from the crowd and Brent Burns, one of Derek's best friends on the Wild, asked him to come over to the dressing room after the game to meet a special guest from the military—the type of meeting that Derek had always enjoyed. Gaborik, Salcer said, came from the Rangers' locker room, but Derek never showed up. He had left with friends for Sneaky Pete's. Burns was upset.

And just the day before, Salcer told Len, he had invited Derek over to his mother's apartment on East 72nd Street. Derek came, but Salcer noticed immediately that he wasn't himself—slurring his words, acting loopy, far from his cheerful self. Salcer wondered if Derek was drunk, high, or something else.

Salcer escorted Derek on a walk through Central Park. Derek began to cry, talking about his loneliness and his depression, about the fits of fogginess that he could not shake from his head. Whatever spell Derek was under seemed to wear off with time, Salcer told Len, but not before he collapsed onto a park bench, weeping uncontrollably.

Once Derek had regained his composure, Salcer said, he told Derek he would have him talk to other clients of his who had battled concussions. Derek then talked about joining the military someday, maybe going to Afghanistan to root out bad guys. On Madison Avenue, Derek stopped at the boutique of Officine Panerai, famous for the stylish dive watches they made for the Italian navy in World War II. Many Panerai watches cost well more than $10,000. Derek wanted one.

"You can spend your money how you want, Derek," Salcer said, "but I think you need to get yourself right first."

Len absorbed what Salcer told him. The next morning, Len noted that six more Ambien pills were gone; there were four left.

Len and Salcer sat Derek down. They saw it as an intervention, and they told Derek they wanted to help. In the dimness of the apartment, New York's afternoon light blocked by the blinds that Derek insisted stay closed, Derek slowly opened up.

He was lonely. He ached for Erin. He felt detached from the Rangers. He felt debilitated by the concussions and frustrated by the drug tests. He felt helpless. He spilled all his problems and bled all his emotions.

Len walked Derek through all that he had overcome to get where he was. He reminded his son of the grade-school teacher who stuck him in the closet. He told him about the parents that he overheard saying that they didn't want Derek on the hockey team. He recalled the kids who picked on him and the coaches who never gave him a chance. They talked about Derek's struggles in Prince George, and how hard he had worked to get drafted into the NHL, and how much he had devoted himself in the minor leagues to make the Wild. They talked about the admiration that Derek had earned from his teammates and legions of fans. They talked about how Derek had overcome his addictions in rehabilitation with his reputation intact and become a prized free agent, signed by one of the league's premier franchises.

The Rangers want you, Len and Salcer told Derek. That is why they gave you a four-year contract worth millions of dollars. And that is why they are giving you the best care, to get you back on the ice so that you can keep doing what you do best. Salcer wanted Derek to understand just how bright his future was, if he was willing to commit himself to staying straight and focused. And Len wanted Derek to remember, always, how far he had come.

For Christmas, Joanne had compiled years' worth of family photographs and created a video album that she gave to her children. The three men sat in Derek's dim apartment, high above New York City, and watched Derek's life unfold in warm images. The photographs showed Derek with his parents and his siblings, during all the happy stages of growing up and deep into the NHL.

Derek had been handed more than he could have imagined, and it was nothing like he had dreamed. And that was the first time that the toughest man in hockey clung hard to his father and sobbed uncontrollably in his arms.

10

E ARLY ON THE JANUARY morning that Len was to fly home to Ottawa after three days in New York, he heard a knock at the door of Derek's apartment. Len was still in bed, and Derek answered. Len heard some indecipherable small talk, and when he rose a short time later, he spotted a small cup and a stick in the garbage. It was the drug test, on schedule, just as Derek had said three days earlier.

Once home in Ottawa, Len received an e-mail message from Ron Salcer, Derek's agent, who wrote that he had spoken to Brian Shaw, one of the co-founders of the NHL/NHLPA Substance Abuse Program. Dan Cronin, the program's lead counselor, was spending the day in New York with Derek.

"He is in experienced hands and we can only hope for the best," Salcer wrote.

The next day, Derek had an appointment with Dr. Macaluso, the neurologist. He prescribed 30 pills of Ambien, records showed. A week later, Dr. Weissman of the Rangers prescribed more Ambien and more Xanax.

Yet the next three drug tests administered to Derek, through most of February, came back negative.

It was up to the administrators of the substance abuse program to determine which drugs should be tested for through the urine samples. For a long time, the test did not search for Ambien, although that was one of the drugs that Derek abused on his way to rehabilitation in 2009.

It was unclear whether Derek was cheating the drug testing system, but such attempts were not uncommon. Brantt Myhres had been in more than 50 NHL fights and violated the substance abuse policy so many times that he received a lifetime ban from the league. His addictions to alcohol and cocaine led him to spend eight months in rehabilitation in 2008.

Myhres said that he sometimes used hockey tickets to befriend specimen collectors, who would then not follow him to the bathroom or would report that he was not home. He stored clean urine and learned to heat it quickly under water to get it to the correct temperature before handing it over. One collector, Myhres said, confided that he only wanted to catch people whose drug use could prove lethal to others—pilots, drivers, and the like. Not athletes.

Derek not only seemed to know ahead of time when the collector was coming to retrieve a sample, but he often managed to avoid the tests for several days. Salcer received calls from the substance abuse program reporting that Derek was being evasive. And Derek told friends that he had learned how to beat the testing system from others in rehabilitation, like prisoners in jail who learn to be better criminals.

By midseason, Derek was a mere afterthought to the Rangers' push toward the playoffs. The Rangers were frustrated and puzzled by his lethargy—concussions rarely kept players out of action for so many weeks—and public updates on his health were rare. When Derek was spotted by reporters at the rink, he referred questions about his health to team management, an unusual deflection from someone usually friendly toward the media.

On the January day that Len arrived in New York at Derek's

request, newspaper reports included a pessimistic and cryptic diagnosis for Derek from Coach Tortorella.

"We're trying to stimulate him and trying to get him moving around," Tortorella said. "But he still doesn't feel well."

Asked if Derek would be ready to play by the end of the season, Tortorella hesitated.

"I can't . . . we'll have to see what happens," he replied. "It's not close."

The relationship between Derek and the Rangers was distant. Derek came to home games, usually watching from the press box, but complained that the bright lights and dizzying movement and loud noises sometimes were too much to bear. He was excused from most practices, which were held a 30-minute drive north of the city in suburban Westchester County.

The remedy for concussions was time, and the Rangers wanted Derek to rest. They tracked him mostly through reports from doctor visits and trainers. ("Remaining at home—still complains of headaches," one recorded on January 18.) Worried about his conditioning and diet, the Rangers delivered healthy food to the apartment. It piled up on the counter or went straight to the trash.

Derek asked if he could travel with the team on road trips, even though he was not playing. He was told no. He began to see it as an insult—the team telling him to keep his distance.

He still might have been better connected to life back in Minnesota. The weekend after Len left New York, before Derek spent the day with Cronin, another visitor arrived: a young woman named Ashley, whom Derek had met at Sneaky Pete's. He bought her a last-minute flight to visit him for a couple of days.

The NHL All-Star Game was on January 30, 2011, in Raleigh, North Carolina. The Rangers played a home game on January 25, then had a week before their next game. Derek asked the Rangers if he could fly to Minnesota during the break, in part to get treatment from O'Brien, the chiropractor whom Derek had used extensively when with the Wild. The Rangers approved. The day before he left, Derek received the Xanax and Ambien prescriptions from Dr. Weissman, records showed. He also withdrew $1,700 in two ATM transactions.

Derek showed up to one appointment at O'Brien's office wearing his Russian fur hat, with the tall front brim and floppy earflaps. O'Brien and his assistant thought it was hilarious.

"It's really warm," Derek said. "You should get one of these."

O'Brien saw Derek several times, for an hour or so each time. And though he never received an explanation for the Christmas Eve brush-off, O'Brien never felt that anything was amiss with Derek.

Derek stayed at the Hotel Ivy in downtown Minneapolis from January 26 to February 6. His bill came to more than $6,200. Laurie, the woman with whom Derek reconnected during his Christmastime trip to Minnesota, was a frequent companion. Unaware of Derek's addiction problems, past or present, she saw pill bottles in the hotel room. On February 2, records showed, Derek picked up a prescription for 30 Ambien pills at a Minneapolis Walgreens, prescribed by Peterson, a Wild team doctor.

"You having trouble sleeping?" she asked Derek.

"Yeah," he said. "But don't tell anybody I'm taking them."

The two weeks in Minnesota were spent getting treatment and visiting familiar haunts. On his first night, Derek spent $648.42 at Manny's Steakhouse. He returned twice more in the next three days. On another day, he spent $68.16 at McDonald's. Sneaky Pete's was a regular stop. Derek charged anywhere from $13 to more than $200 on his credit card there.

There were shopping excursions—$646.50 at Nordstrom's, for example—that were all part of Derek's extended spending spree. He had always spent money loosely, but things had grown out of control in the past year, which is why he now had a financial advisor overseeing his budget. More and more in New York, Derek spent huge sums on spur-of-the-moment merchandise, from a big-screen television at Best Buy to $10,061 from a gun web site. In March, he spent nearly $1,000 to add to the growing collection of Buddhas that he displayed in his apartment. He spent hundreds of dollars on night-vision goggles.

"Retail therapy," Derek joked with old friends when they questioned his erratic buying behavior.

Derek was feeling better, and it seemed that he was serious about working his way back to hockey. Family and friends reported that Derek seemed happier than he had been in months. On February 16, New York newspapers reported that he had resumed light workouts, mostly on stationary bikes. Internal reports from team trainers noted few problems.

Salcer sent Len Boogaard e-mails on February 20.

"I have been talking with Derek these past couple of weeks and have noted a marked change in his attitude/demeanor, all for the better," Salcer wrote. "It is somewhat reminiscent of his former self."

He noted that Derek had been going to the rink every day and was "interacting with teammates. We are not out of the woods yet but certainly the signs are better."

Len and Joanne each noticed the same thing when they spoke to Derek on the phone. Again, maybe the worst was past.

When Derek spoke to reporters in early March, he sounded optimistic about playing again before the playoffs. He told them the concussion he had suffered at the hands of Carkner was the first of his career, and that he was "symptom-free, for the most part." He categorized his season as "very disappointing," and "not the year I wanted to have," especially in the first year of a contract.

The day before, Derek had handed over a urine sample for drug testing. A few days later, about the time that the test came back positive for prescription painkillers, Derek was seen by a friend crushing Ambien pills and snorting them.

ON MARCH 3, 2011, the *New York Times* published a story about the examination of Bob Probert's exhumed brain. Probert had been an inspiration to many young hockey enforcers, including Derek, who chose No. 24 in Minnesota in Probert's honor. Probert had 245 fights in 16 NHL seasons, from 1985 to 2002. A *Hockey News* poll in 2007 named him the greatest enforcer in history.

Probert died of heart failure in the summer of 2010, at age 45. Shortly before his death, he and his wife, Dani, watched a news program about chronic traumatic encephalopathy, or CTE, the degenerative brain disease that scientists believed was caused by repeated blows to the head. CTE could only be diagnosed posthumously, through careful examination of brain tissue. But more than 20 former National Football League players had been diagnosed with it.

"I remember joking with him, 'Wouldn't your brain make a nice specimen?'" Dani Probert told *Times* reporter Alan Schwarz. "He started questioning whether he would have it himself. He told me that he wanted to donate his brain to the research when he died."

Hockey players routinely received potentially damaging hits to the head, most almost instantly dismissed as inconsequential. They came from the shoulders and elbows of opponents, from collisions with the glass and boards that surrounded the rink, maybe the occasional smack of a puck or an inadvertent high stick. Most of those could not be avoided.

But one type of blow could be prevented, if the NHL and other hockey leagues deemed it enough of a safety issue to legislate it out of the game: the blow to the head from the fist of an opponent.

"Hockey's enduring tolerance for and celebration of fighting will almost certainly be tested anew now that Probert, more pugilist than playmaker, has become the first contemporary hockey player to show C.T.E. after death," Schwarz wrote in the front-page story.

Until Probert's brain was examined, the only other hockey player known to have had CTE was Reggie Fleming. But he was a rough-and-tumble player from the 1960s, an era long before helmets were in wide use. His brain was examined after he died in 2009 at age 73.

Probert's litany of personal problems were acknowledged in the story—his long trouble with alcohol, his arrest for cocaine possession, his police record for bar fights and assaults on officers. But the story also listed the symptoms of CTE, usually seen only in the final years of life, understood only with postmortem hindsight: "drug abuse, impulse control and impaired memory."

Back home in Ottawa, Len Boogaard read the story, and it all hit him like a punch to the gut. Probert sounded a lot like Derek. Derek, too, was a hockey fighter who absorbed more blows than he remembered. He became addicted to drugs, including painkillers. He became impulsive and moody, facing bouts of depression. And his memory seemed to be short-circuiting.

What could we have been thinking? Len wondered. It was not the hands, Len realized, that he should have worried about with Derek all those years. It was the head.

AMONG THE 13,724 text messages that Derek sent and received from mid-February to mid-March, detailed in a monthly cell-phone bill that consumed 244 pages, were notes to Todd Fedoruk.

Fedoruk was 32, recently retired from hockey, living with his family in the suburbs of Philadelphia, about 100 miles from New York. He and his wife, Theresa, figured that Derek was lonely, living in a strange city, and sitting out with an injury. Derek said in a text message that the team didn't want him around. Fedoruk replied that he and Theresa would come to New York to see him.

No, Derek said, I'll come down there.

He arrived one morning while Fedoruk was in the garage, doing some woodwork, a postretirement hobby. The garage door was open, and Fedoruk heard Derek arrive and saw him emerge from his Audi with a big Derek smile and a hug for the man whose career he had almost ended with one crushing right hand.

Derek came inside and helped himself to slices of leftover pizza in the refrigerator. He played with the three Fedoruk children, aged seven, five, and just a few months. The oldest, Luke, remembered the Boogeyman from Minnesota—or, at least, the stories often told about his father's giant friend. The older children climbed on Derek as if he were a piece of playground equipment, and Derek laughed his *heh-heh-heh* laugh.

Derek spent hours in the basement, where he and Luke played Guitar Hero on the video-game console. Fedoruk recorded them with his phone. On the toy electric guitar, Derek tried to keep pace with classic rock songs. He had to get this game, he said. His brothers would love it.

Time ticked through the late afternoon, and Derek was in no hurry to return to New York. It occurred to the Fedoruks just what it was that Derek wanted: time out of the city, away from the concrete and the crowds, in the vast expanses of countryside and subdivisions. He wanted to be in a home filled with voices and laughter.

Derek had always felt comfortable around Fedoruk. Maybe it was their similar childhoods and lives as junior hockey players in Regina and western Canada. Maybe it was the way that Fedoruk so easily forgave Derek for shattering his face in the NHL. Maybe it was the late-night conversations on the road as teammates. Or maybe it was that Fedoruk understood the pain as much as anyone else. Probably all of those.

Fedoruk had played his last NHL game less than a year earlier, with the Tampa Bay Lightning, on the last day of the 2009–10 season. Two nights earlier, in a home game against the Ottawa Senators, Fedoruk had briefly fought Matt Carkner—the same man who then beat Derek in December, sending him off with a concussion and a separated shoulder. Carkner was much bigger than Fedoruk, but they exchanged a few punches as the play moved up the ice without them. By the time the whistles blew and the cameras captured them, the two had wrestled each other down.

Fedoruk drank excessively the next night. He said he spent the early-morning hours in a stupor, wandering the streets of Tampa and the sidewalk of Bayshore Boulevard, sometimes called the world's longest continuous sidewalk, stretching nearly five uninterrupted miles.

When the Lightning took the ice that night in the season finale against Florida, Fedoruk still felt unsteady. On one play, he slipped behind the net and slid into the boards. He was not hurt, but he pretended to be, giving him an excuse to leave the game and not return. He later checked himself into rehabilitation—not to save his hockey career, but to save his marriage and his family, he said.

And now here he was, surrounded by the warmth of his wife and their three children, living inside the glow of a gleaming home. For Derek, it must have seemed perfect.

Fedoruk knew about Derek's first time in rehabilitation, at the start of the season before, Derek's last with the Wild. Derek had told him about it, and Fedoruk was struck at the time with one impression: He'll be back. He could tell by how Derek responded to Fedoruk's question about how it went.

"*Pfft*," Derek said. "I've got nothing in common with those people."

Eighteen months later, Fedoruk searched for signs of trouble. He studied Derek's eyes, looking for pupils the size of pinholes or lids that hung at mismatched levels. He listened to Derek's speech and searched for the hidden meaning behind the words he used.

Throughout the day, Fedoruk detected loneliness, and he knew that Derek was in chronic pain, but no other flags were raised in the recesses of Fedoruk's mind. Derek seemed like his usual self—happy and chatty, not medicated, eager to be part of a group.

Todd and Theresa had plans for dinner in Philadelphia, and they asked Derek if he wanted to come, too. He did. They drove from their neighborhood of big brick houses and large lawns, across the Delaware River and into the city. Derek ordered a Jack Daniels and Coke and had chocolate cake for dessert.

While waiting for the valet to bring the car after dinner, out of earshot of Fedoruk, Derek turned to Theresa and told her how much he missed his friend and former teammate. He apologized for the punch that changed everything more than four years earlier. She made Derek make a promise: If Todd comes back to hockey, Derek, you will not fight him.

Derek promised.

The Fedoruks asked if Derek wanted to spend the night, but he declined, saying he was just starting to work out with the Rangers again and had to get back for training in the morning. It was after Derek left, driving back up the New Jersey Turnpike on the 90-minute trip to Manhattan, that Theresa turned to her husband.

Something's not right with Derek, she said. Something's off.

DEREK DROVE FAST, his GPS counting down the minutes to his arrival. Devin Wilson, sitting in the passenger seat of the Audi as it sped through the Queens-Midtown Tunnel and onto the Long Island Expressway, begged him to slow down.

They had spent the weekend at Derek's apartment, Derek's mood shifting like a pendulum. One minute, he complained about headaches and wanted to do nothing but sit on the couch, in the dark. For months, Wilson had been a regular visitor at Derek's apartment, and he had never seen the blinds open. Then Derek would be up, wanting to go to a Duane Reade drugstore for candy or to Best Buy to shop. He was like a kid again, big and energetic and silly, just like the teenager Wilson remembered as a teammate with the Prince George Cougars a decade earlier: kind, non-threatening, quick to laugh. The moods often swung with the painkillers that Derek consumed, and Wilson saw Derek swallow them by the handful.

Like Derek, Wilson was from Regina. He spent four seasons with Prince George, a steady defenseman with a penchant for parties. His hockey career faded after a few minor-league seasons, and he drifted between jobs. In the fall of 2010, he arrived in New York, just as Derek did, with a sales position with the New York Islanders.

Derek and Wilson had not been great friends. They had occasionally crossed paths in Regina during summers after their days in Prince George. But they reconnected at a Rangers game against the Islanders in the fall, and their relationship grew through the winter. By spring, no one spent more time with Derek than Wilson. They planned to move into a different apartment together in Manhattan during the summer.

During the season, though, Wilson still lived on the south shore of Long Island, in Long Beach, a few streets on a narrow, low-lying barrier island. Derek liked it there. He liked going to the beach bars, which reminded him of some of the places he went during the summers in Los Angeles. People came to know who Derek was, and they welcomed him without smothering him. Derek had not had that since he left Minneapolis—the affection of strangers glad to have his company.

Usually, though, Wilson came to Manhattan to stay with Derek.

Derek implored him to come, playfully telling him to "bring girls," and Wilson would arrive to find Derek sitting in the dark. More times than not, they stayed in the apartment, playing video games and filling the long silences with bursts of conversation.

Derek's moods swung with little notice, though, and Wilson's suggestions for things to do would be dismissed because Derek did not feel well, only to be happily overridden by a sudden idea. And, sometimes with little warning, Derek would tell Wilson he needed to leave at that moment to take him back home to Long Island. And they would get in the Audi and speed east across Manhattan and the East River and into Queens, usually stopping at several ATMs along the way. Derek needed cash, and he usually withdrew between $3,000 and $4,000, pulling out the maximum amount the machine would allow before moving on to another.

Once, when a machine denied his withdrawal, Derek entered the bank and made an uncomfortable scene, unable to understand why tellers could not accept his credit card to withdraw cash from his account. Wilson pulled him out of the bank.

Wilson assumed that Derek was getting some pills from team doctors. But he knew that Derek was spending several thousands of dollars a month on prescription drugs bought off the street from at least one supplier.

Derek called the man "The Dude," Wilson said, and he was a sharp-dressed man about their age. Sometimes Derek would drop off Wilson at home and go on his own, but Wilson accompanied Derek now and again. They met the man in a parking lot in Huntington, a sprawling Long Island suburb. At least once, they went to a house. In exchange for the cash he had withdrawn, Derek was handed a Ziploc bag filled with colorful pills. He took them back to his apartment and spent hours organizing them by type and dosage. He placed them in pill organizers and empty bottles from old prescriptions.

And as Easter approached, Derek began a little ritual: he sorted the pills in pastel-colored plastic eggs, the kind used to hold candy or coins for children. He often carried one in a pocket when he left home for a few hours, a dose for when he needed it, no matter where he might be. And he hid the others around the apartment, a one-man game of hide and seek.

ON MONDAY, FEBRUARY 28, the Rangers' trainer noted that Derek had called late on Saturday night, complaining of "severe pain behind his eyes and vomiting." Derek had done some skating and light work with weights on Friday and Saturday without any reported problems. On Sunday, when the Rangers had an afternoon game at Madison Square Garden, records showed that Derek picked up 30 Ambien, prescribed by Weissman, the Rangers' team doctor. He also drove to Long Island, withdrawing $1,600 in cash at two ATMs on the way.

On Tuesday, March 2, Derek provided a urine sample for a drug test. It came back a week later showing a positive result for hydromorphone—a narcotic pain reliever often sold under the brand name Dilaudid. Among its purported effects was a sense of euphoria and stress relief.

Jeremy Clark, Derek's good friend and trainer from Minnesota, arrived on March 3.

The Rangers were on the road that day, without Derek, and the two friends wandered around Manhattan, shopping and eating. Derek charged $237.61 at Caviar Russe, a restaurant on Madison Avenue. He spent $504.16 at Davidoff of Geneva, a high-end cigar store. At some point, he also retrieved $2,700 from his bank account through ATMs.

Derek and Clark went to a movie that afternoon. And they stopped at a Walgreens drugstore on 57th Street, on the same block as Derek's apartment. There was confusion about a prescription, and after a discussion with the pharmacist, Derek made several calls on his cell phone to Weissman, records showed. Derek left with 30 pills of Ambien.

Clark did not think it was strange. He had close ties to many hockey players, and he knew that Ambien was commonly used. And in this case, it was being prescribed by a team doctor. It was only strange when Clark found that Derek crushed the pills and snorted them.

Most thought that Derek was on the mend. On March 15, the day after another trip to Long Island that followed the withdrawal of $3,200, Derek skated with teammates for the first time since the concussion in December. A few days later, Michael Russo of the *Star-Tribune* in Minneapolis wrote an item about Derek for the newspaper.

"Former Wild enforcer Derek Boogaard was so sensitive to sunlight during the early portion of the concussion that still keeps him out of the Rangers lineup, that he stayed in his Manhattan apartment for three weeks at one point," Russo wrote. "He started to get depressed, go stir crazy. 'That's why when [Marian Gaborik] got his concussion this year, I'd call him every day and say, 'I want you to call me and we'll go for lunch and we'll do something for at least an hour just so you get out of your apartment,' Boogaard said."

Through the spring, Derek privately rooted for the Rangers to lose. The team spent much of the season outside the eighth and final playoff spot in the Eastern Conference, and Derek thought that if the Rangers missed the postseason, they might fire the coach, John Tortorella. That is what he hoped. He was optimistic that a new season, with a new coach, would bring him a new start.

Derek tracked all the playoff scenarios, figuring out how many wins and losses, combined with wins and losses of other teams, would keep the Rangers from the playoffs or allow them in. Hopes were dashed when the Rangers went on a hot streak in the middle of March, going 8–1–1 in one 10-game stretch.

Derek flew Laurie in from Minneapolis on March 18. They had spent time together at Christmas, and again during his two weeks in Minneapolis over the All-Star break, and Derek had tried to persuade her to move to New York with him. She demurred, but was falling for Derek's kind, gentle, giving ways.

She barely recognized him this time. The first signal arrived before she did, when she worried about her medication for a respiratory infection. Derek wanted Laurie to bring nothing but a carry-on bag, but she worried that her liquid cough medicine with codeine would be confiscated. He told her to leave it behind.

"I can get you whatever you need," he wrote in a text message. "Whatever you need I can get from the trainers."

When she arrived, he gave her a small Ziploc bag with six or eight oval pills in them. Derek told her that they were Vicodin, a painkiller that no Rangers team doctor had prescribed, according to medical records. Laurie took one that night.

The next day, Derek napped through the afternoon in the dark apartment. He woke up screaming, then jumped to his feet, shaking. Laurie could not tell if he was awake or asleep.

"I'm scared," he said. "Scared about what they'll make me do."

"Who?" she asked.

"The trainers," Derek replied.

He fell back to sleep. But Laurie was shaken. She wondered how a grown man, a man that size, could wake up screaming in terror.

They went out that night with Devin Wilson and another woman. Derek paid the $575.24 bill at Quality Meats, a steakhouse on 58th Street, a block south of Central Park. At bedtime that night, Laurie took a second Vicodin. When she awoke, she spotted the baggie on the kitchen counter. Most of the pills were still there. A bit later in the morning, the baggie was in the bathroom and the last pills were gone.

Breakfast at a nearby restaurant was washed down with Bloody

Marys and mimosas, followed by stops at several bars in midtown Manhattan.

Laurie headed home to Minnesota, confused by the weekend. Derek had always been so happy, so bubbly, so outgoing, she thought. Now he was none of those. He was erratic.

The results from Derek's next test came back positive for hydrocodone and hydromorphone. The next day, he withdrew $4,000 from ATMs. His next drug test revealed hydromorphone. Another test, five days later, showed positive for hydromorphone, morphine, oxycodone, and oxymorphone. On April 2, Derek was screened again. The results took six days to return, and showed a positive test for oxymorphone. By that time, the evidence was too much to ignore.

DEREK NEVER EXPECTED to be told that Mark Messier wanted to talk to him.

Messier might have been the most revered Ranger in history. While he spent most of his career with the Edmonton Oilers, part of a high-scoring dynasty alongside Wayne Gretzky, Messier established permanent residency as a New York sports icon in 1994. He was the 33-year-old captain of the Rangers, a man with his named etched on the Stanley Cup five times from his days with his hometown Oilers. The Rangers had lost Game 5 of the Eastern Conference final to the cross-river rival New Jersey Devils, and Messier was damned if the Rangers would lose again.

"We're going to go in and win Game 6," he said. The New York tabloids splashed his guarantee across their covers, making it the city's most famous victory pledge since New York Jets quarterback Joe Namath promised a win in Super Bowl III.

"I've put my five Stanley Cup rings, my reputation and my neck on the chopping block, boys," Messier said he told his teammates. "Now save me."

The Rangers won Game 6, by a score of 4–1. Messier, nick-named "Captain Courageous," had three goals, perhaps the boldest hat trick in league history. And the Rangers won Game 7, too, back in Madison Square Garden, in double overtime. And then they beat the Vancouver Canucks in the Stanley Cup final, the Rangers' first championship since 1940.

Messier left the Rangers after an acrimonious contract dispute in 1997, but team president and general manager Glen Sather brought him back in 2000. Messier played his final four seasons with the Rangers, and the team retired Messier's No. 11 in 2006. He was inducted into the Hockey Hall of Fame in 2007.

In 2009, Messier joined the Rangers as a "special assistant" to Sather, who had built and coached those Oilers championship teams in the 1980s.

It was a vague title and an unclear role. Messier spent part of one season as general manager of Canada's world-championship team. During the first half of Derek's first season in New York, Messier coached a low-level Canadian national team in a pair of European tournaments. Messier was barely seen or heard in New York. He seldom spoke to the media. The rare times he spoke publicly were usually when he promoted the "Messier Project," with a mission "to address the issue of concussions, which has become an epidemic in hockey, through product development and a public-awareness campaign."

In tandem with his sister, Mary-Kay, Messier worked to develop helmets with better protection and to educate players on the need to wear them properly, with the chin strap cinched.

"The NHL still continues to be our greatest challenge," Mary-Kay Messier told the *Gazette* of Montreal in early March of 2011. "One of the things we're really working on is changing the culture of hockey so that head protection becomes a priority."

Mark Messier, never quoted about the state of the Rangers, was willing to talk about the importance of protecting the heads of players. Helmets, he said, "were designed to stop catastrophic injuries and have done a great job of that. But our game has evolved where now concussions are part of our game, so we have to design our helmets not only to stop catastrophic injuries, but also to help reduce the risk of concussions."

And now, a couple of weeks later, Messier wanted to talk to Derek. Derek was incredulous. *Mark Messier wants to talk to me?*

It was a pep talk, not unlike those that Messier surely used to inspire teammates to rally for the good of the team. The Rangers had put a lot of faith in Derek, giving him a four-year contract and a lot of money to be the enforcer that he had shown he could be. But Derek had been injured since December, out with a concussion for several months, and it was fair to wonder why his recovery was taking so long. Even some of Derek's friends wondered whether he was milking the injury, in no hurry to return to a middling team with a coach he did not like. Messier's intent was to motivate Derek, to scare him into taking responsibility, to push him into becoming the player the Rangers thought they were getting and hoped they would get for the next three seasons.

At the team's suburban practice rink a day or two later, Derek skated with several other teammates who were out of the lineup, too hurt to play but healthy enough to exercise. Derek had been skating with the team for several weeks, but he was still in bad shape—overweight, slow, and unmotivated.

Assistant coach Jim Schoenfeld oversaw the workout. He was 58, a former captain of the Buffalo Sabres during a 13-year NHL career as a sturdy defenseman. He might have been best known, however, for his postgame outburst as coach of the New Jersey Devils in 1988. "Have another donut!" he screamed at referee Don Koharski in the tunnel after a playoff loss.

Schoenfeld had taken a keen interest in Derek. He had coaxed

him into low-impact workouts, including yoga. But Derek complained that Schoenfeld forced him to skate hard in two-minute
intervals. He didn't see the sense in it. His shifts never lasted two
minutes.

It did not take long for Schoenfeld to see that something was
different with Derek this time. Derek fell. He tried to stand up, and
then fell again. He had no coordination. Like a newborn colt trying
to gain footing, Derek could not keep his feet underneath him. It
was obvious that Derek was drunk or on drugs. Other teammates
watched as Schoenfeld ordered Derek off the ice.

Derek, back on his feet, stormed through the gate of the rink and
stumbled into the dressing room. He threw a tantrum, throwing his
equipment to the ground. He sat on a bench and stewed. He clenched
his fists in frustration, a rare display of anger.

Schoenfeld left to call other team officials. In front of team trainers, Derek went through the range of emotions again, unable to
recapture his composure.

"People think I'm a pill head," he screamed, again and again.
And he started to cry.

Within hours, plans were made to send Derek to rehabilitation.

11

From the outside, Authentic Recovery Center was a well-tended two-story Spanish-style house, made of pale adobe and topped with a red-tile roof. It sat on the edge of an elegant neighborhood, surrounded by a high wall and tall hedges on a busy corner of a West Los Angeles intersection.

Derek did not want to be in Malibu again. He hated the isolation. So when he was told he was entering rehabilitation for the second time, he pleaded for something different. The tony recesses of Beverly Hills and Westwood were a mile or two to the north. The glassy office towers and hotels of Century City were a short walk to the east. Trendy Santa Monica was just on the other side of the 405 freeway, the beach a straight shot a few miles to the west.

Derek arrived on Tuesday, April 5, 2011, and filled out paperwork with a counselor. There was a "health questionnaire," and the third question was whether he had "ever had a head injury that resulted in a period of loss of consciousness." Derek checked "no." Another question asked about "back problems, bone injuries, muscle injuries, or joint injuries." Another asked whether he took any prescription medications. Derek replied "no" to both. Asked to list what type of drugs or alcohol that he had consumed in the past seven days,

Derek wrote "3 Ambien." Asked what he had taken in the past year, he wrote "Ambien" and "drank."

The only question to which he replied "yes" was No. 29: "Are you pregnant?"

Since October, when Len told the Rangers that Derek was abusing pills again, a year after he was in drug rehabilitation for abusing Ambien and narcotic painkillers, Derek had been under the watch of the NHL's substance abuse program. He had received at least 12 prescriptions for Ambien, for 274 pills, from team doctors of the Rangers and the Wild, records later revealed. Early in the season, he had received five prescriptions for 64 pills of hydrocodone, or Vicodin. He had been subjected to roughly 20 drug tests, and tested positive in most of them, including for powerful painkillers months after he had been prescribed them. All that was kept private. None of it was enough to send Derek to rehabilitation or get him suspended.

It was a fall on the ice, at a Rangers workout in front of teammates and coaches, that could not be ignored.

In the short time between the episode at practice and being sent to rehabilitation, Derek called his father. Derek told Len that he had fallen several times on the ice and gotten in trouble at practice for slamming a rink gate shut. When pressed, Derek would not say what it was that made him fall. He was cryptic and annoyed.

Len called Ron Salcer to learn what he could. Salcer said that Derek's recent drug tests had been "not good," but he did not elaborate. News that Derek was headed to rehabilitation again came as a surprise to the Boogaards, who had presumed that he was getting better, not worse.

A counselor at the treatment center wrote that Derek's main problem was "opioid abuse" and noted that Derek "continued use despite adverse consequences, illegal procuring of substance." A "biopsychosocial assessment" went into greater detail. The counselor asked Derek a long series of questions and wrote the responses. "Pain meds" were Derek's "main problem," and the cause was "physical pain."

Derek was coy, but began to open up. He admitted to a recent use of Valium—used for flying, he said—but said no to Xanax. He said he first used Percocet after surgeries in 2009, followed by Oxy-Contin, and had recently taken hydrocodone and Ambien. He said he occasionally passed out while drinking and admitted to drinking in the morning, when he was in pain. He said he sometimes felt "guilt" or "shame," and was sometimes depressed, and he wondered aloud if it pertained to his last concussion.

Derek was asked how his chemical dependency affected those close to him.

"Mom gets worried," the counselor wrote as Derek's response. "It's the reason why my fiancée and I split up. My Dad gets pissed."

Derek said he moved eight times as a child and that home life was "crazy, 4 kids, chaos, but not in a bad way, busy, sports." His difficulties in school were attributed to "isolation—dad shunned from the community."

Derek was asked about his relationship with his father.

"Good. I don't lie to him, we're close," the counselor recorded.

In what ways are you like your father?

"Stubborn, independent, loving."

He said he had a good relationship with his mother, too, and that they shared traits of being "independent, strong-willed, caring."

Asked how his parents got along, Derek replied: "Near the end it was crazy. They were fighting."

He described Erin as his "fiancée" for three and a half years. He was asked if chemical dependency played a part in the failure of the relationship.

"Yes," the counselor recorded Derek as saying. "She was suspicious about pain meds and other women." He admitted to "random sex sometimes."

Derek was asked his strengths. He said he was strong-willed and confident. His sole weakness, he said, was pain.

PATIENTS AT THE rehabilitation center were detoxified immediately, and typical treatment mandated at least three drug tests a week.

Its rules required patients to stay in the center—with private, well-appointed rooms, meeting spaces, and offices, and peaceful courtyards to pass the time—for the first three weeks of treatment. The only excuses to leave, the center said, would be emergencies, bereavement, or a work requirement. In all cases, according to the center, patients were required to be accompanied off-premises by a staff member.

Derek appeared to live by a different set of rules. He left the center on most days, sometimes signed out by Salcer, who lived nearby. He went to a local gym to work out and box. His bank records showed that he made nearly daily purchases at nearby stores and restaurants.

On April 7, his third day in rehabilitation, Derek paid for dinner—$93.83 at a restaurant called the Lobster, overlooking the Santa Monica Pier. Within his first week, Derek spent more than $3,800 online at Astor & Black, an upscale clothier in New York. He spent more than $1,000 at Brookstone, the gift company. And he placed a $12,000 deposit on an apartment in Minneapolis that he and Aaron would share over the summer, in the same building in the Warehouse District, near downtown Minneapolis, where he had lived a couple of seasons earlier.

He used his cell phone constantly, calling friends and saying that he was training in Los Angeles. Even some of his closest friends did not know he was in rehabilitation. The media did not know, either, reporting only that Derek's concussion symptoms had kept him from finishing the season. While Derek was in rehabilitation, the Rangers lost their opening-round playoff series to the Washington Capitals, four games to one. He did not care.

Derek sent text messages to close friends and family to tell them what a joke the program was. During counseling sessions, he quoted obscure lines from movies and television shows, inside jokes to amuse himself and laugh about later.

"Client appears to be resistant to treatment protocol," a counselor wrote in the "progress notes" on Derek's second day. "Client is largely non-participatory in treatment curriculum/activities. However, client is compliant in session and views treatment episode as something he must do to comply with NHL."

"Client's referent"—a reference to Dan Cronin, the primary counselor from the NHL substance abuse team—"working closely with program administrator on individualized treatment plan," a counselor wrote on April 14. Derek had been there more than a week. The counselor noted that Derek "demonstrates limited insight into addictive pathology." The same note ended with a cryptic revelation: "Client does report significant closeness to family."

Derek and other patients were encouraged to admit, at the start, that they had substance abuse problems. The center's philosophy shared the first three steps of the familiar 12-step Alcoholics Anonymous program.

On April 20, after about two weeks in the program, Derek was still a reluctant participant. But he seemed to be revealing himself to counselors.

"Client appears to be in positive mood today, but discussed upcoming visits from NHL reps and used time in session to vent about their lack of understanding his physical pain," the day's progress note read. "Therapist notes the conflict/contradiction to client, as client acknowledges abusing pain medication. However, client maintains that pain is excessive and few alternatives have worked."

Again, the notes ended with an unrelated tidbit about Derek's relationships: "Client additionally spoke of ex-fiancée, whom he no longer trusts."

The treatment appeared to be snagged in Derek's own denial.

"Client talked in session today about not needing to be in treatment and his resentment at some of the individuals that facilitated his entrance into treatment," his progress notes read on April 22. "Client maintains that his admission into treatment is 'ridiculous' and that it's 'red-tape.' Client exhibits guardedness when therapist asks clinical questions by smiling, and responding with simple answers and asking therapist 'so what else is up with you?' Client appears to be aware that this question is out of place w/ goal of therapy, but laughs in acknowledgement of it."

Two days later, the counselor noted that Derek planned to go to New York in a couple of days to move into a new apartment, and that he continued to deflect probing questions. The session focused on the issue of pain.

"Client reports that some other athletes are 'babies' when it comes to pain," the counselor wrote. "Client discusses his job with a noticeable delight when he talks about being a professional athlete and appears to take pride in his role on the team."

EARLY ON APRIL 29, a Friday, Derek flew from Los Angeles International Airport to New York's LaGuardia. He landed shortly after 4 P.M. Before heading to Manhattan, to the new apartment on the west side that Derek planned to share with Devin Wilson, Derek headed east, toward the suburbs of Long Island, where he paid a man $4,000.

Derek visited the new Manhattan apartment that he planned to share with Wilson, his old Prince George teammate, who had moved Derek's belongings from his other place. And then Derek drove his Audi to Minneapolis. He arrived well after midnight at the apartment that he and Aaron would share at 415 North 1st Street, a two-bedroom place on the second floor of a complex called Heritage Landing. Before he got to the apartment, though, Derek stopped at Sneaky Pete's.

Aaron saw that Derek had a large Ziploc bag filled with an assortment of pills, dozens of them, including OxyContin, Percocet, and Xanax. Aaron recognized them by now. He placed them into pill bottles from old prescriptions and stashed them out of sight, out of the easy reach of temptation. If Derek needed pills to combat his pain, Aaron was not going to make it easy for him to find them in large quantities.

Derek and Aaron drove to Lawrence, Kansas, to visit their sister, Krysten. Along the way, they stopped at a truck stop because Derek wanted to buy a CB radio.

"Let's screw around with some truckers," Derek said.

He paid $150 for it, thinking he could just plug it into his Audi's cigarette lighter. It was only after the brothers were on the road that they realized it needed to be installed through the fuse box. Derek still liked the idea. He said he would get that done sometime.

Krysten was a graduating senior at Kansas, and the school was holding its end-of-season banquet for the basketball team. A six-foot-five center, as well liked by her teammates as Derek was in hockey, Krysten averaged 8 points and 4.4 rebounds over four seasons. She was the 20th player in program history to score more than 1,000 career points, and was named to the All-Big 12 academic second team as a senior.

The brothers hurried back to Minnesota after the banquet. Aaron was relieved to see how good Derek seemed—clear-headed, not complaining about concussion symptoms. Derek and Aaron had gone most of the fall and winter to February without speaking, the fallout from their arguments the previous summer. Now Derek seemed in high spirits.

The night before Derek was to fly to Los Angeles and report back to the rehabilitation center, Erin sat with a friend in a Minneapolis bar called Bar La Grassa. Erin told the other woman that Derek had been in touch with her now and again, and since she had moved into an apartment building next door to the one that Derek and Aaron planned to spend the summer, she would probably bump into him on occasion. That would be strange.

Just then, Derek walked into the bar. Erin practically jumped.

"I felt like I saw a ghost," she told him.

The two met for lunch the next day before Derek's flight to Los Angeles, and the awkwardness of the breakup and elapsed time faded quickly. Derek told Erin he was going to California to train and see Ron Salcer. Even then—especially then—he tried to keep his drug troubles from her. He was not about to tell her he was back in rehabilitation.

Derek took an afternoon flight from Minneapolis on May 4 and landed back in Los Angeles a little after 7 o'clock in the evening. But before he left, he begged Aaron to come with him. We can hang out together, go to the beach, and work out, Derek said.

Aaron demurred, not wanting Derek to spend money on a last-minute flight for him. But Derek booked one for him, anyway, two days later. He got Aaron a hotel room at a Marriott Courtyard not far from the rehabilitation center.

Derek had rented a Porsche, and he picked up Aaron each morning at the hotel. They spent the days bouncing between the gym and the beach. At the gym, they boxed. At the beach, they worked out and played in the water.

Derek wanted a deep tan—"Brazilian nut" was the tone that he joked he wanted his skin to be—and asked Aaron to put sunscreen on his back. Aaron nonchalantly swiped a few squiggles on Derek. It left Derek with a white *Z* on his otherwise sunburned back.

The two went to movies and to Starbucks. They occasionally saw Salcer and his grown daughters. They ate a few fancy dinners, including at Katsuya in Hollywood, where Derek paid the $579.77 tab. Another night, they went to Supperclub Los Angeles, a restaurant and nightclub in Hollywood where meals were prepared on a stage and diners lay on white beds to eat. Derek spent $2,083.04.

In early May, a woman named Ashley whom Derek liked from Sneaky Pete's—a different Ashley than the one who visited New York in January—called Derek with a problem. She was in Miami Beach, unable to pay a bill at the Fontainebleau Hotel because her credit card was declined. He put the $3,807.32 charge on his American Express card. She promised to pay him back.

At night, Derek dropped Aaron back at the hotel and returned to Authentic Recovery Center. Aaron knew that Derek was being drug tested and undergoing some sort of detoxification. Derek had to check in a time or two every day, but Aaron thought it seemed more like a hotel than a rehabilitation clinic.

The progress reports in Derek's file petered out as the weeks went by. Derek's return on May 4 had been noted, saying that Derek reported that his trip to New York was successful. But the next entry in the notes the center later gave to Derek's family was eight days later.

"Program therapist was informed by Residential Supervisor on 4/12," Derek's file read, with the wrong month written down, "that client left for MN and was due to be away from facility until 5/24/11. Reported purpose of trip was for training."

Shortly after his arrival in April, Derek had received permission from the league's substance abuse program to be gone from the center from May 13 to 24 to attend Krysten's college graduation in

Kansas, according to the Boogaards. (For graduation, Derek gave her a $5,000 gift certificate to Astor & Black, his New York tailor.) In early May, Derek asked Dan Cronin, the lead counselor, if he could book him a flight to Minneapolis on May 12, not May 13.

Cronin told Derek that Dr. David Lewis, the program's co-director, said no.

"Advised by Dan that leaving 5/12 was against my advice," Lewis wrote in his notes on May 6. "Must stick to plan."

Derek bought his own ticket for May 12.

On May 11, the night before he left Los Angeles, Derek went to dinner with Aaron and the Salcers. Ron and his wife and their two daughters, both in their mid-20s, were there, along with the young women's boyfriends.

They ate at Fonz's, a steakhouse in Manhattan Beach. Derek told Salcer that he wanted to come back and stay at a beach house for a few weeks over the summer, as he and Aaron had done the year before, and he gave Salcer a signed blank check for a deposit. Derek was engaging again, comfortable and funny. The group laughed and lingered, and everything seemed right with Derek—not perfect, Salcer thought, but better than it had been in many, many months.

Derek complained about the Rangers, who had recently told him they wanted him to stay in New York over the summer to train—potentially wrecking Derek's summer plans in Minnesota and California. Salcer spun it into a positive. It means they still want you, Derek, he said. Derek said he wanted to make up for the last season, to prove them wrong with a new start. He would show them that he was worth the money. He would regain his crown as the toughest enforcer in the NHL.

The group split after hugs. Derek and Aaron had a flight the next morning. Salcer sent Derek a playful but serious text message: "Have a safe flight. Take care of yourself. Stay out of trouble. And don't go to Sneaky's."

IT WAS THURSDAY, May 12, in the late afternoon of a warm spring day in Minneapolis. Derek showered and prepared to go out. He was in the mood to celebrate. He wore dark jeans, a blue-and-white checked shirt, and black Pumas.

Derek asked Aaron for pills. Aaron knew where they were. He asked Derek if he really thought that was a good idea, given that he had just left rehabilitation, but Derek insisted. Come on, he said. You know one is not going to make a difference.

Aaron gave his brother a Percocet—just one, Aaron said later. It was about 6 o'clock.

Derek left the apartment and went downstairs to let Ashley into the building. She worked at Sneaky Pete's, one of the revolving servers who wore low-cut tops and an alluring smile, and who on busy nights sold beers from a trough of ice or slid through the crowd to sell sweet-tasting shots to keep the patrons well oiled and energized.

They talked with Aaron in the apartment for a while. Derek and Ashley left for Seven, a steakhouse and sushi lounge on Hennepin Avenue, in the heart of downtown Minneapolis's social scene.

Jeremy and Jennie Clark met them there. Dillon Hafiz, part of the family that owned Sneaky Pete's, and another friend had been waiting for Derek and Ashley at Seven for an hour. Aaron declined to go and stayed at the apartment.

At 7:11, Derek called the cell phone of Dan Cronin, the NHL substance-abuse program counselor. The call was not answered. Derek sent a text message. Over the course of 12 minutes, Derek and Cronin exchanged seven text messages.

Derek also called his mother in Regina. Joanne missed the call, and Derek did not leave a message. He called again a short while later, and she missed it again. She called back and left her son a voice-mail message.

At Seven, Derek drank Jack Daniels and Coke, at least a few of them. He excused himself from the table and went to the bar's ATM, where he withdrew $200.

Derek paid the $251.27 bill with a credit card. Ashley drove Derek, in his car, back to the apartment to get Aaron. Ashley left, to go change clothes at home, and agreed to meet Derek later at Sneaky Pete's.

It was about 11 P.M. Derek was visibly drunk.

"Holy fuck," Aaron said to him. "How did you get so banged up at dinner?"

"I didn't even eat," Derek said.

Their travels extended only a few blocks within Minneapolis's Warehouse District, but Derek wanted to keep moving, more than usual. They began at Sneaky Pete's. They moved to a strip club named Augie's, then back to Sneaky Pete's, where Derek had more drinks and called Ashley. She arrived 15 minutes later. The group left and turned right around the corner to take a quick look inside a live-music joint called Bootleggers, but they did not stay long. It was past 1 A.M., and the bars would close within the hour. The group crossed the street to a dance club called Aqua.

Derek squeezed drinks in before last call, and the group rushed back to Sneaky Pete's so that Derek could close his bar tab. When the bars closed at 2 A.M., the group climbed into Clark's car for the short ride, about a mile or so, back to the Boogaard brothers' apartment. Along the way, though, Derek asked for the car to be pulled over. When it stopped, he jumped out and ran. Aaron gave chase.

He caught up to Derek under a bridge. Derek was emotional, complaining that Ashley did not like him the way he liked her. As the brothers walked the mile or so to their apartment, Derek's mood swung from playful to despondent. He spoke of his crippling loneliness one moment. In the next, he belligerently shouted to other night crawlers on the edge of downtown, challenging them to fight.

The others were waiting at the apartment building when Derek and Aaron arrived. Derek went straight into the bathroom. Jeremy Clark followed to offer counseling, and the two spent a half-hour or more inside.

After a time, Derek emerged and went to his bedroom. He lay on the floor for a while, then sat at the foot of the bed, his back to the door, a large window to his left. On the dresser to his right were pictures of his grandparents, whom he called Opa and Oma, who had come to his first hockey games and watched him score his first goal. There were several pictures of the bulldog named Trinity that Derek and Janella had bought in Louisiana but had later given to Len when they realized they could not care for it.

Aaron made pancakes in the apartment's small kitchen, where Derek's Buddha statues lined the counter. Jeremy Clark had a training session with a client early the next morning. He and Jennie left. Ashley left, too, after checking on Derek.

"I went into his room and he was laying on his bed," Ashley told police later. "And I said 'goodnight' and I left."

(The investigator asked her if the two had any disagreement that night. "No," she said. "He was so happy.")

The company gone, Aaron continued to make pancakes. His cooking was interrupted several times by calls from the bedroom.

To Derek, the bed was spinning. He could not lie down. He sat at the end of the bed, his feet on the floor, his sore back hunched. At one point, he threw up on the carpet between his feet.

Aaron moved back and forth down the short hallway between the kitchen and the bedroom. He tried to soothe his brother with words. He tried to get him to eat. He tried to encourage him to fall asleep.

Everything will be okay, he told his brother. Just go to sleep.

Finally, sometime around four in the morning, the calls from the bedroom stopped.

Derek was quiet at last.

HIS BROTHER PRESUMABLY asleep, finally, in bed, Aaron left to spend the rest of the night with a girlfriend. He slept late and was in no hurry to get home, returning to the apartment about 3 P.M. to shower and change clothes. From the hallway, he could see Derek still on the bed, his feet hanging off the end. It was not unusual for Derek to sleep the afternoon away, and he probably had a nasty hangover.

Aaron shouted that he was going to the airport to get Ryan, but Derek did not budge. Let him keep sleeping, Aaron thought.

The Boogaard brothers planned to convene in Minneapolis before heading to Kansas for Krysten's college graduation. Aaron told Ryan that Derek was hungover and still sleeping. In no hurry to return, the two of them stopped at a Potbelly sandwich shop.

They stepped back into the apartment a bit after 6. Derek was still on the bed.

"He still hasn't moved," Aaron said to Ryan.

Ryan glanced into the bedroom. An RCMP member, like the boys' father, he immediately recognized that something was not right. Any nonchalance dissolved immediately, replaced by the slow creep of dread.

Ryan stared at the large body atop the bed, still in his clothes. Derek's chest was not rising and falling.

"He's not breathing," Ryan said.

He stared hard at Derek's face. It was oddly pale. Aaron circled to the other side of the bed. Ryan touched Derek's arm. It was cold.

Ryan was a cop. He knew what a dead body looked and felt like.

Aaron shrieked and began to jump up and down. "What do we do? What do we do?" he shouted.

Ryan, instantly numb, told his brother to call 911. Then he slipped out of the bedroom and collapsed in the hallway.

The call arrived at 6:18 P.M.

"Can you come to 4, 415 North First Street, please, my brother is not breathing," Aaron hurriedly told the operator. "He's pale, his lips are blue, he's . . ."

Aaron's words, shrouded in sobs, became unintelligible.

The phone rang at Len Boogaard's house in Ottawa. Len's wife, Jody, answered and heard nothing but an unintelligible wail. She thought it was a prank call, but something told her to stay on the line. Finally, she realized it was Ryan, and made sense of the words.

Derek's dead.

Len Boogaard was in the backyard. Jody rushed the phone to him.

"I knew this was going to happen," Len cried into the phone.

From the hallway floor, Ryan called his mother in Regina. Joanne was at a friend's house and answered her cell phone. She heard Ryan and Aaron wailing. Derek's gone, Ryan blurted, and Joanne did not understand. What do you mean "gone"? she asked. What is going on? Her spinning mind slowly processed the message through the chaos.

Thousands of miles away in Saskatchewan, Derek's mother was helpless to do anything but offer a reassuring voice. Call 911, Joanne said.

"It's too late," Ryan cried. "It's too late for him."

EPILOGUE

DEREK'S BRAIN WAS CARVED out of his skull by a coroner in Minneapolis. It was put in a plastic bucket and inside a series of plastic bags, then placed in an insulated box filled with a slurry of icy water. The box, marked BIOLOGICAL SUBSTANCE, was driven to the airport and placed in the cargo hold of a plane to Boston. Upon arrival, a courier service drove the box 30 miles to the Bedford Veterans Administration Medical Center in Bedford, Massachusetts.

Building 78 sat among a woodsy, 276-acre campus setting of red-brick buildings, mostly built in the 1920s. At the end of a short driveway was a former ambulance entrance, rarely used anymore for emergencies. Through the door was the basement morgue.

The box was opened and the brain removed. It was vibrantly pink and weighed 1,580 grams, or about three and a half pounds. On a stainless-steel table, Dr. Ann McKee cleaved it in half, front to back, with a large knife. Much of one half of the brain was cut into slices, about the width of sandwich bread.

The pieces of Derek's brain were identified as SLI-76. They were placed in plastic containers and into large refrigerators with glass doors, next to all the rest. There were so many brains, close to a hundred of them, that similar refrigerators lined the walls of another room and an upstairs hallway.

Over the course of several months, parts of Derek's brain were occasionally pulled from the refrigerator. Pieces were delicately shaved thin enough to fit onto glass slides and slipped under the lenses of powerful microscopes. McKee and her team of assistants spent hundreds of hours dissecting Derek's brain, examining every thin strip, looking for tiny clues.

Like everyone else, they wanted to figure out what had happened to him.

THE FUNERAL WAS held in Regina on Saturday, May 21, inside the small chapel at the Royal Canadian Mounted Police Depot Division. It was the same chapel where Len and Joanne were married almost 29 years earlier. The chapel was a simple, barn-like building of whitewashed wood, with a thick, two-story steeple and a gabled red roof. Built in 1883, it was originally the Depot's mess hall, and was converted into a place of worship 12 years later. It faced north

Len, Krysten, and Joanne Boogaard at Derek's funeral.

onto Sleigh Square, a paved space cordoned off from civilians and used for the daily parade of cadets. Len Boogaard marched there, under the watchful eyes of relentless, unforgiving instructors countless times, 30 years earlier. Ryan Boogaard had done the same, just a couple of years before. Derek knew the place well.

Through the rounded, wooden doors was a rich, warm chapel with red carpet and a dozen rows of pews, divided by an aisle, enough to hold about 200. Stained-glass depictions of Mounties, in full red-coated regalia, filtered prisms of daylight from either side of the altar. One showed a Mountie with a bugle. The accompanying inscription, from I Corinthians 15:52, read, "For the trumpet shall sound." The other showed a Mountie, head bowed and hand on the butt of a musket. "Blessed are they that mourn," it read, quoting Matthew 5:4.

The chapel could not hold everyone who came for Derek's funeral. It was Tobin Wright's assignment to bring close friends and family into the chapel and direct others to a nearby theater-style auditorium, where the service would be shown on closed-circuit television.

The bulletin handed to mourners showed a full-color portrait of Derek in his Wild jersey. His back was turned partly toward the camera, showing his nameplate and number, and he looked over his shoulder with little expression. On his right hand was a hockey glove.

The back page, with a photograph of Derek smiling in his Wild uniform, contained the obituary.

"It is with great sadness that we announce the passing of our teddy bear and protector Derek Leendert Boogaard," it began. It cited the relatives and listed all the family moves as a child. It mentioned Todd Ripplinger, the Regina Pats scout. It skimmed over Derek's years in minor hockey and minor leagues and into the NHL.

"Minneapolis was a home away from home for Derek where he made many great friends," it read. "Derek was well loved and a fan favourite for many, making the decision to leave Minnesota a hard one. For the 2010–11 season, he moved to the 'big apple' to play with the New York Rangers. Derek was a strong person who battled many adversities to achieve his dreams. He was a hero to some and a role model to many more. Derek was a larger than life gentle giant that cared for everyone around him providing inspiration as a genuine son, brother, friend and teammate."

It closed by requesting that donations be made to the Boogaard's Booguardians Memorial Fund benefiting Defending the Blue Line, "an organization that supports military families and also donates hockey equipment to children."

Inside the program was a photograph of Derek as a toddler, holding a stuffed bear larger than him. There were several poems. There was also an insert, added at the last moment, with the words from "Amazing Grace." At an impromptu gathering at the Xcel Energy Arena after Derek's death, the atrium filled with fans who had come to pay respect to a former player and the family left behind, those in attendance broke into song: "Amazing Grace."

The Boogaard family entered last and sat in the front two rows on the right side, Len on one end of the first pew and Joanne on the other. Immediately in front of them were large floral arrangements and, on easels, photographs of Derek. Derek's Wild and Rangers jerseys lay folded on a small table, each covering a small box.

Doug Risebrough, the Wild general manager who had drafted Derek, was at the funeral. So was Jacques Lemaire, the longtime Wild coach, and representatives from some of the Western Hockey League teams. Several NHL teammates were there, mostly in dark suits and sunglasses. Marian Gaborik and Brent Burns, who had been in Slovakia with Tobin Wright when they heard the news, were among them.

Janella came. A week earlier, she had been behind the bar at the Rock Rest Lodge in Golden, Colorado, where she worked while attending classes to secure a biology degree from Metropolitan State

College in Denver. She did a double take when she saw Derek's picture on the televisions around her. The screen also showed years—1982–2011—as they do to delicately indicate someone's death. To Janella, the meaning did not register for a moment. She gasped. Customers asked if she was all right.

She had not spoken to Derek for several years, since filing for a divorce from their common-law marriage and receiving a $35,000 settlement in 2008 that infuriated Derek's family. Janella had wanted to ensure that she was free of any complications from their time and tax filings together, but the Boogaards thought it was a ploy for money. Joanne Boogaard sent an e-mail to Janella during the divorce, questioning her motives. Derek, too, sent an angry letter. Janella did not respond to either, on the advice of her attorney. But she sent Derek two text messages after the settlement. One was a promise to pay him back the $35,000. The second told Derek that she loved him, and always would. He never replied.

Every few months, including the weeks before his death, she resisted the temptation to contact him. Someday, she thought. But now her heart was filled with anguish and regret, and the recesses of her subconscious were filled with dreams about Derek that startled her awake in the middle of the night.

She arrived in Regina unsure of how she would be received. Aaron, Ryan, and Krysten gave her hugs. But when she tried to step into the chapel, Wright stopped her. They had known each other since the beginning, having arrived in Derek's life almost simultaneously nearly a decade before. When Derek had first written down Janella's phone number, he'd done it on the same piece of scrap paper on which he'd also written Wright's number.

Only family and close friends, Wright told Janella. Len and Jody Boogaard stood nearby. They stepped over and gave Janella hugs and directed her inside.

Erin came to Regina, too. Aaron had called her.

"You're not going to hear it from Mom or Dad," he said he told her. "You're not going to hear it from anybody. This is about Derek, and I think it would be best if you were there. It's for Derek. Derek would like you to be there."

Derek had texted Erin the day before he died. He had told her it had been good to see her, and she told him to have a good time in California. I always do, he replied.

Then, two mornings later, her phone filled with messages and missed calls. A text message from a friend told her that Derek was dead. It was a shock, if not a complete surprise.

"The addiction got the best of him, and the loneliness—not feeling like he had that companionship to make it better or make it right or push through it," she said months after Derek died. "The pills were his outlet. That's what made him feel better. He never really showed me a struggle, because he never admitted he had an issue. I never saw a desire in him to make it go away. And by the time things got really bad, I wasn't involved anymore. From hearsay, hearing that the night he died he was saying, 'I don't want to be alone, I'm going to be alone the rest of my life,' that hurts to hear something like that. I knew that about him. It seemed like it would be so simple to make that right for him."

Erin did not receive the same reception that Janella did from the Boogaard family. She knew many people there, including Derek's NHL teammates, but was directed to watch the funeral on the television in the auditorium.

THERE WERE FOUR eulogists, and they struck common themes: Derek was a teddy bear of a man who drew people close and then hung tight. He was selfless, quick to donate time and money to friends and charity. He was tireless in his pursuit of his dreams. He was funny and sincere and never wanted to be left alone.

Jeremy Clark tearfully explained that he never intended to become friends with Derek when he arrived as a client at the gym.

"It wasn't long until the size of his love for life and fun overtook the size of his fists," Clark told the congregation. "I never met someone who got more excitement and pleasure from the simple things in life than Derek. That may explain the array of remote-control helicopters, compound bows, gun-cleaning kits, candles, Buddhas, folding knives, camouflage outfits, camping gear, and so on that line my garage. I would shake my head when the array of text messages, pictures, and phone calls would come in, pronouncing the next passion that crossed his path. I would often tell him, 'Boogey, stop spending so much money on this stuff.' His reply was always, 'Clarkie, don't worry about it. I have money now. If I go broke, I'll just live in your basement.'"

He recounted a story of how excited Derek got when he saw Clark and his wife making sandwiches for lunch. It reminded him of childhood.

"Two weeks later, the day before I was leaving to visit Derek for a week in New York, he sent me a picture-text of a grocery cart full of bread, sandwich meats, cheese," Clark said from the dais, "and a note telling me that we were going to make sandwiches all week for meals, just like what we had grown up on.

"The one thing I respected most about Derek," Clark continued, "was that off the ice, you never saw Derek parading his size, or his strength, or his status. He was about the simple things, and the people close to him, and he protected them at any cost."

Risebrough, the longtime Wild general manager who had since become an advisor to the Rangers, recalled Derek's rise through the minor leagues and into the NHL. He told stories of Derek's imposing size, including one in which Derek had a bead on Colorado defenseman John-Michael Liles. Liles ducked at the last minute, avoiding the collision.

"He says, 'Well, I had my head down, and I knew I was in trouble when the building got silent and it got very, very dark,'" Risebrough said.

He said that Derek's career was about getting a chance, and taking advantage of it. Over the course of 10 minutes, Risebrough never used the words "fight" or "enforcer."

"Derek had a way of attracting people," he said. "He had a way of comforting people. A big man with a soft heart. On the ice, players were trying to get away from him. Off the ice, the people were trying to be around him."

Burns spoke next. He and Derek were teammates in the minor leagues and longtime roommates in the NHL. He joked about late-night orders of chicken wings, and the off-season in which the two of them watched the Tour de France and Derek set out to add cycling to his workout regime, surviving a severe road rash when he tumbled over the handlebars.

"We will greatly miss his smirks, his laughs, his little jabs on and off the ice," Burns said. "But most importantly we will miss knowing that when we need something or somebody, he was going to be there for us."

Tobin Wright spoke haltingly about Derek's curiosity.

"I just want everybody to remember the gentle giant that Derek was," he said. "Once you got into his close circle, he was the kindest guy you could ever meet."

The chaplain introduced a country song called "Small Town, Big Dreams," by Paul Brandt. After the chaplain's eulogy, members of Derek's family—Len and Joanne, sister Krysten, brothers Ryan and Aaron, and half-brother Curtis—shuffled to the microphone. The group circled around Aaron as he spoke quietly, reading from sheets of white paper. He was the first to discuss Derek's role as a hockey fighter.

"With the combination of his size, toughness, and downright

meanness at times, who took offense to anyone who dared challenge him or agreed to fight him, was what made him as great as he was at his craft in hockey," Aaron said. "When I think of a definition of a man, I continue to think of my brother. He feared no one and loved everybody."

He thanked the Wild and the Rangers.

Krysten stepped forward to the microphone. She acknowledged all the sympathetic words sent to the family from fans they never met, and said that descriptions of Derek as a teddy bear were correct.

"A teddy bear is, first and foremost, a source of comfort," she said. "And having heard from his teammates, we know how much of a comfort Derek provided on the ice.

"Secondly, a teddy bear is dependable. Derek was dependable to a fault. You could depend on him for anything you needed, any time. Your priority became his priority.

"Thirdly, teddy bears are usually big, and while he would hate to admit it, cuddly. You wouldn't think of Derek as cuddly, but there wasn't a person alive in our lives who had more love to give, or more love to receive.

"Lastly, teddy bears are loyal. They are a constant reminder of what is good in our lives: love, trust, friendship, and selflessness. Teddy bears give but don't ask in return. And this is unconditional. There are no demands in return. Derek was a teddy bear and always will be our teddy bear.

"We aren't here to talk about Derek's hockey career, because his hockey was just a seasonal thing for us. Just an aspect of who he was, what he did. We are here because we have lost a son, a brother, a role model and a friend."

The chaplain directed the family to "receive Derek." In the silence of the chapel, the Boogaards shuffled across the altar. Len grabbed the Wild jersey and the small box it covered. Joanne picked up the Rangers jersey and another box it concealed.

Each box contained half of Derek's ashes. Len and Joanne turned and walked, side by side, slowly up the aisle, the same aisle they once walked as a bride and groom, full of promise and lives never imagined, and carried the remains of their dead son into the bright light.

THE HENNEPIN COUNTY medical examiner in Minneapolis determined that Derek died of an accidental overdose, a lethal mix of alcohol and prescription painkillers.

Derek's blood-alcohol content was 0.18 grams per deciliter, or roughly double most legal limits for drunk driving. Tests found an oxycodone concentration of 0.14 milligrams per liter—enough to surmise that Derek took more than one pill, but probably not enough to be lethal. A Hennepin County study of postmortem cases between 2000 and 2005 involving oxycodone found that seven deaths were caused by oxycodone alone; the mean concentration was 1.06 milligrams per liter, and the lowest in the group was 0.27 milligrams per liter.

There was no way to tell how many pills Derek took that night, but it was certainly more than one Percocet. Over the previous 20 months or so, Derek had allowed very few people to see him gobble painkillers, but he sometimes did so by the handful. Even after his shoulder surgery in April 2009, Derek required twice as many painkillers as Aaron, who had the same surgery, to ease the pain. His appetite for them was initially justified by his size. His increased consumption was explained by his growing tolerance. He needed more to feel the same effect.

But after several weeks in rehabilitation, going through detoxification and being drug tested routinely, Derek's tolerance for the drugs likely shrank. On the night he died, Derek might have consumed what he thought was, for him, a normal amount, not taking into account his reduced tolerance for the pills.

The autopsy report was otherwise unremarkable, with two exceptions. It reported that Derek's brain and brain stem were removed. And it noted heavy scars on his hands.

Inside the apartment in the blurred, scattered minutes after Aaron's 911 call and before the first ambulance arrived, Aaron remembered the pills. He had put them into old prescription bottles and hidden them from his brother, hoping to dispense them in small doses to dull Derek's pain. But he knew they were illegal. And he wanted to protect Derek's reputation.

So Aaron grabbed two bottles—one he kept in his bathroom, one in a bag in his closet—and emptied their contents into the toilet, flushing away any evidence. He later told police that it had been "10 to 15 oxys and 10 or so 30-milligram Percocet and 10 or so more 10-milligram Percocets."

When police investigators arrived at the apartment, Aaron and Ryan Boogaard were there, and so was Jeremy Clark, who received one of the first calls from Aaron.

"I observed V-1 [victim] lying on his back in bed," Minneapolis police officer Timothy Baskin wrote in his report, filled with the misspelled names of prescription medications. "V-1 had a white foam looking cone coming from his lips about ¾″ high. I observed a bottle of Prochlorperazine (10 mg tabs, quantity 12, prescribed 1-15-11 by Dr. Weissman, with 9 remaining) along with a bottle of Ambian (12.5 mg tabs, quantity 30, prescribed on 03-24-11 by Dr. Weissman). The bottle contained 7 pills found to be 50 mg of Tramadall and 11 pills found to be Vicadin 5-500 and no Ambian. This information was determined by calling the poison control center and describing the pills. There was a dollar bill rolled up in V-1's bathroom. There was a small amount of vomit on the floor at the foot of the bed about 6″ round. It appeared the vomit had been partially wiped up."

The subsequent investigation focused on Aaron, and the police, working with the Drug Enforcement Agency, sniffed a broader plot involving renegade doctors. On June 20, 2011, more than five weeks after Derek's death, Aaron was interviewed at length by Minneapolis police investigator Matthew St. George. The report said that Leah Billington of the Drug Enforcement Agency was also present.

Aaron, the son of a cop, wanted to be honest. He told the investigators that he sometimes accompanied Derek to check-cashing places in "shit little areas" of town, sending money in exchange for drugs from New York.

"He would bitch and complain about how doctors wouldn't prescribe him the stuff anymore," Aaron said early in the interview.

"He was on so much shit," he said later.

Aaron explained that he lived with Derek for four summers and always knew when Derek was on the pills or not.

"He'd give the stuff to me and, according to how his back felt or his shoulders or his hands, you know, that's how I'd give him what he kind of needed," Aaron told the investigators. "So last summer around—it was probably the start of August—he, I mean we, worked our asses off up until that point, you know. He had to come in, big year for him, he just showed up at the house with 100 Oxys."

The pills were gone in a couple of weeks, Aaron said, and then there were 100 more. Aaron explained Derek's panicked episode at the airport on the way to New York, and Aaron's refusal to later ship the pills to Derek there, and said that the pills had come from Dillon Hafiz at Sneaky Pete's.

(Hafiz, subsequently questioned by investigators, denied being a drug source, but acknowledged that Derek sometimes came to him in search of them. "No, no, he knows, he hasn't asked me in, in months," Hafiz said, according to the police transcript of the interview. Later, asked why Derek came to him at all in search of prescription painkillers, Hafiz replied, "I mean, I know, I know a lot of people," and "I pointed him in a direction a year or so ago," but he denied being the supplier. "I know and Derek knows that I never—I never gave it to him," he said.)

Four days later, on June 24, the NHL Entry Draft was held at the Xcel Energy Center. The Rangers asked Aaron to announce the team's first choice. When he stepped to the podium, he received a standing ovation from the hometown crowd.

Four weeks later, on July 22, Aaron was in jail, the lone arrest in the case surrounding his brother's death. There were two charges: a felony count for the "sale" of a controlled substance—in this case, officially, one pill of oxycodone that he'd given to Derek the night he died. Aaron "unlawfully sold, gave away, bartered, delivered, exchanged, distributed, disposed of to another, offered to sell, agreed to sell, manufactured or possessed with intent to sell one or more mixtures containing a narcotic drug, to-wit: Oxycodone," the complaint read.

The other charge was for interfering with a scene of death, a gross misdemeanor. Aaron was jailed. Bail was set at $10,000.

"We're being victimized a second time," Len said, distraught. "What is this supposed to prove? Aaron's sitting in the Hennepin whatever the hell it is, being detained, for doing what? Looking out for his brother?"

Aaron's Canadian passport was revoked, leaving him in limbo—unable to cross the border, unable to renew his work visa in the United States. Under de facto house arrest, he stayed in the apartment that he and Derek intended to share all summer, where Derek died, using the complex's gym to stay in shape. He was subject to random drug and alcohol tests. His hockey career was on hold.

The felony distribution charge was ultimately dropped, and Aaron pleaded guilty in October to the misdemeanor charge of interfering with a crime scene. He received probation and 80 hours of community service.

The lease on the apartment ended, and Aaron moved to Regina

and lived with his mother. The Wild offered him a one-year contract and found him a spot with the Rio Grande Valley Killer Bees of the Central Hockey League, a second-level minor league with teams strewn from the Mexican border to South Dakota, from Arizona to Ohio.

Arriving after the season started, Aaron had 6 goals, 6 assists, and 13 fights in 56 games for Rio Grande Valley. He moved on to the Wichita Thunder in 2012, coached by Kevin McClelland, a pugnacious fighter for the Edmonton Oilers through much of the 1980s. Aaron led the team in penalty minutes. He had one goal and 13 fights.

Aaron had seen, more than anyone, the toll that fighting took on his older brother. But he showed none of the symptoms that Derek displayed—no worrisome signs of addiction, erratic behavior, or depression. Still, Joanne Boogaard fretted, wondering what it would take to keep Aaron from fighting in hockey. The game had killed one son, she thought, and her worst fear was that it would take another.

"What else can I do?" Aaron said.

THE SECOND-TOUGHEST call that Joanne Boogaard ever received came a day after Derek died. It was a stranger, a man from Boston, asking for her son's brain.

Chris Nowinski was a former college football player from Harvard who became a professional wrestler. For two years, he performed in the ring as a villain for World Wrestling Entertainment, a muscular blond with a throwback mullet. Much of the wrestling was merely a show. But the folding chairs to the back of the head were real. So were many of the flying elbows and rehearsed pratfalls.

Post-concussion syndrome, the lingering fogginess that Derek encountered and that had prematurely ended the careers or haunted the retirements of many hockey players—Pat LaFontaine, Eric Lindros, Scott Stevens, Keith Primeau, and Chris Pronger among them—forced Nowinski to retire from wrestling in 2004. Looking for answers for his condition, he met Robert Cantu, a clinical professor of neurosurgery at Boston University's School of Medicine. Realizing the lack of awareness and understanding toward concussions in sports, they started the Sports Legacy Institute, dedicated to what they called the "sports concussion crisis."

The two men later partnered with two other doctors at Boston University, Ann McKee, a professor of neurology and pathology, and Robert Stern, a professor of neurology and neurosurgery, to form the Boston University Center for the Study of Traumatic Encephalopathy.

Few had heard of the disease they highlighted—chronic traumatic encephalopathy, or CTE—but it was not new. Long called "dementia pugilistica," and colloquially referred to as being "punch drunk," it had been identified in boxers dating to the 1920s. They had become a caricatured stereotype: the aging ex-boxer who had lost his mind, having been struck in the head too many times. The symptoms were obvious, even if the cause was not: a loss of memory, emotional instability, problems with impulse control, irritability.

Other sports that include persistent blows to the head were beginning to see victims with similar symptoms as they aged, including the early onset of dementia and Alzheimer's disease.

Research showed that CTE was caused by repeated hits to the head. The blows did not have to be severe enough to cause a concussion. Some who were diagnosed with CTE, in fact, had never been officially diagnosed with a concussion. But the repeated blows added up. They seemed to be the root cause.

The team at Boston University had diagnosed CTE in more than 20 former NFL players, even an 18-year-old high school football player. It had been found in dozens of former boxers. And in the previous couple of years, it had been found in two former hockey players: Bob Probert and Reggie Fleming. Months after Derek's death, Rick Martin would represent another.

There was one catch to its discovery: CTE could only be diagnosed by examining the brain after death.

Nowinski had made the delicate pitch dozens of times before. He explained to Joanne Boogaard who he was. He explained the research into CTE, and how it could improve or save the lives of others. And he asked if the Center for the Study of Traumatic Encephalopathy could have Derek's brain.

"This is my child we're talking about," Joanne said.

Nowinski made the same pitch to Len Boogaard in Ottawa. Len did not know much about CTE until he read the stories about Probert a couple of months earlier. But the symptoms, the addictions, the mood swings in the final years of Probert's life, making him someone different than loved ones recognized, hit close to home for Len. He had expected Nowinski's call.

Len and Joanne discussed the matter. There was little debate. Yes, the Boogaards told Nowinski. You may have Derek's brain. Please help explain what happened to our boy.

AS THE BOOGAARDS awaited the results, two other NHL enforcers had died under mysterious circumstances. If their brains were exhumed and examined, the results were not made public.

Rick Rypien grew up in the small town of Coleman, Alberta, in the foothills of the mountains a couple of hours south of Calgary. His father was a boxer, and his older brother, Wes, was a hockey enforcer who, in 2001–02, was second in the Western Hockey League with 32 fights—including two against Derek. Wes Rypien and Aaron Boogaard both played for the Calgary Hitmen the next season.

Rick Rypien was smaller and more skilled, but he still fought often. He scored 47 goals and racked up 493 penalty minutes over three seasons with the Regina Pats. While there, his girlfriend was killed in a car crash.

Rypien reached the NHL with the Vancouver Canucks during the 2005–06 season, Derek's rookie year. He scored on the first shift of his first game, but injuries took their toll over the years as he settled into a role as a hardscrabble fourth-line center. A leave of absence from the team for most of the 2008–09 season was not fully explained. It was only later that it was acknowledged that Rypien had been diagnosed with depression.

The Canucks re-signed him, and Rypien fought a career-high 16 times. In a game at the Xcel Energy Center in October 2010, after Derek had left the Wild for New York, Rypien was restrained before getting into his second fight and he pushed an official. On the way to the locker room, he reached into the crowd and grabbed a Minnesota fan who had taunted him. Rypien was suspended for six games. In late November, he was granted another personal leave of absence, fueling speculation about his mental state.

Rypien returned in the spring and was assigned to the Manitoba Moose, a minor-league affiliate. On July 1, 2011, he signed a $700,000 contract with the NHL's Winnipeg Jets.

On August 15, he was found dead in his home in Crowsnest Pass, Alberta. He had committed suicide. The family insisted it had nothing to do with fighting or brain trauma.

Wade Belak died on August 31. He was 35 and recently retired when he was found in a Toronto apartment, having hung himself.

Belak was born in Saskatoon, like Derek, and grew into a six-foot, five-inch, 225-pound defenseman and a first-round NHL draft choice. Belak was that rare combination—a sturdy, minute-gobbling top-line defenseman who fought more than 100 times in the NHL.

His opponents included Derek. It was Belak who, in October

2008 while playing for the Florida Panthers, knocked a tooth out of Derek's mouth with a punch, leading to the first in a stream of prescriptions for narcotic painkillers.

Few knew that Belak increasingly battled depression. He kept it disguised with an effervescent smile and a reputation as a happy-go-lucky prankster. He was married and had two daughters. From the outside, everything seemed fine with Belak.

Waived by the Predators, he retired from hockey in March 2011. He had started a career in broadcasting and, at the time of his death, was preparing for the Canadian reality-television series *Battle of the Blades*, in which hockey players took part in a figure skating competition. While his mother said that Belak was relieved not to have to fight anymore, the family did not publicly link his role in hockey to his depression.

Like that of Rick Rypien, Wade Belak's brain was not examined after his death.

The self-inflicted deaths of three hockey enforcers in less than four months prompted a heated debate over the role of fighting. Tradition collided with tragedy. Columnists and commentators who had long questioned the rationale for hockey fights and wondered aloud about the damage to those who took part suddenly sounded less extreme than those adamantly in favor of the status quo.

"While the circumstances of each case are unique, these tragic events cannot be ignored," the NHL's commissioner, Gary Bettman, and the NHL Players Association's executive director, Don Fehr, wrote in a joint statement following Belak's death. "We are committed to examining, in detail, the factors that may have contributed to these events, and to determining whether concrete steps can be taken to enhance player welfare and minimize the likelihood of such events taking place."

It was more than two years later, in December 2013, that NHL deputy commissioner Bill Daly gave an update on the findings. No changes to the program were noted. "We commissioned jointly with the Players' Association and cooperated with them on an independent review of our program and I reported on the results of that review today," Daly said following a meeting with the league's board of governors. "The bottom line is the report was good, that the program is doing what it is intended to do, it is helping players and former players in times of need."

Three years after Derek's death, David Lewis and Brian Shaw still oversee the substance abuse program. And the team doctors who treated Derek during his years with the Wild and season with the Rangers, and who prescribed him medicine leading to his two trips to rehabilitation, remain employed by the teams.

In late November 2011, in an interview with the *New York Times*, Bettman was asked whether he thought that enforcers were more prone to addiction or off-ice problems.

"I've never seen any evidence to that effect," he said.

He said that fighting served as a "thermostat" to prevent worse forms of violence on the ice, and noted that statistics showed that fighting was declining in the NHL. But the league, he said, had little interest in driving the enforcer out of hockey.

"We don't allow fighting," he said. "Fighting's punished, penalized. The issue is whether or not you increase the penalties further, but the game's at a point where people who aren't inclined to fight, don't fight, and don't have to.

"The issue is do we increase the penalty because it is penalized now. And there doesn't seem to be an overwhelming appetite or desire to go in that direction at this point in time."

Much as the National Football League did for years before the data became too overwhelming to ignore, Bettman dismissed the brain research into CTE.

"I think it's been very preliminary," he said. "There isn't a lot of data and the experts who we talked to who consult with us think that it's way premature to be drawing any conclusions at this point because we're not sure that any, based on the data we have available, is valid."

Early the next season, the Wild honored Derek with a pregame tribute. The team sold No. 24 Boogaard jerseys and autographed memorabilia that it had stored from two seasons earlier. Len and Joanne and all of Derek's siblings—Ryan, Aaron, Krysten, and Curtis—were escorted onto the ice at the Xcel Energy Center. They were presented with flowers, a painting of Derek, and a framed game-worn Wild jersey of his. Fans serenaded Derek's family with a standing ovation.

In 277 regular-season NHL games, all but 22 with the Wild, Derek had scored three goals and 13 assists. He accrued 589 penalty minutes and fought at least 61 times. Before reaching the NHL, starting at age 16, he fought well more than 100 times. He never scored more than twice in a season.

The arena was darkened. A 4-minute, 45-second tribute to Derek was shown on the arena's giant video boards. Fans watched in silence as the tribute showed Derek barging into opponents, smiling with fans, and talking to children. It showed each of the three NHL goals he scored.

It did not show a single punch.

DR. ANN MCKEE sat at her computer at the Bedford Veterans Administration Medical Center in Massachusetts, clicking through digital photographs of Derek's brain.

A professor of neurology and pathology at Boston University, she worked independently of the other doctors studying Derek, like Dr.

Robert Stern, who was building a file of Derek's history through interviews with his parents and medical reports from doctors. Independence was crucial. The findings of one doctor would not somehow influence the findings of another.

McKee knew nothing of the person she was examining, other than that he was a 28-year-old hockey player.

In the photographs, the thin slices of brain tissue looked a bit like two-dimensional cross sections of cauliflower, off-white and ragged around the edges. Unlike some of the brains she had examined, Derek's tissue was not shriveled or darkened. Reddish-brown dots and splotches, telltale signs of brain damage, were few, not sprinkled thickly around the edges the way they were on many brains she had seen. The evidence was not obvious to anyone but McKee. But to her, the signs were clear and shocking: Derek had CTE, classified as Stage 2 of the four stages of the progressive disease, more severe than McKee had seen before in a person that young. A "wow" moment, she called it.

The biggest spots were in the frontal cortex, the part of the brain that controls organization, planning skills, and inhibition. When she saw the damage, she wondered if this particular hockey player was prone to impulsiveness and nonchalance.

The medial temporal lobe, the part of the brain behind the ears, also showed extensive damage. There was damage to the hippocampus, where memory is formed and stored. McKee presumed that memory had become a growing issue for this particular specimen.

"This is all going bad," McKee said as she pointed out the damage, difficult for the untrained eye to ascertain. "You just don't expect that much in a 28-year-old. It is already showing substantial destruction."

It was impossible to know how much the damage would spread, if at all, but that was how CTE was thought to work. Damage to the brain could be hidden for years, maybe decades, until it manifested itself in the form of symptoms: memory loss, impulsiveness, mood swings, disorientation, even addiction.

"The association between Boogaard's brain pathology and his clinical symptoms, specifically the behavioral changes and memory problems he experienced in his last two years, is unclear," the researchers wrote in a news release. "For example, his clinical symptoms occurred during the same time period he was exhibiting narcotic abuse. CTE has been found in other deceased athletes who have died from overdoses or who had problems with substance abuse. It is unknown if that substance abuse is caused by the impulse control problems associated with CTE or if they are unrelated."

As Stern later put it: "What's the chicken, and what's the egg?"

The release quoted the co-directors of the Center for the Study of Traumatic Encephalopathy.

"It is important not to over-interpret the finding of CTE in Derek Boogaard," Cantu wrote. "However, based on the small sample size of enforcers we have studied, it does appear that frequently engaging in fistfights as a hockey player may put one at risk for this degenerative brain disease."

The group was careful not to leap to conclusions.

"Boogaard's clinical history was complex, so it is unclear as to if or how much CTE contributed to his behavior, addiction, or death," Stern wrote. "However, CTE is believed to be a progressive disease, so even if it was not directly affecting Boogaard's quality of life and overall functioning before he died, it likely would have in the future."

That news had already been broken to the Boogaard family on a private conference call that linked Boston with Ottawa and Regina. Len and Joanne listened carefully, but were numbed by the news and overwhelmed by the medical jargon. All they really heard was that Derek had CTE. And that there was a possibility, if not a likelihood, that Derek would have been fighting off the effects of dementia, maybe as early as in his 30s.

That is when Derek's father stopped listening. For months, Len had been tormented by regret and haunted by what-ifs. Suddenly, his mind was numbed by the thought of something he had not considered—the kind of life his son might have been left to live.

ACKNOWLEDGMENTS

IT WAS ON THE SUNNY patio of a Minneapolis coffee house a
few blocks from where Derek died that Len Boogaard started to
talk about the life and death of his son. I had never met Derek. But I
planned on writing a story about him for the *New York Times*, a deep
look into his life and death, and hoped that the family would be willing to cooperate. Len agreed to meet for an informal conversation, a
chance for me to explain my intentions and a chance for us to get to
know one another.

Aaron, Derek's brother, sat at Len's side, quiet and deferential.
It had been five weeks since Derek's death, and there remained the
thick pall of grief and fatigue that might never fade entirely. Len, the
Canadian Mountie, answered questions without meandering asides,
like someone careful not to reveal too much. But it quickly became
clear that Len appreciated direct questions and believed in direct
answers. He spoke unflinchingly about Derek's childhood, his unexpected rise in hockey, and his unimaginable fall. After more than
two hours, we stood and parted, promising to be in touch. I would
continue to report, and he would consider his level of cooperation
with whatever it was I was doing.

Fifteen minutes later, while I was driving to another interview in another coffee shop, this one at the other end of the Twin Cities, in Saint Paul, the phone rang. It was Len.

"One other thing," he said, in the straight-talking baritone that soon became recognizable with the first syllable of every conversation. "We found some notes of Derek's in his belongings—16 pages or something about his childhood, in his handwriting. Would you be interested in seeing those?"

It would have been possible to write what became a three-part series on Derek, titled "Punched Out," without the cooperation of Len and Derek's mother, Joanne Boogaard, and their other children. The loose idea of telling the story behind and beyond the death of one of the National Hockey League's scariest enforcers was conjured with or without the family's input. But the story would have been emptier, void of the feeling and context and humanity that only parents and siblings can provide. By extension, this book likely would not have been written without their help and trust.

With no promise other than to have Derek's story told as fully and honestly as possible, even if the findings or the material proved painful or embarrassing, Len and Joanne never blanched in their willingness to help. Len, living in Ottawa, and Joanne, living in Regina, dug through files and scrapbooks and the deep recesses of their memories. They answered all the calls and e-mails, and they welcomed me into their homes for long stretches over many days, with patience, kindness, and good humor, qualities that they could have been forgiven for forfeiting in light of the enduring heartache.

Len, especially, was instrumental in turning a newspaper story into a book. He followed Derek's death with a police-style investigation, a one-man mission to assemble the puzzle pieces of his son's final months and years. He gathered cell-phone and banking records. He requested, and mostly received, medical reports from team doctors, prescription records from pharmacies, notes from rehabilitation clinics, and results from drug testing companies—bits and bytes that only a next of kin could request and receive. And when Len put them together, answering questions and raising more, he shared them. In a lot of ways, I think Len saw it as the last gift—the only gift—he could give Derek after he was gone.

Ryan Boogaard and his longtime girlfriend, Lisa McCormick, (they married in 2013), provided both help and shelter. Ryan, a Royal Canadian Mounted Police member like his father, was stationed at Deschambault Lake, many hours north of Saskatoon and into the deep woods of Saskatchewan. He and Lisa opened their home over the course of two days and one night. Ryan provided his vast collection of Derek's hockey fights, which he had archived as a sort of scout and curator for his older brother from the time they were teens. Ryan also willingly described his life with Derek, from their first childhood memories to the afternoon when Ryan entered Derek's Minneapolis apartment to find him dead on the bed.

Aaron, four years younger than Derek, became Derek's best friend in his later years, the two of them on similar arcs in careers as hockey players expected to fight. Aaron was the last to see Derek alive and, with Ryan, the first to discover his death, and the fallout included his arrest for his role in hiding and dispensing prescription painkillers to his brother when he demanded them. Aaron, over many interviews, provided candid snapshots of Derek, including the episodes that, in hindsight, leave scattered, serpentine trails of destruction.

Krysten Boogaard, six years younger than Derek, deserves special mention for her openness, as well. So does Curtis Heide, the half-brother that Derek did not know he had until the men were grown, and who became the sort of big-brother figure Derek never had.

The help and trust of all the Boogaards was extraordinary. They made things infinitely easier and, I hope, feel some sense of warmth that Derek's name will continue to live, and inform, through these printed and electronic pages.

But, now, a step back: this book never would have happened

without Joe Sexton, the former sports editor of the *New York Times*. It was Joe who, a couple of weeks after Derek's death in May 2011, asked if I wanted to take a deeper look into the late enforcer's life. The Boogaard family had donated Derek's brain to scientists at Boston University, and the *Times*, especially reporter Alan Schwarz, had published groundbreaking stories about concussion research, particularly among former National Football League players.

Sexton recognized that Derek's story was one that we at the *Times* needed to follow. But he wanted to go beyond any sense of obligation. Enforcers represented a small and misunderstood fraternity, as we both knew from years of covering hockey. Perhaps this was a chance to delve into that world beyond the commotion of their theatrics. What is the toll?

It was Sexton and deputy sports editor Jason Stallman who kept me steered straight into the unknown, coaxing me to keep reporting and to keep writing. As the project grew in scope and size, absorbing the magical touches of wizards in the photo, video, and graphics departments, Sexton and Stallman also steered the project deftly through the barriers of newsroom convention. The story became one of the longest published by the *Times*, broken into three parts, each roughly 5,000 words. The online version was accompanied by a 37-minute documentary, shattering the preconceived confines of video for a newspaper web site (and earning an Emmy nomination), and included such a bevy of multimedia components that its complex design was immediately lauded and quickly copied.

Those with the veto power to stop such an audacious project, most notably executive editor Jill Abramson, instead gave it a clear runway. Her appearance at my cubicle shortly before the story was published is a career highlight—a warm handshake and the words that will never leave me: "I would be proud to publish this wonderful piece of journalism."

There are too many others at the *New York Times* to thank, but the top of any list includes photographer Marcus Yam and video journalist Shayla Harris. They accompanied me during the reporting of the newspaper story on an odyssey that included a 2,000-mile route through Saskatchewan and many other trips in the hope of illuminating Derek's world and the people in it. They are two of the finest journalists I know, but I now consider them friends first.

Among those who read the story and saw the potential for a book, none showed the enthusiasm of literary agent Luke Janklow at Janklow & Nesbitt, whose first e-mail to me included a memorable line: "I would almost kill a man to represent you." Luke saw potential in me that I did not see in myself—namely, an ability to write a book, an idea I usually dismissed as beyond my means, patience, and capability. His confidence, advice, and enthusiasm have been welcoming mileposts on this long highway. His assistant, Claire Dippel, showed a knack, intended or not, for eliciting a smile with every phone call or e-mail exchange.

I am forever grateful for two editors who enthusiastically expressed their desire to publish a book by a first-time author about the life and death of Derek Boogaard: Matt Weiland at W. W. Norton & Company and Jim Gifford at HarperCollins Canada. Theirs was an unusual partnership, co-editing one book to be published in two different countries. They made it seamless. If there were wrinkles of philosophical differences, they were ironed out before I knew. Both supplied guidance and ideas. Matt, the point man, patiently read every draft, then subtly wielded a red pen full of suggestions that made the next draft better. Writers and editors are not meant to get along as well as Matt and I do. His assistant, Sam MacLaughlin, ably and kindly kept the process going to the end. And sharp-eyed copy editor Lloyd Davis saved me, I hope, from a litany of grammatical errors and embarrassing mistakes.

It would have been easy to turn Derek Boogaard into a one-dimensional character, a caricature, as he was so often portrayed.

But Matt and Jim never saw this project in absolutes—not as a sports story, not a hockey story, not a goon story, not a story about fighting or drugs or concussions. It is all of these, to be sure, but they shared my belief that it was something both simpler and more complex. It was a story about a boy.

The gears that quietly go to work to publish a book are extraordinary. The teams at W. W. Norton and HarperCollins Canada were nothing but gracious and professional. They are well-oiled machines, and deserving of my utmost appreciation.

And, finally, I owe the biggest debt of gratitude to my family— my wife, Cathy, and our children, Joe and Ally. The reason I had not written books in the past, when receiving occasional interest from those asking if I would, was my great concern over the toll it would take on the three most important people in my life. I worried about what kind of husband and father I could be when hidden in some quiet corner of the house or hunched at the table behind a laptop and stacks of papers and notebooks, answering their innocent questions with a far-off stare.

Writing a book, I know, is not for the timid; writing a book while working full time for the *New York Times* and raising two grade-school children might only be for the delusional. Without their support and understanding—and suggestions for a title and the occasional bragging about this endeavor to classmates—this project never had a chance. I nearly did not write this book because of you. In the end, you were the exact reason I did. I hope you're proud.

A NOTE ON
SOURCES

THIS IS A WORK OF nonfiction, based on interviews, archival research, and documents. The difficult part about crafting Derek Boogaard's story is that he could not contribute directly to its telling. That some details of his life began 30 years before the publication of this book meant that it depended heavily on the recollections of those who knew Derek deeply.

No people contributed more than Len Boogaard and Joanne Boogaard, Derek's parents, who should be applauded for their patience, honesty, integrity, and trust in helping this story be told. It should be noted that this was a journalistically independent endeavor, in no way an authorized biography subject to oversight. The Boogaards and their children, like the many dozens of others who answered persistent and pointed questions about Derek's life and death, were willing contributors, but not editors. No one was paid to provide information.

Vital to the search into Derek's childhood were 16 pages of handwritten notes found at his apartment after his death. In the years before his death, he had written down memories of his youth, presumably for a potential book. Those notes, used liberally in this book, offer the only first-person accounts of Derek's childhood and memories of youth and junior hockey beyond newspaper clippings or television news clips in which he was quoted.

Both Joanne Boogaard and Len and Jody Boogaard shared troves of scrapbooks, photo albums, and memorabilia. Ryan Boogaard, one of Derek's brothers, provided photographs and video clips of most of Derek's fights, including those in junior hockey. Janella D'Amore, Derek's live-in girlfriend for several years while Derek worked his way from junior in Canada to the minor leagues in the American South to his NHL debut in Minnesota, supplied countless photographs, pieces of memorabilia, and letters she and Derek had traded and that she had long kept locked privately in a safe.

Vital to the research were the archives of many newspapers, including the *New York Times*, particularly stories written by respected journalists who covered Derek closely, such as Rob Vanstone of the *Leader-Post* in Regina, Jim Swanson of the *Prince George Citizen*, and Michael Russo of the *StarTribune* in Minneapolis. Many other newspapers, including the Saint Paul *Pioneer Press*, the *Houston Chronicle*, the *Advertiser* of Lafayette, Louisiana, the New York *Daily News*, and the *New York Post*, were invaluable to the reporting.

During much of the reporting and writing of this book, my computer had windows open to several websites. A couple, HockeyDB.com and Hockey-Reference.com, provided statistics on games, goals, assists, penalty minutes, and the like. Sites devoted to hockey fighting, primarily HockeyFights.com, run by David Singer, but also DropYourGloves.com, helped immensely in compiling statistical records of Derek's fights, often with accompanying video and analysis.

Among the proud tradition of hockey-themed books that served as both inspiration and guide, foremost was *The Code: The Unwritten Rules of Fighting and Retaliation in the NHL*, Ross Bernstein's excellent and exhaustive book filled with history and voices of many of the men who have played the role of enforcer. Another was *Tough Guy,* the insightful autobiography of the late Bob Probert (written with Kirstie McLellan Day), one of Derek's NHL enforcer heroes and the reason he wore No. 24 with the Wild.

Formal, exhaustive interviews were conducted with roughly 60 people with firsthand, intimate ties to Derek. Most of those people were interviewed subsequent times, ranging from on-camera interviews for the *New York Times* documentary that accompanied the original newspaper series to follow-up sessions that delved more deeply into particular aspects of Derek's life. Countless other people provided smaller glimpses into Derek's life or the world of hockey and enforcers. Those with close connections to Derek mentioned in the book either were interviewed or were provided the opportunity to be interviewed and declined, including officials of the New York Rangers, Minnesota Wild, and their team doctors.

People in Melfort and Herbert were interviewed, including Derek's former coaches, teachers, friends, and teammates—none more helpful than former coach Floyd Halcro and childhood friend Evan Folden. Coaches and executives of the three teams that Derek played for in the Western Hockey League—the Regina Pats, Prince George Cougars, and Medicine Hat Tigers—were interviewed at length. They included then Pats scout Todd Ripplinger and general manager Brent Parker; Cougars general manager (and assistant coach during Derek's tenure) Dallas Thompson and former general manager Daryl Lubiniecki; and former Tigers coach Willie Desjardins.

Also interviewed were several of Derek's teammates and rivals, from Brett Condy and Devin Wilson to Mat Sommerfeld and Mitch Fritz. Several billet families willingly shared their thoughts, including Doris Sullivan in Medicine Hat. Mike and Caren Tobin in Prince George, who grew closer to Derek than any other adults during his formative years in their home, were vital contributors and wonderful hosts.

Several NHL enforcers, past and present, were giving of their time and insight, including John Scott, Georges Laraque, D. J. King, Brantt Myhres, and Ryan VandenBussche. A special commendation goes to Todd Fedoruk, Derek's one-time rival and longtime friend, who was consistently gracious with his time and insight, particularly as someone who shared many of Derek's struggles yet remains steadfast in his belief that fighting has a reasoned place in hockey.

Especially helpful were mostly former officials of the Minnesota Wild, including assistant general manager Tom Lynn, assistant general manager Chris Snow, scout Tommy Thompson, coordinator of player development Barry MacKenzie, and assistant equipment manager Rick Bronwell, one of Derek's best friends when the two were employed by the minor-league Houston Aeros.

National Hockey League commissioner Gary Bettman was interviewed, on camera, at league offices in New York City on November 29, 2011, in the presence of NHL vice president of media relations Frank Brown. Deputy commissioner Bill Daly was interviewed in his office in July of that year, also in Brown's presence.

Derek's agent, Ron Salcer, provided a wide range of information, none more poignant than his eyewitness accounts of Derek's downfall, the struggles to keep a star client on his feet, and the decisions to send him to rehabilitation. Also instrumental in helping explain Derek's rise and fall were Tobin Wright, who worked for Salcer and was a business manager and confidant of Derek's in Minneapolis; Rob Nelson, Derek's financial advisor, one of several friends who visited Derek in New York; and Pat O'Brien, Derek's trusted friend and physical therapist.

Jeremy Clark, an athletic trainer who became one of Derek's best friends in Minnesota and was with Derek the night he died, was interviewed several times at his gym. He was always accommodating and forthright.

Derek's two primary girlfriends, the two loves of his life, deserve special recognition. Janella D'Amore and Derek were together for about three years, stretching from his stint in Medicine Hat through his first season in Minnesota. Janella shared intimate memories of two young people in love, on a crazy journey from obscurity to wealth and fame.

Erin Russell and Derek became intimately involved early in Derek's second NHL season, about the time of his knockout punch to Todd Fedoruk. They had several years together, through the ups and downs of fame, fortune, and the tangled web of personal problems that Derek encountered, including substance abuse. In his final year, Derek hoped to win Erin back, and the two had their most pleasant exchange of many, many months shortly before he died. Erin, reluctant to participate in the story, eventually provided a two-hour phone interview after I inadvertently discovered her waiting tables at a Minneapolis bar and restaurant and introduced myself.

With the permission of the Boogaard family, the doctors and experts at Boston University's Center for the Study of Traumatic Encephalopathy opened their files on Derek and showed me Derek's brain. Dr. Ann McKee, Dr. Robert Cantu, Dr. Robert Stern, and Chris Nowinksi helped educate me on brain science, the mystery behind concussions, and the precise damage Derek's brain absorbed during his 28 years.

Finally, Len Boogaard deserves a special section, because so much of this book could not have been written without his help. In the wake of his son's death, the longtime Royal Canadian Mounted Police member began his own investigation. He tirelessly uncovered a paper trail of Derek's final year or two, lined with the types of documents mostly available only to next of kin, and shared it for the purposes of telling Derek's story.

He requested—and, in most cases, received—Derek's medical reports and files from team doctors of the Wild and Rangers, including notes from trainers and prescriptions from doctors. He requested and received Derek's pharmacy records from drugstores in Minnesota and New York, mostly various outlets of Walgreens and Duane Reade that Derek frequented.

He painstakingly combed through Derek's phone records, making a directory of contacts by calling numbers he did not recognize and seeing who answered. He collected Derek's bank records and credit-card reports. He received copies of Derek's drug tests, which showed which drugs the league's substance abuse program was testing for, and the results. He received Derek's file from Authentic Recovery Center, the Los Angeles rehabilitation clinic where Derek spent most of his final few weeks. (Founder and program administrator Cassidy Cousens was among those I interviewed.)

By overlaying the data—doctor's notes, prescriptions received, drug tests taken, and bank records—Len's research created a deeply woven arc of highs and lows and, ultimately, the death of his son. It also became the foundation of a wrongful-death lawsuit that the family filed against the NHL in 2013, which was slowly wending its way through the American court system at the time of publication.

For those people, and all the others with a stake in Derek's life and an aching from unanswered questions, their trust and insight will forever be appreciated.

PHOTO CREDITS

FRONTISPIECE: Courtesy Joanne Boogaard

PAGE 14: Courtesy Joanne Boogaard

PAGE 19: Courtesy Joanne Boogaard

PAGE 35: Courtesy Joanne Boogaard

PAGE 76: Brent Braaten/*Prince George Citizen*

PAGE 140: Bruce Kluckhohn/Getty Images

PAGE 150: Bruce Kluckhohn/Minnesota Wild

PAGE 157: Andy King/Bruce Kluckhohn Photography

PAGE 188: Andy Devlin/Getty Images

PAGE 227: AP Photo/Jim Mone

PAGE 259: Andre Ringuette/Getty Images

PAGE 306: AP Photo/*The Canadian Press*, Mark Taylor

INDEX

Page numbers in *italics* refer to illustrations.